PRAISE FOR *MANAGING LUXURY BRANDS*

'The new insights and scientific approaches detailed in this book are a powerful guide to understanding cultural trends and global patterns that will impact fashion and luxury businesses in the coming years. How will luxury shape the way to our future? And how will products be developed, marketed and sold to ultra-high-net-worth individuals?'
Stephen Morgan, Managing Director, Vogue Business

'For those who want to understand the current and emerging state of the intricate tapestry that is the luxury industry, this brilliantly researched work, written by true scholars and practitioners, is a must read. If you are a lifelong learner and are passionate about the fascination that is the luxury industry, you will read it several times and learn many new things each time.'
Milton Pedraza, CEO, Luxury Institute

'Provides insights into the emerging topics that the industry faces today, backed up by well-researched current business cases. From a deep analysis of the role that luxury brands play in the lives of customers and society, and the forces that are shaping the future of luxury businesses (sustainability, digital, AI, China, evolving customer trends), to the special art of reaching the unreachable, *Managing Luxury Brands* is essential reading.'
Charlotte Keesing, Director, Corporate Partnerships and International, Walpole

'One of the most comprehensive takes on what makes the world of luxury tick. With its clear-eyed look, this book is a must read for executives in luxury and those poised to enter the ecosystem.'
Mickey Alam Khan, Founder, Luxury Daily

'Offers an insightful perspective into the key challenges and opportunities for a sector that has specific peculiarities and has proven to be in continuous evolution. *Managing Luxury Brands* is useful reading for any current or future luxury manager thanks to its interdisciplinary approach and the quality of the contributors.'
Filippo Cavalli, Partner and Director, Style Capital SGR Spa

'A must-read for anyone working in, or looking to enter, luxury brand management. J P Kuehlwein's insightful "dream-do-dare" framework is a key reference guide to this ever-evolving industry.'

Tennille Kopiasz, Global Chief Marketing Officer, fresh/LVMH

Managing Luxury Brands

A complete guide to contemporary luxury brand strategies

Edited by Eleonora Cattaneo

KoganPage

First published in Great Britain and the United States in 2023 by Kogan Page Limited

2nd Floor, 45 Gee Street	8 W 38th Street, Suite 902	4737/23 Ansari Road
London	New York, NY 10018	Daryaganj
EC1V 3RS	USA	New Delhi 110002
United Kingdom		India

www.koganpage.com

Kogan Page books are printed on paper from sustainable forests.

ISBNs
Hardback   978 1 3986 0674 6
Paperback   978 1 3986 0640 1
Ebook   978 1 3986 0673 9

British Library Cataloguing-in-Publication Data
A CIP record for this book is available from the British Library.

Library of Congress Cataloging-in-Publication Data
Names: Cattaneo, Eleonora, editor.
Title: Managing luxury brands : a complete guide to contemporary luxury
  brand strategies / edited by Eleonora Cattaneo.
Description: London ; New York, NY : Kogan Page, 2023. | Includes
  bibliographical references and index.
Identifiers: LCCN 2022050013 (print) | LCCN 2022050014 (ebook) | ISBN
  9781398606401 (paperback) | ISBN 9781398606746 (hardback) | ISBN
  9781398606739 (ebook)
Subjects: LCSH: Luxury goods industry–Management. | Brand name
  products–Management.
Classification: LCC HD9999.L852 M37 2023 (print) | LCC HD9999.L852
  (ebook) | DDC 658.8–dc23/eng/20221019
LC record available at https://lccn.loc.gov/2022050013
LC ebook record available at https://lccn.loc.gov/2022050014

Typeset by Integra Software Services, Pondicherry
Print production managed by Jellyfish
Printed and bound by CPI Group (UK) Ltd, Croydon, CR0 4YY

CONTENTS

PART TWO Managing luxury brands today

**12   Future industry developments: Experiential luxury,
extreme personalization and bringing back the human
factor in luxury branding** 313
Alessandro Brun

ABOUT THE CONTRIBUTORS

Matteo Atti is the Chief Marketing Officer at Vista, the largest private jet on-demand group in the world, leading a global marketing team in charge of the entire customer journey, harnessing insights about its UHNWI to introduce exciting innovation programmes. In the past few years his projects have been featured in the *WSJ*, *Robb Report*, *NYT* and *Business Insider*, and he has been a contributor to *Forbes* magazine. His ideas won the 'Legends Award' from *Departure* magazine in 2019 and 2020. He has created books on fine wine and private dining and contributed to several innovation books.

Glyn Atwal is Associate Professor of Marketing at Burgundy School of Business (France). His teaching, research and consultancy expertise focuses on marketing and strategy within the affluent and luxury space. He is co-author of *Luxury Brands in China and India* (Palgrave Macmillan) and a regular contributor to *Jing Daily*. Prior to academia, Glyn worked in industry for Saatchi & Saatchi, Young & Rubicam, and Publicis.

Alessandro Brun has a PhD in Management Engineering and is Full Professor at the School of Management of Politecnico di Milano. He is a teacher of Quality Management, and Director of two Master in Luxury Management programmes at POLIMI Graduate School of Management.

Eleonora Cattaneo (ed) is Professor of Luxury Management and Director of the MSc and Executive Masters in Luxury Brand Management at Glion Institute of Higher Education in Switzerland. She holds a PhD in Management from the University of Pavia and is Senior Fellow of the Chartered Management Institute in the UK and fellow of The Swiss Center for Luxury Research.

Roberta Crespi is Associate Professor of Business Management & Economics at the Catholic University of the Sacred Heart, Milan, Italy. She is also the Scientific Director of Emlux Master in Luxury Goods. She is the co-author of several books on luxury management and supply chain management.

Alessandro Donetti is Senior Adviser for Consumer-Centric Transformation and lecturer at POLIMI Graduate School of Management, with over 30 years' experience as an adviser to global brands. His main fields of activity are brand strategy and consumer behaviour. In his consulting work he has helped iconic brands position themselves in consumers' minds and in their growth projects, both in physical and metaverse markets.

Nicoletta Giusti began her career in academia as an assistant professor at the University of Bologna, where she spent 18 years conducting research and delivering courses at undergraduate, graduate and postgraduate level. She was granted tenure in 2010. From 2014 to 2018, Nicoletta also served as Programme Director of the MSc in Fashion, Design and Luxury Management at Grenoble Ecole de Management (GEM). In 2018, she was named Professor Ambassador for the INSIDE LVMH Programme. From 2018 to 2022 Nicoletta created and directed the MSc in Luxury Management and Guest Experience, as well as its Executive online version, at Glion Institute of Higher Education. In addition to her academic experience, Nicoletta has worked as a consultant for several fashion and luxury firms. Her interest in luxury can be traced back to her family business, Giusti, a luxury menswear store founded in Bologna in 1887, that she also is trying to steer to the next century.

Alice Guzzetti, PhD Management and Innovations at the Catholic University of the Sacred Heart, Milan, Italy. Her fields of research are luxury management, digital transformation, new business models and brand management.

Klaus Heine works as a marketing professor at Emlyon Business School (Paris and Shanghai) and runs the MSc in High-end Brand

Management programme. He has worked and cooperated with a wide variety of luxury houses and high-end brands from Europe and Asia and helps entrepreneurs to build high-end brands with a higher purpose. His main interest is the creation of brand meaning, to give a brand an aura and soul, and a personality all of its own.

Phil Klaus is Professor of Customer Experience Strategy at the International University of Monaco. He is widely considered one of the leading global CX management, strategy and practice experts. His award-winning work has appeared in numerous books and a wide range of top-tier academic and managerial journals. He is the author of the best-selling book *Measuring Customer Experience* as well as a frequent keynote speaker at public and in-company seminars and conferences around the world.

J P Kuehlwein is principal at Ueber-Brands, an advisory firm that helps 'elevate brands to make them peerless and priceless'. He has also served on the board of Smith & Norbu, a luxury eyewear start-up in Hong Kong and was named International Marketer of the Year 2016 by The Internationalist and Association of National Advertisers (ANA). J P teaches at the Columbia University, NYU Stern and EMLyon schools of business, is a Senior Fellow at The Conference Board and serves as an industry advisory board member at the Fashion Institute of Technology, New York. J P has co-authored the books *Rethinking Prestige Branding: Secrets of the ueber-brands* and *Brand Elevation: Lessons in ueber-branding*, both published by Kogan Page.

Yan Sun leads specialist modules for PG International Luxury Marketing at Oxford Brookes Business School. Supported by industrial contacts including the luxury sectors, she has successfully introduced business engagement to module delivery on campus. Dr Yan Sun is also the lead tutor of the Institute of Direct and Digital Marketing (IDM) at Oxford Brookes University.

Annalisa Tarquini-Poli is Director of the MSc in Luxury Management at the International University of Monaco. Annalisa has vast managerial and academic experience in human resources, luxury fashion and yachting. In her recent publications she has analysed the UHNWI customer experience, talking with more than 100 billionaires. Her upcoming research explores what drives UHNWI purchasing behaviour and how the UHNW customer experience could evolve in the near future. She is also the founder and director of The Mark Challenge, a business plan competition on luxury products and ser- vices for students and alumni from all over the world that has reached its 10th edition. Before joining IUM, Annalisa worked for more than a decade as a human resource manager in the luxury industry, advis- ing companies such as Fendi, part of the LVMH group, and success- fully managing recruitment processes such as Corporate Headquarters, the Plant, the European Offices and Retail Network.

Tiziana Tini is a Senior Lecturer at Polimoda in Florence, ranked in the world top 10 best fashion schools by the Business of Fashion. With more than 15 years of professional experience in the luxury business, she is a Professor at Glion Institute of Higher Education as well as a consultant for international luxury companies. Among her multiple passions (as a gamer, a manga lover and an haute cuisine taster), she has been focusing on the relationship between the internet and people living with disabilities, for more than five years.

Rachel Wang is a Senior Lecturer at Oxford Brookes Business School, Oxford Brookes University. Her primary research interests lie in business analytics, application of Big Data in business and organizational management, especially in the hospitality and tourism context, and sustainable luxury hospitality and tourism. Rachel is a member of the editorial board for the *Journal of Tourism and Hospitality* and a member of the scientific committee of ICHRIE, EuroCHRIE and APacCHRIE. She also peer-reviews for several journals, including but not limited to *Annals of Tourism Research*, *International Journal of Contemporary Hospitality Management*, *Journal of Vacation Marketing* and *Management Decisions*.

Definitions of luxury and key facets of luxury branding

ELEONORA CATTANEO

LEARNING OBJECTIVES

- To acquire a clear understanding of the debate on the meaning of 'luxury'.
- To be able to discuss different views on luxury.
- To be able to define and discuss key facets of luxury branding today.

What is luxury? A never-ending debate...

Traditionally luxury has been associated with conspicuous consumption. Veblen (1899) theorized that the wealthy chose to display their status by wearing items that were both expensive and would make physical labour impossible – a man's high hat or a woman's high heel signalled that the wearer did not have to perform manual tasks. In subsequent decades luxury brands developed a similar culture of 'exclusion' which, to some extent, can still be observed today (Cattaneo, 2022). Mauss (1954) linked conspicuous consumption to gift-giving, showing that gift exchanges were used to gain status in the 'prestige economy'. Eastman et al (1999) focused on the relationship between status and conspicuous consumption for luxury products, defining it as a 'motivational process by which people strive to improve their social situation'. However, a consensus on what makes a product a luxury product or what makes a brand a luxury brand (Kapferer and Michaut, 2016) is the subject of constant debate. Vigneron and Johnson (2004) define luxury brands as those which are at the pinnacle of their respective product categories. Fionda and Moore (2009) suggest that luxury goods have status symbolism, high quality, exclusivity and artistry. Dubois and Paternault (1995) proposed that luxury should have 'dream value' and Bjorkmann (2002) suggested that it should be characterized by an 'aura'. Chevalier and Mazzalovo's (2008) definition is more precise, indicating a truly exclusive brand as: 'almost the only brand in its product category, giving it the desirable attributes of being scarce, sophisticated and in good taste'. On the other hand, Ko et al (2019) propose that luxury is a relative concept, 'a specific kind of sign value, produced in specific narratives and used in processes of stratification'. This suggests that any product or service can be considered luxurious in a particular context by an individual.

Practitioners are not unanimous on what constitutes 'true' luxury (Brun and Castelli, 2013). Some focus on product quality: 'once you start compromising, once you start trying to keep cost lower, this is not luxury. Luxury is wanting the best and using the best materials with which to do that' (Doig, 2015). Others consider the experience more relevant: 'luxury is the necessity that begins when the necessity ends' (Coco Chanel). Bonnie Brennan, President of Christie's Americas suggests that 'the greatest luxuries are based in extraordinary experiences' (Christies, 2021). Bernard Arnault, President and CEO of LVMH, has a more down to earth view – 'my relationship to luxury goods is really very rational. It is the only area in which it is possible to make luxury profit margins' – whereas Karl Lagerfeld stated that 'there are many different types of luxury. Luxury also means having the time for yourself without having to live under continual pressure' (Kumar, 2019).

Consumers also have different approaches. Han et al (2010) found four luxury segments based on financial means and the degree to which status consumption is a motivating force in the customer's behaviour. The 'patricians' category, willing to pay a premium for inconspicuously branded products, view luxury very differently from the 'parvenus', who crave status and look for explicit brand signals in their purchases. Kuksov and Xie (2012) suggest that some consumers want to identify as members of a 'desirable' type and buy luxury goods in order to conform with a group they wish to be associated with – similar to the concept of 'bandwagon luxury consumption behaviour' proposed by Kastanakis and Balabanis (2012). Differently, consumption motives associated with individual style are those in which the ultimate objective is to express a personal orientation (Tsai, 2005), fulfilling individual needs and perceptions, independently from interpersonal judgements or social pressure. In this case, customer satisfaction is purely subjective (Wiedmann et al, 2009).

In the course of this book we will discuss a definition of luxury brands 'as distinct for their potential to offer extraordinary levels of hedonistic pleasure or of symbolic, socially elevating, or self-expressive value, for a cost that is generally understood to be extravagant compared to the level of utility obtained or to possible non-luxury alternatives' (Kuehlwein, 2022). Chapter 2 discusses the relevance of luxury brands to the economy, society and human psychology, exploring how they have become desirable to humans across generations and geographies.

The evolution of luxury

The market for personal luxury goods has been growing consistently over the past two decades; at the turn of the century, it was valued at €116 billion, growing to €288 billion in 2021 (Bain, 2022) with only minor dips in 2008 and 2009 as a result of the financial crisis and in 2020 during the Covid-19 pandemic. In the first quarter of 2022, growth reached 17–19 per cent at current exchange rates (13–15 per cent at constant exchange rates) over the same period in 2021 (Bain, 2022). The luxury travel and tourism market was valued at €222 billion in

2021 and expected to reach €393 billion by 2028, driven by rising Millennial and Gen Z spending, and tourism sector expansion, which are all contributing to its growth (Valuates, 2022). The market for hard luxury is also on track for growth according to several studies. Valued at €56 billion in 2020, it is expected to reach approximately €92 billion by 2028, with a CAGR of 7.1 per cent during the forecast period.

Although it has always been associated with wealth, rarity and aspiration (Brun and Castelli, 2013), luxury today is no longer the reserve of a minority elite. Luxury in all its dimensions is accessible for viewing, with many brands making shows, product presentations and launches available online. Entry-level items, the rise of rental and pre-owned, and now NFTs are making luxury accessible to a wider and increasingly younger audience (Cattaneo, 2022). Chapters 7 and 11 will provide insights into these emerging trends.

The desire for luxury continues to grow but there has been a significant change in consumer profiles and relative expectations. At the end of the last century, luxury consumers were a small segment of the global population, based mainly in Europe, North America and Japan. In the last three to four decades, however, a vast amount of wealth has been accumulated in other markets and legacy luxury brands have expanded their offers and presence to meet the requirements of emerging demand. Moreover, a significant number of emerging luxury brands have been launched and are enjoying considerable success. Chapter 10 examines the world of ultra-luxury niche brands, discussing how they can leverage their strength to develop unique products, moving from aspirational to inspirational, communicating only at times and in ways that are meaningful to their hyper-targeted markets.

Millennials and Gen Z luxury buyers focus particularly on memorable experiences rather than material possessions because of the deeper emotional connections (Girardin, 2020). Health, happiness and mindfulness, more inwardly focused ideals, are quickly replacing material goods as the new pinnacle of affluence. Luxury brands are adapting to the shifting priorities of today's younger consumers by offering immersive experiences. Luxury flagship stores are developing into blended physical and digital spaces which invite customers to discover immersive shopping. Chapter 6 will discuss how advances in digital are creating new opportunities for luxury retail.

Is luxury an industry?

An industry is defined as a group of firms that have the same primary business activity, which would exclude luxury which has an offer spanning from apparel to jewellery, automotive, hospitality and more. However, although luxury offers vary in terms of their functional uses, they provide consumers with comparable symbolic and experiential benefits – such as prestige and social status – that mostly come from the intangible attributes of their brands (Kapferer and Bastien, 2009). It is this shared brand identity which targets a customer with similar needs that has resulted in researchers and practitioners grouping luxury brands into a single industry (Okonkwo, 2009). Kapferer and Bastien (2009) argue strongly that the 'identity' is what distinguishes a luxury brand from premium or fashion alternatives and therefore that positioning is irrelevant for luxury brand management. Identity, according to Kapferer and Bastien (2009, p 122), 'expresses the tangible and intangible specificities of the brand' that are 'nurtured from the brand's roots, its heritage, everything that gives it (brand) its unique authority and legitimacy in a specific territory of values and benefits'. The luxury brand industry can therefore be referred to as an exclusive group of brands across different product segments that are distinguishable by their ability to convey unique elements of characteristics that consumers perceive as luxurious (Vigneron and Johnson, 2004), representing luxury in their respective product categories (Okonkwo, 2009).

The contemporary luxury paradigm

In the late 1990s the luxury industry was still characterized by many small, family-owned businesses with a strong product focus. The quality and aesthetics of their offer were of primary importance and brand extensions approached with circumspection:

> In a world of consumerism often focused upon disposable goods machined from synthetics at low price, Loro Piana has blazed a steadfast trail of success by engineering natural fibers and finishing

impeccable Italian-made garments regardless of the cost so as to demonstrate to the world the pinnacle of what can be achieved when quality and quality alone is the driving force of creativity and connection. (Alps and Meters, 2021)

Over the next decade the industry underwent progressive consolidation led by powerful brand-driven luxury corporations (Jackson, 2002). Multi-brand groups such as LVMH and Kering made substantial investments in product design, marketing and retail capabilities in order to build and maintain the luxurious appeal of their brands (Okonkwo, 2009). With the emergence of large multinational conglomerates, the luxury market underwent some major changes (Okonkwo, 2009) in particular. While some conglomerates continued to emphasize their heritage and superiority of products, aligning themselves with their most affluent consumers (Kapferer, 2006), others combined a perceived high prestige with reasonable prices to attract new luxury buyers and more price-sensitive customers (Truong et al, 2009). Many luxury brands targeted new international markets with the objective of increasing their customer base (Chadha and Husband, 2006). As a result, the luxury sector has not only significantly increased its market size, but also its customer diversity (Jackson, 2002; Okonkwo, 2009).

The increased desire for luxury brands worldwide has been influenced by a number of macro-environmental trends, such as globalization and cultural convergence (Chadha and Husband, 2006); the emergence of new segments of affluent customers (Okonkwo, 2009); and a growing interest for luxury from the media (Mandel et al, 2006). China has become a key market for luxury brands, with its share of the global luxury market up to about 21 per cent in 2021 (Bain, 2021). 'We anticipate this growth to continue, putting the country on track to become the world's largest luxury goods market by 2025 – regardless of future international travel patterns' (Bain, 2021). Chinese luxury buyers born between 1990 and 2000 now account for 50 per cent of total luxury consumers in the country (Tencent Marketing Insight, 2021). Chapter 9 discusses the importance of the country of origin for luxury brands and how they can develop strategies to leverage their origin in key markets such as China.

Culture has been shown to drive buying behaviour: consumers in different markets may purchase similar brands for different reasons. Consumers from individualist cultures buy luxury for self-indulgence and hedonism, whereas those from collectivist cultures are more interested in the status value of their luxury purchase (Jain et al, 2021). Research on Indian consumers has shown that interests and values are quite different from those of Western customers (Jain and Khan, 2017). Whereas consumers in Western countries are more likely to judge a brand based on their personal values and principles, their counterparts in India and China are more likely to look to their reference group for confirmation. 'Purchasing luxury items is a symbol of prestige, social status and accumulated wealth. The more you take care of your appearance and lifestyle, the more you show to the world you succeed' (GMA, 2021).

Luxury is constantly evolving but the Covid-19 pandemic had a significant impact on the industry over only two years. On the one hand, it accelerated digital interactions between customers and brands; on the other, it focused attention on global issues such as sustainability and social responsibility. A number of luxury brands turned retail staff into personal shoppers for key customers who received personalized online assistance. Others sent curated collections to the homes of their most loyal customers. Online transactions doubled in 2020, reaching 22 per cent of total luxury consumption which, should the trend continue, would make digital the first channel by 2025 (Bain, 2020). 'Urgency for social impact is growing, with younger generations increasingly valuing diversity, equity and inclusion when choosing what to buy' (Bain 2020). Chapter 3 discusses how the accelerating forces of consumer behaviour will reflect the 'new normal' or 'next normal' in a post-pandemic world, and Chapters 4 and 5 look at sustainability and luxury, discussing how luxury brands are tackling the paradox of 'repair, reuse, recycle' versus extravagance. Chapter 11 will focus on the two main collaborative consumption business models in luxury: resale and renting. Both these practices rely on the redistribution of existing items, but while resale gives the customers the opportunity to acquire ownership of unwanted or underused products, through renting the consumer pays to access the use of products owned by others.

Technology has changed the way individuals purchase and interact with luxury products and services. Luxury customers, traditionally driven by direct interactions with brands and their ambassadors, now embrace technology in all its facets. Chapter 7 explores how AI is increasingly becoming part of luxury brand management, showing how for the luxury customer convenience, reliability and time savings will always be more important than aspiration, social and hedonic value (Klaus et al, 2021).

Evergreen issues in luxury

Luxury brand extensions

Most luxury brands have leveraged growing demand by extending into new categories, seeking to attract new customers and new sources of revenue. For many luxury apparel brands, developing a sneaker line has provided an entry point for Millennial and Gen Z customers. Gucci introduced the leather Ace low-top sneaker in 2016. The shoe is embellished with the gold embroidered bee against the traditional red/green stripe. The bee is an archival code first introduced in Gucci ready-to-wear in the 1970s and Gucci Ace sneakers became an overnight success. The range has expanded far beyond the classic 'bee' design to incorporate more bold accents such as spikes, sequins and seasonal prints. Alessandro Michele, the creative director of the fashion house, chose to pay homage to tradition and enter the emerging sneakers market, managing to satisfy both customers and fashion critics. Extensions that are a poor fit, on the other hand, will risk equity built up over time and dilute the essence of the brand, resulting in a loss of investment and customers. Reddy et al (2009) warned against overextending: 'a luxury brand's profitability will rise as the perceived premium degree increases only if the brand is extended along adjacent product categories'. The cautionary tale of Pierre Cardin has been quoted as an example of overextending a luxury brand. Whereas initially the brand's extensions into perfumes and cosmetics were successful, the brand diversified into a series of downmarket categories, from cigarettes to baseball caps.

There was even a table wine launched under the Pierre Cardin label, which was a failure (Ries et al, 1982). In the end, the adjacency of the extensions – or their consistency – is what makes the difference (Mergen et al, 2009).

Remaining exclusive

Luxury brands lose much of their allure if they become commonplace and yet the drive to grow is built into most business models. As a result, luxury brands need to achieve a seemingly impossible balance of acquiring new customers while maintaining a high level of customer exclusivity. Luxury brands should avoid sales, price reductions and related 'special offers'; high perceived worth, social prestige, an affluent way of life and a cultural signifier are some of the essential things luxury consumers seek in a brand today. What characteristics give a brand its symbolic value? The impression of being excluded from something is a significant issue. All high-end labels work to give their clientele a feeling of being part of an exclusive group. One's perception of scarcity may be based on factors such as a high purchase price, a remote location, a difficult path to ownership, or restricted quantities available. These processes of producing perceived exclusivity provide loyal customers with a feeling of superiority while also giving the impression that there is a heightened demand for the product among the general public. Brands that succeed in cultivating a sense of scarcity are better equipped to weather significant external shocks, including increased competition, regulatory shocks, and economic downturns. CEOs and brand managers with an eye towards creating luxury brands should take great care in developing strategies and implementing the next tactics that will give their products and services an air of exclusivity. Potential customers of the Birkin bag cannot purchase it on the Hermès website and the many Hermès boutiques around the world would not have any on display. It is also not possible to order a Birkin bag unless the customer is a Hermès VIP who is personally invited to custom order, and even long-term customers who make requests for a specific Birkin may wait years for the item to be delivered.

Maintaining the integrity of a high-quality brand promise at all costs

Making good on all of a brand's promises at all times is a formidable task. Successful companies build solid organizational and operational foundations to fulfil their customers' expectations. However, in the case of luxury companies, executing on brand promises entails numerous aspects. In addition to reliably delivering on the promise of symbolic worth, luxury businesses must also present a sense of continuity and stability across all conceivable customer contact points. Global luxury brands all go to considerable lengths to guarantee that every customer interaction runs smoothly across their worldwide operations. Ritz-Carlton hotels, for example, empower every employee, from housekeeping to management, allowing them to spend up to $2,000 per guest, per day, to resolve a problem without consulting their manager. When facing an issue, staff members are entrusted with the responsibility to manage it directly.

Heritage and innovation

In their storytelling, luxury brands often associate their creations with the preservation of traditional craft skills, with a history of excellence and an iconic founder. For luxury brands, heritage in all its different facets is a badge of honour because it defines their identity and adds to the aura of the brand. In addition, heritage is a promise to the stakeholders that performance is secure because of the value and authenticity of the brand (Scarpi, 2021). Chanel still capitalizes on Coco's personality and values; on the website, Chanel N° 5, one of the best-known fragrances in the world, is described as 'the very essence of femininity… the epitome of Gabrielle Chanel's request: "a women's perfume, a scent of woman"' (Chanel). Cartier used a retro-themed campaign recalling the 1980s to successfully relaunch the Panthère de Cartier watch, which had previously been discontinued (Liu et al, 2017). A brand with a heritage can increase the perceived value of the products or services it offers and, in some cases, motivate purchase (for products specifically) as the customers consider them an investment. Luxury buyers define this as 'monetary appreciation', 'potential to become vintage' and 'inheritance value' based on their perceptions of a brand (Halwani, 2020).

Heritage needs to be carefully managed in order to avoid the negative connotations of 'old' and 'irrelevant' that can be associated with it. Moreover, because continuity is a tenet of brand heritage, change is not always easy to implement. The positioning of heritage brands is dependent on their ability to seamlessly relate their past to their present without being viewed as outdated; therefore any innovation needs to be carefully managed. According to some, memory is the key to executing innovation: 'To keep the memory of the past is crucial. It's true that everything changes but it is also true that everything is related. Memory helps in finding the right inspiration in order to encourage change and innovation' (Nicoletti, 2019). Heritage and innovation therefore need to co-exist in luxury brands as their customers expect them to provide cutting-edge offers. Luxury fashion brands are market-driving in terms of launching new shapes or colours. The renowned 'cerulean' clip from 'The Devil Wears Prada' (2006) is an excellent example of this. There is also an expectation that luxury will keep abreast of market changes, hence Gucci developed Demetra, an animal-free, leather-like material after two years of research and development. In this case luxury was not first to market but showed sensitivity in adopting innovative materials.

Luxury Brand Management seeks to provide insights in the emerging topics the industry faces today and opportunities to learn from current business cases.

References and further reading

Alps & Meters (2021) Loro Piana: A history of first-class quality, https://journal.alpsandmeters.com/journal/2021/11/9/loro-piana-a-history-of-first-class-quality (archived at https://perma.cc/J7Y8-GVKN)

Atwal, G and Williams, A (2017) Luxury brand marketing–the experience is everything! In *Advances in Luxury Brand Management*, pp 43–57, Palgrave Macmillan

Bain & Company (2020) The future of luxury: bouncing back from Covid-19, www.bain.com/insights/the-future-of-luxury-bouncing-back-from-covid-19/ (archived at https://perma.cc/WT4G-6ZUX)

Bain & Company (2021) From surging recovery to elegant advance: The evolving future of luxury

Bain & Company (2022) Luxury 2022 Spring Update – 'Rerouting the Future'

Bjorkman, I (2002) Aura: aesthetic business creativity, *Consumption, Markets and Culture*, **5** (1), pp 69–78

Brun, A and Castelli, C (2013) The nature of luxury: a consumer perspective, *International Journal of Retail & Distribution Management*, **41** (11/12), pp 823–47

Cattaneo, E (2022) Sustainable Luxury. In S Studente (ed) *Contemporary Issues in Luxury Brand Management*, Routledge

Chadha, R and Husband, P (2006) *The Cult of the Luxury Brand: Inside Asia's love affair with luxury*, Nicholas Brealey Publishing, Boston, MA

Chanel (nd) Chanel N°5, www.chanel.com/gb/fragrance/women/c/7x1x1x30/n5/ (archived at https://perma.cc/H84L-NCHS)

Chevalier, M and Mazzalovo, G (2008) *Luxury Brand Management*, Wiley, Singapore

Christies (2021) The definition of luxury: Experts and tastemakers have their say, www.christiesrealestate.com/blog/the-definition-of-luxury-experts-and-tastemakers-have-their-say/ (archived at https://perma.cc/D59Y-JXFB)

de Azevedo, R C (2012) Luxury today – key factors for success, Doctoral dissertation, unpublished PhD thesis, University of Lisbon, Portugal

Doig, S (2015) Joining Loro Piana in the seventh annual superyacht regatta, *Telegraph*, www.telegraph.co.uk/luxury/mens-style/joining-loro-piana-in-the-seventh-annual-superyacht-regatta/ (archived at https://perma.cc/W7WS-DU4W)

Dubois, B and Paternault, C (1995) Understanding the world of international luxury brands: the 'dream formula' (Special Issue: Research Input into the Creative Process), *Journal of Advertising Research*, **35** (4), pp 69–77

Eastman, J, Goldsmith, R and Flynn, L (1999) Status consumption in consumer behavior: scale development and validation, *Journal of Marketing Theory and Practice*, **7** (3), pp 41–52

English, B (2013) *A Cultural History of Fashion in the 20th and 21st Centuries: From catwalk to the sidewalk*, A&C Black

Fionda, A M and Moore, C (2009) The anatomy of the luxury fashion brand, *Journal of Brand Management*, **16** (5), pp 347–63

Girardin, F (2020) An insight into the state of luxury branding today, *Hospitality News & Business Insights by EHL*, https://hospitalityinsights.ehl.edu/an-insight-into-the-state-of-luxury-branding-today (archived at https://perma.cc/2CKX-7GC8)

GMA (2021) China Luxury Marketing Guide, https://marketingtochina.com/china-luxury-market-guide/ (archived at https://perma.cc/P555-NCQL)

Gutsatz, M and Heine, K (2018) Luxury brand-building and development: New global challenges, new business models, *Journal of Brand Management*, **25** (5), pp 409–10

Halwani, L (2020) Heritage luxury brands: insight into consumer motivations across different age groups, *Qualitative Market Research: An International Journal*, **24** (2), pp 161–79

Han, Y J, Nunes, J C and Drèze, X (2010) Signaling status with luxury goods: The role of brand prominence, *Journal of Marketing*, **74** (4), pp 15–30

Jackson, T (2002) International Herald Tribune fashion 2001 conference review, *Journal of Fashion Marketing and Management*, **6** (4), www.emeraldinsight.com/doi/full/10.1108/jfmm.2002.28406dac.001 (archived at https://perma.cc/AM2E-C7FR)

Jain, S (2020) Assessing the moderating effect of subjective norm on luxury purchase intention: A study of Gen Y consumers in India, *International Journal of Retail & Distribution Management*, **48** (5), pp 517–36

Jain, S and Khan, M (2017) Measuring the impact of beliefs on luxury buying behavior in an emerging market: Empirical evidence from India, *Journal of Fashion Marketing and Management*, **21** (3), pp 341–60

Jain, S and Mishra, S (2020) Luxury fashion consumption in sharing economy: A study of Indian millennials, *Journal of Global Fashion Marketing*, **11** (2), pp 171–89

Jain, S et al (2021) Critical success factors for luxury fashion brands in emerging markets: Insights from a qualitative study, *Journal of Global Fashion Marketing*, **12** (1), pp 47–61

Kapferer, J N (1998) Why are we seduced by luxury brands? *Journal of Brand Management*, **6** (1), pp 44–49

Kapferer, J N (2006) FAQ: la marque (No. hal-00786818)

Kapferer, J N (2012) Abundant rarity: The key to luxury growth, *Business Horizons*, **55** (5), pp 453–62

Kapferer, J N and Bastien, V (2009) *The Luxury Strategy: Break the rules of marketing to build luxury brands*, Kogan Page, London

Kapferer, J N and Bastien, V (2017) The specificity of luxury management: Turning marketing upside down. In *Advances in Luxury Brand Management*, pp 65–84, Palgrave Macmillan

Kapferer, J N and Michaut, A (2016) Pursuing the concept of luxury: A crosscountry comparison and segmentation of luxury buyers' perception of luxury, *Journal of International Marketing Strategy*, **4** (1), pp 6–23

Kastanakis, M and Balabanis, G (2012) Between the mass and the class: Antecedents of the 'bandwagon' luxury consumption behavior, *Journal of Business Research*, **65**, pp 1399–1407

Kernstock, J et al (2017) Introduction: Luxury brand management insights and opportunities. In *Advances in Luxury Brand Management*, pp 1–24, Palgrave Macmillan

Klaus, P, Tarquini-Poli, A and Park, J (2021) (Priceless) time: The UHNWI's most precious possession: implications for international marketing theory and practice, *International Marketing Review*, **39** (2)

Ko, E, Costello, J P and Taylor, C R (2019) What is a luxury brand? A new definition and review of the literature, *Journal of Business Research*, **99**, pp 405–13

Kuehlwein, J P (2022) An ueber to take your brand to the next level, Luxury, http://doi.org/10.1080/20511817.2022.2095480 (archived at https://perma.cc/4989-DCXT)

Kuksov, D and Xie, Y (2012) Competition in a status goods market, *Journal of Marketing Research*, **49**, pp 609–23

Kumar, I (2019) Karl Lagerfeld's definition of luxury, *Euronews*, www.euronews.com/culture/2019/02/19/this-is-how-karl-lagerfeld-defined-luxury (archived at https://perma.cc/ZL9L-8R2N)

Liu, M T, Wong, I A, Tseng, T H, Chang, A W Y and Phau, I (2017) Applying consumer-based brand equity in luxury hotel branding, *Journal of Business Research*, **81**, pp 192–202

Mandel, N, Petrova, P K and Cialdini, R B (2006) Images of success and the preference for luxury brands, *Journal of Consumer Psychology*, **16** (1), pp 57–69

Mauss, M (1954) *The Gift: The form and reason for exchange in archaic societies*, Cohen & West, London

Mergen R, Terblanche N, Pitt L, Parent, M (2009) How far can luxury brands travel? Avoiding the pitfalls of luxury brand extension, *Business Horizons*, **52** (2), pp 187–197

Nicoletti, S (2019) Opinion: Heritage and disruption rule in luxury, but is there a third path to success? *Luxury Society* (quoting interview with Barbara Curti, fashion expert)

Okonkwo, U (2009) Luxury fashion branding – trends, tactics, techniques, *Journal of Brand Management*, **16** (5), pp 413–15

Paul, J (2019) Masstige model and measure for brand management, *European Management Journal*, **37** (3), pp 299–312

Reddy, M, Terblanche, N, Pitt, L and Parent, M (2009) How far can luxury brands travel? Avoiding the pitfalls of luxury brand extension, *Business Horizons*, **52** (2), pp 187–97 www.sciencedirect.com/science/article/abs/pii/S0007681308001675 (archived at https://perma.cc/43EQ-B8WS)

Ries, A L L, Trout, J and Ampudia, G P (1982) *Positioning*, McGraw Hill

Risitano, M et al (2017) Critical success factors in strategic brand management in luxury fashion markets: the case of Isaia. In *Advancing Insights on Brand Management*, Intech

Scarpi, D (2021) The importance of consumer engagement in brand heritage advertising: How Feeling close to a brand can increase willingness to pay more, *Journal of Advertising Research*, **61** (3), pp 334–45

Tencent Marketing Insight (2021) How China's post-90s consumers are reshaping the luxury market, www.tencent.com/en-us/articles/2201262.html (archived at https://perma.cc/4297-DBUS)

The Devil Wears Prada (2006) Directed by David Frankel [Film]. Los Angeles, CA: 20th Century Fox

Truong, Y, McColl, R and Kitchen, P J (2009) New luxury brand positioning and the emergence of masstige brands, *Journal of Brand Management*, **16** (5), pp 375–82

Tsai, S (2005) Impact of personal orientation on luxury-brand purchase value, *International Journal of Market Research*, **47**, pp 429–54

Valuates (2022) Global Luxury Travel Market Insights and Forecast to 2028

Veblen, T (1899) *The Theory of the Leisure Class*, BiblioLife, Charleston SC, United States

Vigneron, F and Johnson, L (2004) Measuring perceptions of brand luxury, *Journal of Brand Management*, **11** (6), pp 484–506

Wiedmann, K P, Hennings, N and Siebels, A (2009) Value-based segmentation of luxury consumption behavior, *Psychology and Marketing*, **26**, pp 625–51

PART ONE
Luxury: a changing paradigm?

The evolving meaning of luxury brands and a framework for creating modern prestige

02

J P KUEHLWEIN

LEARNING OBJECTIVES

- To understand how the phenomenon of luxury brands relates to the economy, society and human psychology.
- To understand what makes these brands desirable to humans across generations and geographies, in particular.
- To understand when, why and how building luxury brands evolves and how it stays the same.
- To understand one framework that can help research, assess or develop a modern luxury brand.

Introduction

This chapter explores the role luxury brands might play in the life of individuals and in society, what can make these brands very desirable, how the shape of this desirability might differ depending on the good, geography, generation (or not), and how to elevate a brand to acquire prestige based on this understanding and in the current context. It starts by looking at luxury brands as part of the economy, society and of the modern-day quest for identity. A definition of what is understood by 'luxury brand' is provided. The chapter then investigates how changes in time, technology, market or culture might change the manifestation or impact of luxury brands. To illustrate the points, a spotlight will be turned on whether 'loud luxury' is dying or how 'Gen Z' might impact what luxury brands are or how they act. This will lead to a review of a framework – Dream-Do-Dare – that can help us understand, assess and build brands fit for the modern prestige market.

Luxury brands as part of the economy, society and providers of identity, distinction and ecstasy

Luxury is a very subjective, personal idea, but it is also a social construct. Luxury takes on different meanings in different situations and cultural contexts. It is associated with things and experiences that have been commercialized and branded and which evolve over time.

A quick review of some of the ways in which researchers have sought to frame the unique roles and attributes of luxury and associated brands will provide a definition of the 'ideal' luxury brand and help define the criteria by which successful luxury brand building could be judged.

It also serves as an acknowledgement that the project of understanding the power of luxury and of how brands might harness it to be wanted is not a new one and will remain 'work in progress' for as long as humanity evolves in its search for meaning and companies in their efforts to create it.

'And what about the product?' one might ask. Products certainly are a central manifestation of any luxury brand. But it is the associations that go beyond the material or functional benefits of the 'thing' that make it meaningful and transform it into that 'icon' of a brand, desired beyond reason. After all, most of us don't really need another skincare cream, handbag or pair of shoes. And those complicated analogue watches, turntables or sports cars are impractical at best.

Luxury, evolution and economics

Some psychologists and evolutionary theorists link our desire for luxury goods and the brands that signify them with such fundamental desires as procreating or securing a powerful position in a tribe. For example, the conspicuous consumption of luxury brands has been interpreted as a 'wasteful signal', employed by males to appeal to potential mating partners (Saad and Gill, 2000; Griskevicius et al, 2007; Miller, 2009) or by females to attract preference over intra-sexual competitors in being chosen by a mate. Hudders et al (2014) summarize it from a woman's point of view: 'The rival wears Prada'.

Whether such signalling actually works is a matter of scientific debate (Saad and Gill, 2000; Miller, 2009). Either way, brand managers in the luxury and lifestyle industries certainly believe in it judging by ads that illustrate the seductive powers of their products. And their customers seem to 'buy into it', judging by elaborate and expensive dress-up or make-up routines that seem exaggerated compared to their utilitarian value.

Social media provides ample documentation of how people use luxury brands to project their status. Ostberg researched an example of such signalling by youngsters and how they use luxury brands to find and differentiate their tribe – in this case the 'Stockholm Brats' (Ostberg, 2007). The 'Rich Kids of Instagram' (RKOI) is a US-born example that illustrates the perceived value some 'rich kids' associate with posting on the platform to show off. They are reported to pay several thousand dollars to be featured with their latest luxury acquisitions (Hewitson, 2020).

Social capital

Kapferer and Bastien, in their popular 2009 book *The Luxury Strategy*, emphasize the need for luxury products or services to deliver a social statement on top of individual pleasure to be a lasting financial success. And so it comes as no surprise that the way in which people use luxury 'to impress others' is the most researched theme in this brand tier (Wiedmann et al, 2009). In his 1984 book *Distinction*, sociologist Pierre Bourdieu talks about how the upper social classes bring up their children to adopt certain aesthetics, tastes and rituals, and promote them as virtuous and sophisticated, while making access to this 'social capital' difficult for lower classes. In this context, luxury goods and experiences can serve as objectified symbols of high social as well as financial capital that class peers share and lower classes might miss.

This value-creating role and the profit-making potential behind it was not lost on luxury brands. Beyond providing the goods, luxury brands have been providing the young with education when it comes to the appreciation of 'the finer things' and related rituals of Old Money and the New Rich alike through their stores or concierge services, as Dion and Borraz have shown (2017). Take the Bourbon House by Dunhill in London or the Global Swann Club events by LVMH's Berluti shoe brand, for example; they can be seen as training grounds for the (aspiring) high class to hone their luxury aesthetics and practise symbolic consumption (Ings-Chambers, 2008).

Extravagant cost – beyond the price

As signals of financial capital luxury goods are not only associated with steep price tags but with the unusual phenomenon of being more desired and in higher demand, the higher their price is. Such goods are labelled 'Veblen goods' after the economist that gave 'conspicuous consumption' its name (Veblen, 1899; Dubois et al, 2001; Heine, 2012).

However, blatant displays of wealth are sometimes frowned upon. And this is no longer just by a small group of above-it-all patricians and sophisticates but a broader base of affluent and educated consumers, as we will see later. Thus, to avoid negative perceptions, elites often make a point to display connoisseurship rather than money as a mark of distinction, investing significant time and effort in the education offered by luxury brands (often about themselves), on associated rituals and their appreciation.

Perception of self and personal pleasure

Researchers like Russell Belk (1988), using human psychology and anthropology as a point of departure, have theorized goods to be used as 'extensions of self'. Grant McCracken (1990) talks about brands as meaningful building blocks of the 'cultural project' individuals are engaged in, 'the purpose of which is to complete the self'. He points out luxury consumption, in particular, as a point of access to our ideals. Later, quantitative experiments by Vigneron and Johnson (2004) show how 'the supposed luxury of a brand enables a consumer to express his or her own self, an ideal self, or specific dimensions of the self', while those by Wiedmann et al (2009) establish how 'congruity of a luxury product or service with their self-image or intended self-image' creates 'Self-Identity Value', which they find to be a key driver in the overall value perception of a luxury good.

While helping to satisfy the need for social stature seems a primary function, the satisfaction of cravings for hedonistic pleasure – intimate or shared – has also been called out as an important attribute of much consumption of luxury brands (Dubois et al, 2001; Kapferer and Bastien, 2009). Few are those who would not associate a champagne-fuelled party on a superyacht with pleasant feelings or even states of ecstasy.

Myth and un-marketing

In their aforementioned, seminal study, Vigneron and Johnson (2004) drew on both the 'personal-oriented perceptions' (i.e. self-identity building) and socially relevant perceptions of luxury goods (conspicuousness, uniqueness and quality) in an attempt to develop and statistically determine a holistic 'brand luxury index'. Wiedmann et al (2009) added functional and financial values striving for a holistic definition of 'Luxury Value'.

Attempts to consistently predict the perceived value or luxurious-ness of brands applying the proposed methodologies have mostly failed, however. (Read about a failed attempt by Christodoulides et al (2009) to replicate Vigneron and Johnson's Australian-born Brand Luxury Index (BLI) in Taiwan, for example.) To many, the nature of luxury cannot be expressed in an algorithm or a luxury brand built by following the reason-based marketing models of mass merchandisers.

Dion and Arnould (2011) 'propose that successful luxury brands are auratic', that they need to acquire a charisma and create excite-ment that comes with something uniquely 'other' and which we crave deeply. Kapferer and Bastien (2009) suggest that this otherness can only be created by following the 'anti-laws of marketing' which ig-nore concepts of competitive positioning or catering to consumers' needs. Instead, they emphasize the need to 'dominate the client', to be inaccessible, rare, perceived as expensive and to play the 'role of advi-sor, educator and sociological guide'.

The constants are meaning and mystery

Looking across all the theories and research, some key differences of luxury brands vs others emerge:

- Luxury brands are meaning-full to humans – far beyond their utility. But with meaning also comes mystery.

- Luxury brands have an aura that radiates out from a mythical core versus a rationally superior proposition. Kapferer and Bastien (2009) even talk about luxury cars as 'sacred products'.

- In the past decade and post the pandemic, people's cravings to construct identities, find meaning and experience spirituality have only increased, as we will illustrate next. In that respect, quasi-religious objects and experiences will be as desirable as ever and the framework proposed below appropriately starts with 'Dream' as the first step in elevating a brand but also its central promise.

- However, the socio-cultural developments observed will also point to the fact that ideas of brand-centred domination or of brand-worth being derived primarily from price, provenance and precious crafts and materials will need some adjusting, particularly as brands 'do' and 'dare' to create desire.

How to define luxury brands?

For the purpose of this chapter (and book) we will follow this approximation for what is a 'luxury brand':

> Luxury brands are perceived as distinct for their potential to offer extraordinary levels of hedonistic pleasure or of symbolic, socially elevating or self-expressive value. They are generally understood to have a cost that is extravagant for the level of utility obtained or compared to non-luxury alternatives available.

The characteristics listed above are reflected in many definitions by academics who have studied luxury over time, such as Veblen (1899), Bourdieu (1984), Kapferer (1998), Vigneron and Johnson (2004), Keller (2009), Tynan et al (2010) or Heine (2012). And, admittedly, they are also dimensions that are pertinent to our review of how the perception of luxury is evolving and of a strategy framework for brand elevation that accounts for those changes. Of course, luxury and brands are subjective ideas that exist in people's minds but also have shared connotations in various cultural, commercial, academic or other contexts. This makes it likely that some readers might consider the above definition too imprecise – missing other attributes often cited as essentially 'luxury', like provenance or craftsmanship – or too narrowly defined.

The starting point of the brand elevation framework proposed below is to 'dream', which aims at accruing meaning to the beholders of the brand that goes beyond functionality or material value. One can argue over the level of dreaming at which 'true' luxury happens or whether it should be rooted in inspiration or aspiration. The framework posits that dreaming, doing and daring are essential phases when it comes to elevating a brand through meaning. It lets the user be the judge as to whether a sufficient level or desired kind of prestige has been attained to call something luxury rather than lifestyle, premium, masstige or other.

Does luxury branding need a 'total reinvention'?

Marketers and their consultants have called for nothing short of a 'total reinvention of luxury' for a few years now, in the face of social media accelerating and democratizing the consumption and sharing of news and interpersonal information and of digitally based technologies transforming the way businesses source, make, market or deliver their wares – which might be entirely virtual, by now (Au, 2017; Luxury Institute, 2020; Kurzke, 2020). A recent concern has been how brands and luxury might exist in a near future where most of our existence is expressed virtually and which some are eager to brand as the 'Metaverse' (Hermann and Browning, 2021; Business of Fashion, 2021).

And while consultants or the media have always had a vested interest in warning their audiences about 'gamechangers' and have created waves of more or less game-changing management and marketing methodologies over the years, there are two aspects of change that are likely to impact humanity more than in decades past: the ever-accelerated speed at which technological innovation but also environmental degradation change the way we live. The global pandemic of 2020 made that very clear to most and was a further accelerator in itself.

Futurist Ray Kurzweil wrote in 2001, 'We won't experience 100 years of progress in the 21st century – it will be more like 20,000 years of progress', and we have already met some of his predicted technology milestones on the way to a world where man and machine – or rather artificial intelligence – become one. Unfortunately, though, that does not apply to the climate crisis being resolved.

So, what impact might these fast changes have on luxury brands? How can they respond to it? Or better still, be part of the change? Looking at some recent, salient trends in the evolution of society, economy, technology and ecology will provide some criteria to test the relevance and flexibility of the proposed brand elevation framework against.

Luxury markets are maturing

At the beginning of the millennium, US business consultants Michael Silverstein and Neil Fiske (2005) were observing a 'democratization of luxury' by serving the significant 'middle market' that had emerged from years of sustained economic growth – particularly in the cities.

Baby Boomers were 'trading up' to premium propositions in areas they considered core to – and reflective of – their ever more privileged lifestyle. David Brooks (2000) described the most affluent and intellectual crust of the (ex-) hippie generation as concurrently demonstrating their riches and their disdain for the 'mass consumption' of the middle. They develop what he termed a Bourgeois-Bohemian or 'Bobo' lifestyle and caste, which relied on more subtle signals of wealth like high-end clothes or furniture carefully 'stressed' to look lived-in and vintage. This, in turn, made the 'Old Money', WASP class reinvent a distinctive kind of 'preppiness' to differentiate from all those parvenus rising up.

Since then, we have seen similar growth and transformation patterns in the high-end brand markets across Europe, Japan and emerging markets. China's cities, in particular, have become the main growth engines of the luxury industry and the biggest market for many brands. Uniquely favourable drivers were steep, sustained and board-scale economic growth mixed with many exceptional fortunes being made fast and a culture that favours signalling good fortune, respect and class belonging through conspicuous luxury consumption or gifting.

The continuous 'sophistication' at the high end of these markets can also be observed with 'ageing money' moving on from their 'loud' expressions of wealth (now associated with parvenus or poseurs in their minds) to more 'silent' luxury brands or less obviously 'logoed' (and counterfeited) version, for example (see, for example, Wilson et al, 2013, and Han et al, 2010).

Being able to read the more subtle or complex codes of this silent luxury is what elevates one to connoisseur status. Knowledge of idiosyncratic values and beliefs associated with select brands lets the owners make them their own and join an exclusive tribe that shares them (Morency, 2021). Consumption is experienced as more meaning giving and meaning projecting.

Note, however, that the ageing of 'old' money happens much faster nowadays, with some 'unicorn' fortunes being amassed in a few years rather than generations, and that 'sophistication' is taking on a much younger, less traditional character and aesthetic than was the case just a few decades ago (Frasier, 2018). In that context, having an axe made by hipster brand BestMade ($400) handy at your cabin and a vintage Ford Bronco that has been fitted with an electric engine ($185k) parked in front is a modern expression of sophistication (Fearon, 2021).

Is loud luxury dying?

Jing Daily reports that the *Little Red Book* now censures ostentatious display of luxury (Nan, 2021). The Red Book in question is not the 1964 'Mao Bible', but the 2021 guidelines to the Chinese version of Instagram, which is highly popular among Gen Z. That said, there certainly is a link to the latest leader of China – President Xi Jinping – having an aversion to ostentatious displays of wealth which contradicts the rediscovered mantra of 'common prosperity' (Mullen, 2021).

How did the display of – often pretended – excessive wealth become so prevalent in China that the Communist leadership feels compelled to intervene in the first place? Will 'The Bling Empire's Christine Chiu' (Thomas, 2021) become one rare survivor... because she lives in California?

Those seeking to explain the 'China Bling' phenomenon often point to high collectivism but also high power distance and uncertainty avoidance as being Hofstedian cultural characteristics of China (Hofstede et al, 2010). Combined, these cultural markers are assumed to motivate people to display brands that are clearly recognized and broadly understood as status-giving to signal their belonging to the higher, more powerful class (Naumova et al, 2019). Similarly, the important Chinese cultural concepts of 'face' (aka面子 or miànzi), which is much more relational and community oriented (e.g. representing the family or work team), and 'guanxi' (关系 or social relationships) play into items that are strong status signals being used to acknowledge or bestow 'face'. Hence 'gifting' making up a large share of many luxury brands in China (Atwal and Bryson, 2017).

Finally, one might argue that the rise of luxury in China in the past 40 years is a consequence of the behavioural changes that come hand-in-hand with a society developing capitalist and post-modernist traits. Modern, Western-styled societies being 'other-directed' (rather than the pre-modern, inner-directed tribal societies), impressing on others who you are is an essential part of having a place in that society (Mason, 1981). Possessions and their perceived nature (value, sophistication, etc) are a shortcut used to signal or assess social rank.

In early 'capitalist' or 'achieving' societies, those now enabled to accumulate wealth exhibited it to gain acceptance or even distinction over the old, aristocratic elite (which had founded its elite status on 'God-given' privileges and exclusive possessions), to acquire social acceptance from their perceived peers and social superiority and admiration over the less fortunate. The advancements and the spreading of industrialization, communication and education brought conspicuous consumption within the reach of the masses, though. And with it came a change in behaviours.

As Galbraith (1984) observed, 'simple forthright display is now out of fashion and is often referred to as vulgar; required instead is a showing of what may be called obtrusive good taste. That, unlike the conspicuous consumption of earlier times, requires a certain measure of artistic and even intellectual effort.'

The now larger group of educated people who have incomes high enough to selectively own or rent themselves into the world of the rich are looking for more tacit signifiers of wealth to not be mistaken for people who 'try too hard'. And that includes categories not immediately associated with luxury consumption, like investing in an Ivy League education for their offspring. In the United States, for example, education represented 6 per cent of household spending among the richest 1 per cent of households in 2007, vs 1 per cent for medium-earning households. In contrast, spending on material goods is trending down among the top 1 per cent while it is flat or up among the rest (Currid-Halkett, 2017).

While still desirous of status and prestige, today's elite is strongly motivated by a pursuit of social and group acceptance. Affluent societies tastefully consume to denote belonging to a particular group (Rassuli and Hollander, 1986). For example, being subscribed to or citing from the 'right' news source, like The Economist (see more on how that brand image is built below), is one of the rites of passage into the aspirational class (Currid-Halkett, 2017).

Veblen's depiction of ostentatious display solely for reasons of invidious distinction seems to be dismissed by these post-affluent societies... as it is by the Chinese Communist Party.

Does that mean ostentation and celebration of wealth will disappear?

For one, it seems irresistible to the super-rich of today to establish privilege by showing off hyper-yachts, private space ships or country-sized real estate that are out of reach to the onlooking 99.9 per cent of humans. And the admiration and envy of those onlookers seems equally unabated.

There are also those, like historian Arthur Schlesinger Jr., who contend that history and associated human behaviours oscillate. Schlesinger described 30-year cycles of ostentatious consumption and hedonistic self-indulgence (for the United States, the Roaring Twenties, the Eisenhower years, the Materialism of the 1980s) alternating with periods of benevolence and activism (the New Deal era of the Thirties, hippie activism of the Sixties) (Schlesinger, 1986). Another period of strong demand for bling luxury items would not come as a surprise to those taking a long view.

A case in point. *Wallpaper*, one of the lifestyle magazines for the modern, intellectual, aspirational consumer, reported on 'The ostentation of the Roaring Twenties' being brought back by fashion houses in 2021. The interpretation offered is that 'excess is a signal of aesthetics excellence' (Hawkins, 2021).

Also, an item can be understood as rich or ostentatious in its inner sophistication but 'silent' in its outer expression and discriminating in that way. Take the absurdly expensive but – to the untrained eye – inconspicuous and obscure Alvar Aalto Savoy concrete doorstop by Tobias Wong (Maldre, 2009) or an all-organic vegetarian soup consumed at a neo-rustic farm-to-table tavern. The owner and consumer can be assured of the approval or even admiration of those 'in the know' and thereby of their belonging to this modern elite.

More in the 'loud' vein of luxury, there is talk of the overtly aggressive, muscle- and money-signalling Hummer SUV coming back – in a socially more acceptable electric version (Korn, 2020).

The bottom line: 'Loud Luxury' is a question of perspectives and of periods in time. But no matter whether something is labelled as refined or as a frivolity, the humans seeking out those goods are in search of meaning through what they consume.

Cultures keep evolving

The spreading and growth of brands that are more intellectually demanding or ideologically involving is not only a sign of luxury markets maturing. First and foremost, demand for such brands is driven by the steady march of societies through modernity and post-modernity towards a yet fully to emerge post-industrial... virtual existence?

Jettisoned or lost along the way were many of the traditional institutions that guided (or straight-out told) people how to labour, live or love and provided the structures, rules, rituals and codes that made it work. Luxuries that used to be formally reserved to signify nobility or, later, pointed to an accepted bourgeois hierarchy, have long been abolished (for a historic perspective see Turunen, 2018).

Today, modern markets revere the fully emancipated self-made individuum that guides itself through a unique set of ethics and aesthetics. But many people are struggling with creating an identity from scratch and giving life meaning. And the scope feels ever broader and the burden heavier the more money, time and knowledge people have to invest into their personal culture projects and broader societal issues.

Today, the educated classes, from the HENRYs – the 'High Earners but Not Rich Yet' – to the high-net-worth individuals, have a desire to express and, if convenient, live their ideals when it comes to matters of self-awareness, body positivity, diversity, ecology, equality, inclusion, sustainability, spirituality and so forth through their discretionary spending (Frasier, 2018; Lewis, 2020; Danziger, 2021). Living in a pristine environment while feeling protected from the elements has graduated from the bottom of the needs pyramid to become part of living in luxury.

Companies see a high-margin opportunity behind delivering on these higher-order needs. They assist in the meaning-finding mission by becoming ready symbols of desirable ideologies or offering the platforms where people with shared beliefs and passions can meet. Luxury brands, in particular, have an opportunity to fill a void when it comes to our desire for spirituality by playing the roles of quasi-sacred objects, rituals and experiences in life (Maffesoli, 2018; Ott, 2018).

In contrast to the passive 'consumer' of yesteryear, the customers of today demand that brands are either convenient commodities or are worthy of their attention, time, effort and money by offering meaning that goes far beyond the material (Schaefer and Kuehlwein, 2015). From the emphasis on 'owning', then 'experiencing', those who can afford it are stepping up along Pine and Gilmore's value creation ladder to seek out brands that can assist in the 'transforming' towards an ideal self – or even fantasy self (Pine and Gilmore, 1999).

And tech as a turbo charger... keeps accelerating

As journalist Virginia Hefferman (2021) relates, 'the manipulation of undigitized, offline objects, stuff with mass' has stopped being a promising field of endeavour at the factory as well as office level – at least for those who have a choice. The new elite deals in information, ideas and ideals, looking to create or join tech-fuelled 'unicorn' ventures that generate billions in value – seemingly overnight – based on data and virtual realities rather than tangible goods. In fact, authors and artists are imagining us living our lives in a mostly virtual future and today's digital entrepreneurs are not far behind them, seeking to have a stake in that new world, if they do not succeed in owning and shaping it entirely.

Already today, remote workers spend countless hours interacting on Zoom, Team or Slack, and some transform themselves into e-gamers, living in the universes Roblox or Fortnite in their time off.

This, of course, has spawned new rituals and ways to practise conspicuous consumption as well; people strut 'their' stuff in aspirational environments on social media – which might really be theirs, or rented, or a digital filter – an augmentation and idealization of reality. In some cases, the messaging and digital augmentation a brand enables have become more important than its physical materiality.

Given the unstoppable proliferation of media and deep-reaching marketing technologies, audiences have become dispersed, their attention spans shortened to seconds and their base attitude defensive, doubting or indifferent. In other words, for luxury brands to matter in today's context, they also need to be able to break through and elevate themselves above what looks like a sea of meaningless chatter and not get lost but rather get noticed in the virtual universe.

Does Gen Z hold the key to the future? What do that key and future look like?

Only 'Gen Z' (people born between around 1996 to 2012) might top some form of new technology in being the likely focus of a discussion about the future of luxury brands – or of almost any industry or brand for that matter.

And, judging by how long the preceding 'Millennial' generation took centre-stage for marketers, the mining for – and minting of – 'unique Gen Z traits' and of strategies to satisfy their needs might last for another six to nine years. By which time, 'Gen Alpha' will likely move into focus. But is this somewhat obsessive attention to the latest generation of shoppers warranted? Are the ways in which these generations are clustered and attributes attached to them of use?

Gen Z's share of luxury consumption was estimated at less than 10 per cent in 2020, but forecasters think they might make up 40 per cent of the category by 2035 (Danziger, 2019; BoF Studio, 2021). Rather than their current spending power, what draws attention is that they are seen as the arbiters of what luxury should become.

The netizen-consumers

Without doubt, Gen Z is the first to grow up with their fingertips on a mobile screen, interacting with Web 2.0 sites, 'googling', communicating via social media or shopping via e-commerce from as soon as, and for as long as, their parents would allow them to. It comes naturally to them.

In that way, Gen Z are a natural testing ground, if not a window to the digital future. They approach the virtual world with few reservations and are eager to try the latest offerings, thereby helping to select and fine-tune winning propositions. With their help, app, website and online game designs have become so intuitive and engaging and the algorithms of shopping and social media platforms so refined at serving up ever more emotionally arousing content that an increasing number of young users, in particular, are starting to struggle with digital addiction (Dauk, 2021).

Gen Z is observed to have a seemingly insatiable appetite to match the unlimited information and entertainment the web has on offer. To achieve this, these 'digital natives' have a preference for convenient access, easy juggling between apps, and information in the form of ultra-short stories, videos and pictures. And they are reported to have an average attention span of some eight seconds or less (Vizcaya-Moreno and Pérez-Cañaveras, 2020).

Getting entangled in networks of desire

Of course, these preferences translate to where Gen Z meet brands, how they learn about them and shop for them. They are more likely to notice and get seduced by brands that get raved about by popular peers and celebrities, in different contexts, across multiple platforms, in engaging snippets of information – like a Snap (on Snapchat), as a prop on Instagram or a skin on Fortnite, being unboxed on YouTube, discussed on Discord or as part of a meme on TikTok, and so on.

Robert Kozinets (2021) talks about the emergence of 'Algorithmic branding through platform assemblages'. He thinks that marketers who understand the opportunity will seek to 'use engagement practices as well as algorithmic activation, amplification, customization and connectivity to drive consumers deeper into the brand spiral, entangling them in networks of brand-related desire'.

Transforming physical brand manifestations

Over in the physical world, retail brands react by consolidating stores and transforming flagship locations to become stages where customers are engaged in ways not possible online (PWC, 2021). This 'IRL' (in-real-life) engagement is devised to create a desirable brand image and a relationship that leads to sales anywhere within the brand's omnichannel web. It can also take the form of experiences that add new dimensions to the brand and yield new sources of income and bonding: LEGO producing movies, biking accessory brand Rapha creating cycling clubs (see below) or REI organizing hands-on tutorials in nature are some examples.

To 'bring the brand's dream to life' is central to elevating a brand, as is posited below. And luxury brands have traditionally done so for the select few – be it having a saddle custom-made at the Hermès atelier, a private fashion show on the second floor of the Chanel boutique, or a bespoke fitting and even an overnight stay at the Maison Dior (see insert below).

What is different with the youngest generation is that they want to dip into a multitude of dreams, immediately, briefly and 'shareably' to feed their personal brand assemblage across social media platforms. This is where luxury brands have observed and then obliged this trend-setting consumer. Dresses become theirs for an Instagram minute out of the changing room at Gucci; showrooms are now staged specifically to be Instagram-friendly, and the most influential peers are invited to the fashion shows.

The development is part of what is described as the 'democratization' of luxury. Furnishings company RH (formerly Restoration Hardware) invites people to slumber in its living rooms; Tiffany's makes experiencing 'Breakfast at Tiffany's' possible at their flagship store's café. And part of the payout – beyond the affordable appetizers in luxury – is that it all feeds into social media. The posts generated add to that branded message spiral which is expected to bind senders and their followers emotionally to the brand and make them long to consume 'for real'– once the means are available.

But, of course, Gen Z is not the only or the first generation to post images of their dreams on social media. Millennials were called the 'selfie generation' before them and over 70 per cent of those aged 30 to 60 years use at least one social media platform regularly (Statista, 2019).

Emerging technologies adopted by any (age) group and the resulting changes in their consumption behaviours should serve as inspiration to explore how these behaviours might spread and how they might serve to make the brand more meaningful. It's just that the youngest often play with the latest innovations and joining them holds the potential to keep a brand young.

Demanding environmental sustainability, social equality and transparency!

If being 'tech savvy' (or 'tech addicted') is portrayed as the top trait of Gen Z, then being deeply concerned about protecting nature and creating a socially just environment must be close behind. Images of Greta Thunberg speaking at 'Fridays for Future' rallies come to mind or teens organizing protests to show that Black Lives Matter. They declare themselves 'gender fluid' through their clothing or choice of restroom and violate traditional beauty norms by celebrating their acne zits with sparkles rather than trying to suppress them with creams. Companies that claim to do good get favourable attention, but news about missteps spreads equally fast among the 'communaholics' and requires quick corrective action (Francis and Hoeffel, 2018).

On the luxury front, second-hand platforms are highly popular. Reuse saves the environment and the vintage pieces are perfect for the kind of high-low fashion mix from which they curate a uniquely 'me' style (Danziger, 2019). Eating big steaks, wearing fur, owning fat cars (at least the combustion engine type) or donning diamonds (at least the mined type) are big no-no's. 'Eat the Rich!' We are told that Gen Z prefers experiences and access over ownership and socialism over capitalism (Jones, 2021).

Or are they?

On the other hand, Gen Z is also a key driver behind the growth of ultra-fast-fashion, where garments are made to last but a few wears (not years) before falling apart (Nguyen, 2021). And those acne sparkles are one-use plastic film – how can that be?

Quite simply, 'generations' are not composed of identical clones. Greta Thunberg and the Bling Cling Girls – a K-Pop dance troupe – are both labelled 'Gen Z influencers', but they couldn't exhibit more different personalities and behaviours. And the reasons behind those behaviours are usually more complex than the trend-tellers or survey results capture.

Going against the grain might be more a trait of the young, rather than the character of a generation. Many Boomers certainly evolved from being free-spirited hippies to becoming dedicated capitalists. The 'no to ownership' attitudes might have more to do with Gen Z-ers being 'CARLYs' – people who 'Can't Afford Real Life Yet' – rather than not wanting to do some of those things (Schott, 2021).

Humans with different DNA and backgrounds

The need for a more differentiated view applies even more when seen globally. Even at the macro level, the differences in circumstances are vast.

Consider the economic and socio-cultural differences between Gen Z-ers in China and the UK, for example. In China, the youngest generation is described as the richest and most pampered yet – at least for the dominant Han majority (over 90 per cent according to the 2020 census) living in the cities. They have grown up in a time of sustained, fast economic progress and growing national power and pride. They get to spend 15 per cent of the household budget they depend on and have a predilection for luxury items, according to a 2019 global survey (Bloomberg, 2019).

Compare that to the UK where Gen Z grow up with more siblings and as a radically more diverse cohort than their Chinese peers (or parents) but also in the context of several severe economic and political crises, the most recent being Brexit and the Covid-19 pandemic. The generation-to-generation income progression has reversed for the first time in 100 years as the first of them entered the workforce in 2017 (Edwards, 2017). The economic situation not being as rosy, it might be no surprise that they get to only spend 4 per cent of the household budget, according to that same survey.

And while both young populations lean heavily on tech, and the platforms and infrastructures at their disposal are similar, the freedoms afforded are markedly different when it comes to sharing political opinions, for example (Wang, 2020).

The key lies in harnessing shared dreams – across generations

So, what is a luxury marketer to do with all this techno-cultural complexity and ambiguity? What is the key to ensuring a brand stays relevant and desirable? 'Cherchez-le-rêve!' (Seek the dream!)

Brands elevate themselves by becoming a shared dream – or myth, as Joseph Campbell defines it (Campbell and Moyers, 1991). Humans are dreaming about a pristine nature, or about a society where all are equal or young or wise or beautiful, or about having super-human powers – or some combination thereof.

The young might be particularly creative in this regard and the technologies they shape and embrace might enable them to manifest ideas in new ways. But the hard work to capture those aspirations and harness those tools that grow the attraction of the dream that is the luxury brand is that of the owner. For we expect luxury to seduce and guide us, not to mimic and sell.

Dream-do-dare – a framework to understand how modern prestige brands create meaning

How then can brands elevate themselves above the rest and accrue value and meaning beyond the material? How can they be experienced as peerless by an audience over-exposed to advertisements and lend prestige without being perceived as pretentious?

Based on empirical study, own practice and in-depth interviews with other practitioners, Schaefer and Kuehlwein (2021) summarize the actions that drive the sustained desirability and pricing power of modern luxury brands as follows: 'They dream, do and dare' (Figure 2.1).

Starting with a dream that unites brand mission and myth

The brand dream is where the previously described soulful 'aura' of luxury meets emotional and (post-) rational reasons to buy 'into' the brand. Brand stories mined from the brand's 'DNA' – history, culture, business model, product development and so forth – are elevated to take on mythical proportions. The brand's mission is determined,

Figure 2.1 The three phases of brand elevation

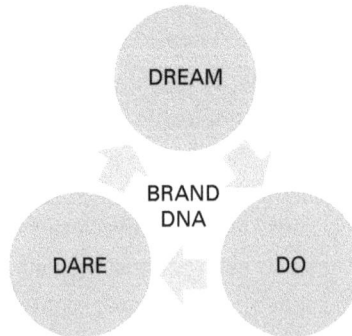

SOURCE Schaefer and Kuehlwein (2021)

reaching beyond the money and material for a reason for being, a higher calling that seduces customers, employees, suppliers and other key stakeholders alike.

Of note is that this starting point of luxury brand creation is centred on the brand and emphasizes the ethereal, where ordinary brands usually start with the rational: consumer needs.

Thus, the story of Chanel, for example, centres on the myth of the ever-rebellious, creative free spirit that was Coco Chanel. A woman who liked to dress in men's clothes to tease her many and mostly married but always high-society lovers. It forms a meta-story that also serves the 'luxury education' mentioned above through more literal recounting in books, films and expositions and, more importantly, that serves as a guide in expressing the brand across all touchpoints and in reinterpreting and evolving it into the future.

The internal mission statement of Chanel is purported to be about 'defining style and creating desire, now and forever'. With this understanding of the brand myth and mission, we can understand seemingly bewildering but 'legendary' and trend-setting moves by the then high-priest of the brand, Karl Lagerfeld, fitting his models in tweed jackets and bikinis (1993) or sports sneakers (2000) or having them stage a fantasy feminist protest (2014). The company buying up ever rarer flower fields in Grasse, France (latest in 2021) is an example of the business steps taken to secure both mission and myth. The high-altitude fields are said to yield the rare jasmine that is characteristic of the seductive fragrance of that fifth vial Coco supposedly chose to become the first perfume of the brand (Gaillard, 2021).

Does a powerful brand myth require a long history and be steeped in traditions? No. Tesla, the e-car brand, was dreamed up by Elon Musk in 2008. Initially, it attracted an elite Hollywood and Silicon Valley crowd through now-legendary pronouncements by Musk about how to 'change the way the world uses energy', 'spread [...] humanity to other planets' (Schaffer, 2015; Mosher, 2018) and by spectacular stunts like sending one of the cars onto a trip into the galaxy. The brand has since reached down with popular models (priced at $40–60k) to live up to its gospel while also staying aspirational, for example by promising a new version of its roadster at the top end (rumoured to start at $200k).

Does having a brand mission force a brand down to dream-busting reason? No. Chanel has made making us dream part of its mission. And Hermès provides the example that one of the most venerable luxury brands can gain new relevance and audiences by extending its myth and mission: Hermès is all about preserving and spreading the joy of craftsmanship – 'les joies de l'atelier'. And its little daughter – 'Petit h' – sitting under the atelier's table, so the legend goes, extends this joy by reimagining the precious scraps into beautiful toys, accessories or objets d'art (Schaefer and Kuehlwein, 2015). What a magical, yet mission-driven way to approach what could also be described as 'upcycling'.

Always do rather than declare: living the mission and myth

The easiest way to recognize a pretender is by their 'luxury' label. True luxury is not proclaimed, it is felt by its beholder.

Certainly, the product has to live up to the dream through all the detail in design, use, ritual and rhyme. Particularly in today's social media-powered world, any deviation from the brand's promise will be called out and disappointments will be shared quickly and broadly. But this does not mean that a luxury product must be perfect and please everyone in every way. Rather, the brand proposition needs to be perfect in 'its own way' and stay true to itself. Here, again, the luxury brand is expected to delight by teaching, inspiring and making our taste rather than 'deliver on expectations' as ordinary brands do.

Ferraris are famously difficult, uncomfortable, uneconomical and even unsafe to drive – at least for the average driver on normal roads in normal traffic. But then, being a 'daily driver' – even a fast, luxuriously equipped one – is not the Ferrari dream. In a similar fashion, the 'falcon wing' doors on the Tesla Model X SUV create a lineage with iconic supercars like the 1955 Mercedes-Benz 300 SL, while also manifesting the futuristic promise of the brand. The feature would be questionable if convenience, cost, maintenance or safety were primary concerns (Lambert, 2017) – just like shooting one of the cars into outer space would.

This does not mean that luxury brands ignore that modernity has 'made man God', putting the individual at the centre of everything, as philosopher Luc Ferry argues (2002). But rather than following the popular credo of 'customer is king', the luxury brand ensures product and experience are 'fit for the Gods'.

A big part of experiencing luxury comes not just from experiencing the unique object or service but from sensing the dedication to the dream by the people behind the brand.

At Hermès, artistic director Pierre-Alexis Dumas is certain the customer 'feels the presence of the person who crafted the object, while [...] the object brings him back to his own sensitivity, because it gives him pleasure through his senses' (Anaya, 2014). The company lets this feeling radiate from the inside out by making the atelier and its artisans the source of its manifestations, be it in the form of tours of the archives and workshops (in person, virtual, in books or on film), through personalization or bespoke services, audacious designs crafted for special clients or auctioned at charity events during the 'Festival des Métiers' (craft fair) touring the globe. Meanwhile at 'Petit h', Dumas's cousin Pascale Moussard showcases the 'Alibaba cave' of Hermès manufacturing scraps which she and her artisan associates reimagine into ingenious and precious creations (Hermès, 2022). A bracelet woven from scrap silk by Petit h is priced relatively modestly, yet the distinguished provenance thus created imbues it with the power to convey sophistication or even social standing.

The same applies for *The Economist*, a uniquely created product worthy of the intellectually discriminating reader. Here, the 'Do' is journalism executed in ways that often go against the grain of common news media; the choice of topics is serious, and the articles are authoritative and take mostly a long form. The language is an idiosyncratic mix of high-brow-yet-witty British. One of the details proving an authenticity that comes from within the organization is the absence of a 'byline' stating the author(s) of an article. It is an expression of the organization's belief – maintained for some 175 years – that it is the backroom collaboration between its journalists resulting in a coherent and consistent voice that provides a unique product (*The Economist*, 2013). There is no place for superficial or sensational, ego-centric journalism in *The Economist*'s world – and for that, a price needs to be paid.

Dare to inspire disciples and create desire

Daring is the way in which modern luxury brands interact with the world. They are courageous and confident leaders, inspired by and inspiring their targets – above all influential super-fans or the 'ueber-target'.

At the most literal level, the provocation comes in the form of deeds or communications that surprise and shock, not because you are desperate for attention but rather because you have arrived, are emancipated and simply 'can'. Recall Coco showing up in a man's outfit, Karl putting models in sneakers or Gisele Bündchen playing a photo model, mom… and mistress (?) in an ad for Chanel N° 5? And this after Gisele had led a 'faux feminist protest' at the Paris Chanel fashion show a week earlier (Gibson, 2014) and N° 5 had mainstream audiences puzzled by choosing Brad Pitt as a spokesperson for the women's fragrance. That said, to the initiated Chanel connoisseur and ueber-target, these will feel exciting, if not intuitively right.

The same applies to the late Virgil Abloh sending psychedelic, half-animated, half-human travellers on a virtual and somewhat psyche-delic trip around the world for Louis Vuitton during the Covid-19 pandemic. To the initiated, it is a provocative, yet appropriate spin on the mythical journey the brand has sent us on through the years.

A direct and traditional dare by luxury brands is gatekeeping through high prices or by playing 'hard to get' through limiting quantities or access.

A more modern dare – in the sense of being more acceptable to a culture that prides itself in rejecting blatant discrimination – is the balancing of access that is based on more than money or celebrity. The above-mentioned Louis Vuitton Men's Summer '21 tour is a good example. Granted, the tour also had some exclusive in-person elements, but the main shows could be accessed live by any dedicated fan 'in the know', while everybody else could watch outtakes diffused – many by those fans – on social media later.

Increasingly, access and prestige are gained by 'knowing', 'getting' and 'living' the brand intellectually or aesthetically as much as or more than by being able to afford it.

True luxury doesn't pay influencers, it makes 'ueber-targets' rave

A brand and its 'ueber-target' are in a symbiotic relationship. The ueber-target is the brand's muse, inspiring its products and actions, but it also represents people who are in love with the brand and yearn to pass their knowledge and passion for it on to others. They help the brand 'radiate from the inside out' (Schaefer and Kuehlwein, 2015).

In contrast to paid 'influencers' or 'celebrities', the ueber-target will readily spread the gospel without getting compensated – at least not in cold cash. True luxury brands have the power to seduce and feed their ueber-target with creations the latter might have inspired, through limited-edition collaborations with partners they admire or by cultivating the kind of connoisseur talk and rituals the ueber-target likes to use to distinguish themself from the rest.

This doesn't mean that luxury brands do not or should not hire celebrities, brand ambassadors or social media influencers to deliver specific communication messages in a timed and controlled way to get things started or fan the flames. But when it comes to presenting a brand as truly desirable, few messages can top the authentic and enthusiastic testimonial of fans who are also people or groups admired by the larger target audience.

The ueber-target helps the brand balance distance and proximity, longing and belonging, which is essential for luxury brands that want to grow but not feel too accessible. If active or 'activated' on social media, the ueber-target's behavioural profiles can also be used as filters to target events, and conversations can be promoted to those most likely to engage and act. The objective is to create a virtuous cycle with fans, feeding high-potential future fans while also feeding back new ideas to the brand.

At Berluti, the premium shoe brand owned by LVMH, select customers and gentlemen tastemakers get invited to 'Swann Club' soirées at which they enjoy good food and drink and… a lesson on how to tie and polish their shoes properly – sometimes by Olga Berluti herself. Apparently, Italian linen, a good dose of champagne and a full moon help shine those precious shoes. Most importantly, perhaps, those who have the privilege of attending are equipped with the mythic knowledge and some social media footage to initiate those they find worthy of being let in on the secrets.

Over at Dior, another LVMH brand, an ueber-target magnet of sorts has been created in the iconic *Maison* that is Dior at 30 rue Montaigne, Paris. The 'hotel particulier' that Dior loved so much has been extended and transformed into a brand experience firework that is partly accessible to most – the store, the museum, the café – at least by day (Holevas, 2022). The after-hours or the upper floors, however, are reserved for very special guests who can roam around at their leisure, be fitted with elegant couture to wear for a drink or dinner, play, shop and even sleep at the place. All while being tended to by an army of discreet valets, concierges and couturiers in case of need. In other words, these chosen few get to live the Dior dream. And they will return the favour – and enjoy the experience even more – by letting everyone who has not had the privilege know about it. This is how branded aspiration spreads (Cavanagh, 2022).

An equally lifestyle-related but recent and down-to-the-road example is the high-end bike apparel brand Rapha. Founded in 2004 in London, it was inspired by the gritty but suave world of road bike racing back in the 1960s. Rapha features a mix of high-performing apparel with a modern-vintage aesthetic and a uniquely high price point to match. Style and price are two ingredients of an imaginary 'velvet rope' drawn, separating those who are 'in' from those who are 'out'– just like the physical rope and bouncer in front of an exclusive club, but more subtle and sophisticated. Definitely 'in' are Rapha's ueber-target, the 'gentleman cyclist'. Bikers who are athletic and cultured, who love to combine physicality with worldliness and do things full-on, but in style and with an *esprit de corps*. Those admitted are Rapha's strategic target: road bikers who are willing and able to spend not only on the functionality but also the looks of their gear and outfits. Core among this target are upper-middle-class men with an urge to rekindle their youthful self, athletically and aesthetically. 'Out' are those who do not care for biking but also those who see it solely as a sports activity rather than an expression of lifestyle.

The brand creates an intricate web of degrees of access based on merit and money alike, to allow new members in while preserving the desirability to the hard-core pros – the 'Raphia'. Beyond the gear, bikers can buy more fully into the brand philosophy, symbols and rituals: the motto is *ex duris gloria* ('glory through suffering') and it can be practised through a paid membership in the 'Rapha Cycling Club' which regularly meets up in shop-clubhouses and at races around the world. The various sub-tribes can be recognized by exclusive caps on their handlebars and on their heads and a custom of pushing struggling comrades over the hill (Richardson, 2017).

The 'other bike riders' comment on all of this, and the associated 'eyewatering prices', as eccentric at best and subversively elitist at worst (Chandler, 2021). When asked to comment, 'Raphia' mostly show themselves above what they consider envious chatter.

A final note on execution and style: it's substance

Beyond the dreaming, the doing and the daring, luxury brands need to pay close attention to how they execute within this framework: their style, attitude and tone.

The dream forms a guiding narrative, but it has to be retold and creatively transformed and evolved again and again to stay relevant and fresh. Luxury brands can only hold social and cultural significance as long as they maintain resonance and significance – beyond their history. And that is an ongoing exercise in style.

Chapter summary

This chapter discussed how luxury evolves with society in its role as socio-cultural signs and with the needs of humanity in its role of satisfying hedonistic desires. Luxury also responds to technological, ecological and other developments that surround and power it. The constant is that luxury is in the business of creating meaning that is desirable and that goes beyond the material.

A framework was presented for building modern luxury brands that are responsive to their environments in their own, unique way, which is being perceived as peerless and priceless. It starts with a dream which can be shared and desired. The doing – manifestations of the dream through products and experiences – is perceived as iconic and mythical, offering customers soulful transformations of their selves. But the brands cannot let the dream or its icons become outdated or stale. They need to constantly dare to be different and distinctive, inspired by and dedicated to an inner circle, whose actions radiate out and create a longing among the broader target audience to belong. In sum, modern luxury brands dream, do and dare.

Key questions to ask

- What is a brand's reason for being – beyond quality, enjoyment and a sign of riches? How does it satisfy intellectually, ideologically and spiritually?

- What is the meta story that guides saying, being and doing? Is there a myth that is 'flexible in its manifestations, triggering ecstasy, but coherent'?

- What are the brand's icons? How does it elevate and evolve the product, the associated coaching and experiences to keep them fresh and remain socially and culturally relevant?

- What tribes are/can be attracted through shared passion and aesthetic? What is their motivation? How does a brand ignite them to spread the word?

References

Anaya, S (2014) The humanity of Hermès, www.businessoffashion.com/articles/news-analysis/humanity-hermes/ (archived at https://perma.cc/AM2E-C7FR)

Atwal, G and Bryson, D (2017) *Luxury Brands in China and India*, Palgrave MacMillan, London

Au, K (2017) Why we need to recycle, reinvent, and revive the luxury goods market, https://www.forbes.com/sites/outofasia/2017/09/14/why-we-need-to-recycle-reinvent-and-revive-the-luxury-goods-market/?sh=7dc6751b78fc (archived at https://perma.cc/P87E-W6FV)

Belk, R W (1988) Possessions and the extended self, *Journal of Consumer Research*, **15** (2), pp 139–68, https://doi.org/10.1086/209154 (archived at https://perma.cc/E9BY-2XTN)

Bloomberg (2019) China's Gen Z teenagers spend more and worry less than you do, https://www.thejakartapost.com/life/2019/02/01/chinas-gen-z-teenagers-spend-more-and-worry-less-than-you-do.html (archived at https://perma.cc/7ZW8-SR34)

BOF Studio (2021) How Gen-Z buys Luxury, https://www.businessoffashion.com/articles/news-analysis/how-gen-z-buys-luxury/ (archived at https://perma.cc/CZY2-UCRP)

Bourdieu, P (1984) *Distinction: A social critique of the judgement of taste*, Harvard University Press, Cambridge, MA

Brooks, D (2000) *Bobos in Paradise: The new upper class and how they got there*, Simon & Schuster, New York, NY

Business of Fashion Podcast (2021) Transforming Luxury Episode 5: Can luxury maintain its relevance in the metaverse? https://www.businessoffashion.com/podcasts/luxury/transforming-luxury-episode-5-can-luxury-maintain-its-relevance-in-the-metaverse (archived at https://perma.cc/L62Z-TW8G)

Campbell, J and Moyers, B (1991) *Power of Myth*, Bantam Doubleday Dell Publishing Group, New York, NY

Cavanagh, A (2022) Keys to the Dior – a night at the fabled flagship store, *Financial Times*, https://www.ft.com/content/c92717d6-e883-4719-85e7-879dfa3d2847 (archived at https://perma.cc/78E8-WPQX)

Chandler, M (2021) Is Rapha worth it (and why do some cyclists hate them)? *Discerning Cyclist*, https://discerningcyclist.com/is-rapha-worth-it/ (archived at https://perma.cc/A5EB-BHVX)

Christodoulides, G, Michaelidou, N and Li, C H (2009) Measuring perceived brand luxury: An evaluation of the BLI scale, *Journal of Brand Management*, **16** (5–6), pp 395–405

Currid-Halkett, E (2017) The new, subtle ways the rich signal their wealth, *BBC*, https://www.bbc.com/worklife/article/20170614-the-new-subtle-ways-the-rich-signal-their-wealth (archived at https://perma.cc/5H3S-MJWP)

Danziger, P N (2019) Three ways Millennials and Gen-Z are radically transforming the Luxury market, *Forbes*, https://www.forbes.com/sites/pamdanziger/2019/05/29/3-ways-millennials-and-gen-z-consumers-are-radically-transforming-the-luxury-market/?sh=6899f3f7479f (archived at https://perma.cc/5EJL-XVYF)

Danziger, P N (2021) Luxury turns from conspicuous to conscientious in 2021, *Forbes*, https://www.forbes.com/sites/pamdanziger/2021/01/10/luxury-turns-from-conspicuous-to-conscientious-in-2021-challenges-and-opportunities-ahead/?sh=2d3ba4d85a9b (archived at https://perma.cc/VJZ6-VDRH)

Dauk, N (2021) Is internet addiction a growing problem? *BBC*, https://www.bbc.com/news/business-58979895 (archived at https://perma.cc/JPQ2-QWFW)

Dion, D and Arnould, E J (2011) Retail luxury strategy: Assembling charisma through art and magic, *Journal of Retailing*, **87**, pp 502–20

Dion, D and Borraz, S (2017) Managing status: How luxury brands shape class subjectivities in the service encounter, *Journal of Marketing*, **81**, pp 67–85

Dubois, B, Laurent, G and Czellar, S (2001) Consumer rapport to luxury: Analysing complex and ambivalent attitudes, Working paper 736, HEC School of Management, Jouy-en-Josas, France

Edwards, J (2017) An economic trend that ensured British prosperity for the last 136 years just went into reverse, *Business Insider*, https://www.businessinsider.com/millennials-uk-first-generation-1800s-do-worse-than-parents-resolution-foundation-2017-2 (archived at https://perma.cc/9APQ-8DC5)

Fearon, R (2021) Retrofitting older cars with electric motors could transform transport, *Discovery*, https://www.discovery.com/motor/retrofitting-older-cars-with-electric-motors-could-transform-tra (archived at https://perma.cc/8YST-E96U)

Ferry, L (2002) *Man Made God: The meaning of life*, University of Chicago Press, Chicago, IL

Francis, T and Hoeffel, F (2018) 'True Gen': Generation Z and its implications for companies, *McKinsey*, https://www.mckinsey.com/industries/consumer-packaged-goods/our-insights/true-gen-generation-z-and-its-implications-for-companies (archived at https://perma.cc/3EK7-DWF8)

Frasier, F (2018) Gemic Whitepaper: The rise of new Luxury, https://gemic.com/the-rise-of-new-luxury/ (archived at https://perma.cc/7HNP-TA9A)

Gaillard, E (2021) Chanel buys up more jasmine fields to safeguard famous No. 5, *Reuters*, https://www.reuters.com/lifestyle/chanel-buys-up-more-jasmine-fields-safeguard-famous-no-5-2021-08-27/ (archived at https://perma.cc/225H-AYBJ)

Galbraith, J K (1984) *The Affluent Society*, Houghton Mifflin Company, Boston

Gibson, M (2014) Chanel closes fashion show with faux-feminist protest, *Time*, https://time.com/3449319/chanel-feminist-protest/ (archived at https://perma.cc/QXN5-TMXC)

Griskevicius, V, Tybur, J M, Sundie, J M, Cialdini, R B, Miller, G F and Kenrick, D T (2007) Blatant benevolence and conspicuous consumption: When romantic motives elicit strategic costly signals, *Journal of Personality and Social Psychology*, **93**, pp 85–102

Han, Y J, Nunes, J C and Drèze, X (2010) Signaling status with luxury goods: The role of brand prominence, *Journal of Marketing*, **74** (4), pp 15–30

Hawkins, L (2021) How to embrace the ostentation of Roaring Twenties fashion, *Wallpaper*, https://www.wallpaper.com/fashion/roaring-twenties-fashion-womenswear (archived at https://perma.cc/RS8K-UHFQ)

Hefferman, V (2021) When you're living in an immaterial world, what's for sale? *Wired*, https://www.wired.com/story/influencers-turbo-capitalism-immaterial-world/ (archived at https://perma.cc/JLK3-YQV5)

Heine, K (2012) *The Concept of Luxury Brands*, 2nd ed, www.conceptofluxurybrands.com (archived at https://perma.cc/UD2F-SWN8)

Hermann, J and Browning, K (2021) Are we in the metaverse, yet? *The New York Times*, 10 July

Hermès (2022) Petit H, https://www.hermes.com/us/en/story/22741-us-petit-h/

Hewitson, J (2020) How James Isan started the Rich Kids of Instagram, *The Times*, https://www.thetimes.co.uk/article/how-james-ison-started-the-rich-kids-of-instagram-5mvsz9cq7 (archived at https://perma.cc/MU8W-988F)

Hofstede, G, Hofstede, G J and Minkov, M (2010) *Cultures and Organizations: Software of the mind*, 3rd ed, McGraw-Hill Professional, New York

Holevas, C (2022) Dior restores an iconic address at 30 Avenue Montaigne, *W*, https://www.wmagazine.com/fashion/dior-30-avenue-montaigne-paris-restored (archived at https://perma.cc/3LUV-UQRM)

Hudders, L, De Backer, C, Fisher, M and Vyncke, P (2014) The rival wears Prada: Luxury consumption as a female competition strategy, *Evolutionary Psychology*, July

Ings-Chambers, E (2008) Membership: Brand fan? Join the club, *Financial Times*, https://www.ft.com/content/5b556216-292e-11dd-96ce-000077b07658 (archived at https://perma.cc/7JZB-C2MA)

Jones, O (2021) Eat the rich! Why millennials and generation Z have turned their backs on capitalism, *Guardian*, https://www.theguardian.com/politics/2021/sep/20/eat-the-rich-why-millennials-and-generation-z-have-turned-their-backs-on-capitalism (archived at https://perma.cc/C6CJ-9N6D)

Kapferer, J N (1998) Why are we seduced by luxury brands? *Journal of Brand Management*, 6, pp 44–49, https://doi.org/10.1057/bm.1998.43 (archived at https://perma.cc/9NKG-BH72)

Kapferer, J N and Bastien, V (2009) *The Luxury Strategy: Break the rules of marketing to build luxury brands*, Kogan Page, London

Keller, K L (2009) Managing the growth tradeoff: Challenges and opportunities in luxury branding, *Journal of Brand Management*, 16 (5–6), pp 290–301, http://dx.org/10.1057/bm.2008.47 (archived at https://perma.cc/8MUJ-L5QR)

Korn, M (2020) Gas-guzzling Hummer could make its comeback as an all-electric truck, *ABC News*, https://abcnews.go.com/Business/gas-guzzling-hummer-make-comeback-electric-truck/story?id=68434413 (archived at https://perma.cc/PRV2-RUFN)

Kozinets, R V (2021) Algorithmic branding through platform assemblages: core conceptions and research directions in for a new era of marketing and service management, *Journal of Service Management*, 33 (3) pp 437–52, https://doi.org/10.1108/JOSM-07-2021-0263 (archived at https://perma.cc/MF4C-FCMB)

Kurzke, C (2020) New Luxury: Re-inventing luxury & premium brands for the new normal, https://www.linkedin.com/pulse/new-luxury-re-inventing-premium-brands-normal-dr-christian-kurtzke/ (archived at https://perma.cc/YAQ6-W9Y3)

Kurzweil, R (2001) The law of accelerating returns, https://www.kurzweilai.net/the-law-of-accelerating-returns (archived at https://perma.cc/D24E-BDXH)

Lambert, F (2017) Tesla Model X door gets torn off by truck as it automatically opens, owner and Tesla argue over what happened, *Electrek*, https://electrek.co/2017/09/26/tesla-model-x-door-gets-torn-off-by-truck/ (archived at https://perma.cc/SKN4-3TX8)

Lewis, H (2020) How capitalism drives cancel culture, *The Atlantic*, https://www.theatlantic.com/international/archive/2020/07/cancel-culture-and-problem-woke-capitalism/614086/ (archived at https://perma.cc/93FB-TEAY)

Luxury Institute (2020) The 7 rules for reinventing your luxury business model post pandemic, *GlobeNewsWire*, https://www.globenewswire.com/en/news-release/2020/04/28/2023285/20215/en/Luxury-Institute-The-7-Rules-For-Reinventing-Your-Luxury-Business-Model-Post-Pandemic.html (archived at https://perma.cc/R3UT-XXTD)

McCracken, G D (1990) *Culture and Consumption*, Indiana University Press, Bloomington, IN

Maffesoli, M (2018) *Être Postmoderne*, Editions du Cerf, Paris

Maldre, E (2009) Aalto Doorstop, *Unlikely Moose*, https://www.unlikelymoose.com/blog/aalto-doorstop/ (archived at https://perma.cc/QJT7-K2PF)

Mason, R S (1981) *Conspicuous Consumption: A study of exceptional consumer behavior*, St. Martin's Press, New York

Miller, G F (2009) *Spent: Sex, evolution, and consumer behavior*, The Penguin Group, New York

Morency, C (2021) Highsnobiety Insights: New Luxury New Normal, https://drive.google.com/file/d/1O4FJNKVBhFXWB59nYNR5BE4tbrY61QHZ/view (archived at https://perma.cc/329P-DUKP)

Mosher, D (2018) Elon Musk explains why he launched a car toward Mars – and the reasons are much bigger than his ego, *Business Insider*, https://www.businessinsider.com/why-elon-musk-launched-tesla-mars-falcon-heavy-2018-3 (archived at https://perma.cc/PU46-N8XS)

Mullen, A (2021) What is China's common-prosperity strategy that calls for an even distribution of wealth? https://www.scmp.com/economy/china-economy/article/3146271/what-chinas-common-prosperity-strategy-calls-even (archived at https://perma.cc/ENC4-BKQG)

Nan, L (2021) Luxury lifestyles banned on Little Red Book, *Jing Daily*, 27 April

Naumova, O, Bilan, S and Naumova, M (2019) Luxury consumers' behavior: a cross-cultural aspect, *Innovative Marketing*, **15**, pp 1–13

Nguyen, T (2021) Gen Z doesn't know a world without fast fashion, *Vox*, https://www.vox.com/the-goods/2021/7/19/22535050/gen-z-relationship-fast-fashion (archived at https://perma.cc/LW8U-A67J)

Ostberg, J (2007) The linking value of subcultural capital: Constructing the Stockholm Brat enclave. In B Cova, R V Kozinets and A Shankar (eds) *Consumer Tribes*, Butterworth-Heinemann, Oxford, pp 93–106

Ott, D (2018) How consumers relate to luxury brands in the 21st century: the changing concept of sacredness and its importance, *Business Administration*, Université Paris sciences et lettres

Pine, B J and Gilmore, J H (1999) *The Experience Economy: Work is theatre & every business a stage*, Business School Press, Boston, Harvard

PWC (2021) Global M&A trends in Consumer Markets: 2022 Outlook, https://www.pwc.com/gx/en/services/deals/trends/consumer-markets.html (archived at https://perma.cc/53WH-YZ5Q)

Rassuli, K M and Hollander, S C (1986) Desire – induced, innate, insatiable? *Journal of Macromarketing*, **6** (2) pp 4–24

Richardson, B (2017) Why Rapha is the new Harley-Davidson, *People & Company*, https://research.people-and.com/why-rapha-is-the-new-harley-davidson-3981832d83b8 (archived at https://perma.cc/H4HK-CMVM)

Saad, G and Gill, T (2000) Applications of evolutionary psychology in marketing, *Psychology and Marketing*, **17**, pp 1005–34

Schaefer, W and Kuehlwein, J P (2015) *Rethinking prestige branding: Secrets of the ueber-brands*, Kogan Page, London

Schaefer, W and Kuehlwein, J P (2021) *Brand Elevation: Lessons in ueber-branding*, Kogan Page, London

Schaffer, A (2015) Tech's enduring great-man myth, *Technology Review*, https://www.technologyreview.com/s/539861/techs-enduring-great-man-myth/ (archived at https://perma.cc/A29U-XJJ2)

Schlesinger, A M (1986) *Cycles of American History*, Houghton Mifflin Company, Boston

Schott, B (2021) Generation Z, You're Adorkable, *Bloomberg*, https://www.bloomberg.com/opinion/articles/2021-01-24/the-gen-z-brand-aesthetic-is-both-disruptive-and-adorkable (archived at https://perma.cc/8LLB-6EY6)

Silverstein, M J and Fiske, N (2005) *Trading up: Why consumers want new luxury goods--and how companies create them*, Portfolio, New York

Statista (2019) Percentage of adults in the United States who use social networks as of February 2019, by age group, https://www.statista.com/statistics/471370/us-adults-who-use-social-networks-age/ (archived at https://perma.cc/NT3R-CQ3Z)

The Economist (2013) Why are the Economist's writer anonymous? https://www.economist.com/the-economist-explains/2013/09/04/why-are-the-economists-writers-anonymous (archived at https://perma.cc/ZY4S-MXBW)

Thomas, C (2021) How Bling Empire's Christine Chiu spends her millions: Private jets, superyachts, high jewellery, haute couture and – of course – Lunar New Year red packets filled with cash, *South China Morning Post*, https://www.scmp.com/magazines/style/luxury/article/3119084/how-bling-empires-christine-chiu-spends-her-millions-private (archived at https://perma.cc/9SWN-UUKK)

Turunen, L L M (2018) Concept of luxury through the lens of history. In *Interpretations of Luxury*. Palgrave Advances in Luxury, Palgrave Macmillan, Cham, https://doi.org/10.1007/978-3-319-60870-9_2 (archived at https://perma.cc/82JP-S4JL)

Tynan, C, McKechnie, S and Chhuon, C (2010) Co-creating value for luxury brands, *Journal of Business Research*, **63** (11) pp 1156–163

Veblen, T (1899) *The Theory of the Leisure Class*, Macmillan, New York, NY

Vigneron, F and Johnson, L (2004) Measuring perceptions of brand luxury, *Journal of Brand Management*, **11**, pp 484–506, https://doi.org/10.1057/palgrave.bm.2540194 (archived at https://perma.cc/26RH-24PW)

Vizcaya-Moreno, M F and Pérez-Cañaveras, R M (2020) Social media used and teaching methods preferred by Generation Z students in the nursing clinical learning environment: A cross-sectional research study, *International Journal of Environmental Research and Public Health*, **17** (21), p 8267 https://doi.org/10.3390/ijerph17218267 (archived at https://perma.cc/SS6V-EBAD)

Wang, Y (2020) In China, the 'Great Firewall' is changing a generation, *Human Rights Watch*, https://www.hrw.org/news/2020/09/01/china-great-firewall-changing-generation (archived at https://perma.cc/J9RB-C37M)

Wiedmann, K-P, Hennigs, N and Siebels, A (2009) Value-based segmentation of luxury consumption behavior, *Psychology & Marketing*, **26** (7), pp 625–51

Wilson, J, Eckhardt, G and Belk, B (2013) The rise of inconspicuous consumption, *European Advances in Consumer Research*, **10**, pp 202–03

Luxury trends accelerated by the Covid-19 pandemic

03

GLYN ATWAL

LEARNING OBJECTIVES

- To analyse the external luxury market environment.
- To critically evaluate strategic options in order to achieve a competitive advantage.
- To develop an effective post-pandemic strategy.

The Covid-19 pandemic brought unprecedented challenges that continue to impact the way consumers engage with luxury products and services. The pandemic affected every level of society and nearly every facet of everyday life. Although the future is still uncertain, it is an understatement to view the pandemic as merely disrupting the global luxury market. Fundamental shifts have had and will have long-lasting effects. The pandemic has transformed consumer societies and has not only accelerated but also unlocked pre-existing consumer trends.

As such, luxury executives need to understand the seismic shift in the psychology of consumer behaviour and align strategies to changing consumer values and behaviours. The objective of this chapter is to outline how the accelerating forces of consumer behaviour is reflecting the 'new normal' or 'next normal' in a post-pandemic world. Although the implications vary according to the defined product or service category and market geography, the transformation in consumer behaviour is defining the future of the global luxury landscape.

Brand purpose

The outbreak of the first wave of the pandemic resulted in luxury companies committing significant resources to support coronavirus relief efforts. For example, LVMH converted its perfume production lines to make hand sanitizer for French hospitals, while Prada manufactured 80,000 medical overalls and 110,000 masks to distribute to healthcare workers in Italy. Such measures received wide acclaim and there is indeed evidence that consumers were willing to reward or punish companies for their coronavirus-related marketing initiatives (Atwal & Kaiser, 2020). As argued by Rambourg (2020, p 73), Covid-19 'has become an accelerator as it enhanced consumer perception of which brands were doing good – repurposing production sites to manufacturing hand sanitizers or masks, making donations to hospitals or charities, cutting management pay and dividends – and which were simply not part of the conversation, or came across as untrustworthy'. According to a 12-country online survey, 65 per cent of respondents agreed that how brands responded to the coronavirus crisis would have a significant impact on future purchase intention (Edelman, 2020).

This sentiment is reflected in how attitudes are rapidly changing towards ethical issues: 'One of the silver linings of the crisis is that it will undoubtedly make consumers think differently about how and where products they consume are made and whether they can trust the brands that manufacture them' (Rambourg, 2020, p 200). A shift in consumer priorities can be attributed to heightened awareness of a wide range of sustainable issues. This is underlined by an eight-country survey that found that 70 per cent of survey participants said they were more aware now than before Covid-19 that human activity threatens the climate and the degradation of the environment threatens humans (BCG, 2020). As a result of the Covid-19 crisis, 65 per cent of UK and German respondents are planning to purchase more durable fashion items (McKinsey & Co, 2020).

This puts the resale luxury business model in the frame for consumers who wish to support the development of a circular economy. McKinsey research data revealed that approximately 50 per cent of Gen Z-ers and Millennials expect to purchase more items secondhand (McKinsey & Co, 2020) and 40 per cent of respondents said that sustainability was a key factor when making a pre-owned instead of a new-product purchase (McKinsey & Co, 2021a).

Brands such as Lululemon, Hugo Boss and Steve Madden have launched their own resale programmes. Indeed, the luxury resale market is set to experience phenomenal growth. According to a 2021 resale report by GlobalData and ThredUp, the second-hand market is projected to grow 11 times faster than the broader retail clothing sector between 2021 and 2025 to reach £67 billion by 2025 (ThredUp, 2021). Indeed, The RealReal, the world's largest online marketplace for authenticated, resale luxury goods, announced Vision 2025 financial targets that include gross merchandise value of $5+ billion, total revenue of $1.5+ billion, and positive adjusted EBITDA of $100+ million in 2025 (The RealReal, 2022).

This market phenomenon has also given rise to a series of rental services. For example, the #BreitlingSelect rental service allows US subscribers to choose three different watches over 12 months with an option to purchase one of them. Similarly, Ralph Lauren's rental service, The Lauren Look, enables subscribers to receive unlimited monthly box exchanges for a flat fee with the option to purchase items.

Within a wider context, consumers globally want companies to take a stand on a range of social issues, aligning their own personal values and beliefs with those of the brands they buy. This is not an entirely new phenomenon. A 2017 Edelman Earned Brand survey of 14,000 people in 14 countries found that 57 per cent of consumers claim they will boycott a brand solely because of its parent company's perceived position on a social or political issue (Edelman, 2017). This is consistent with the critical trend, 'conscious', which determines if consumers perceive luxury companies as being trustworthy (HSBC, 2021).

As a result, luxury companies are no longer merely launching ad-hoc initiatives but integrating corporate social responsibility (CSR) as part of their corporate strategy. The pandemic highlighted the need for luxury companies to integrate 'good citizenship' within their corporate governance model (Maignan and Ferrell, 2000) as their moral commitments can enhance their perceived value as well as their economic value creation (Pies et al, 2009).

As Black (2022, p 599) notes, 'Due to the conflation of environment issues and the coronavirus pandemic, consumer priorities are changing fast and new, more responsible ways to experience and enjoy luxury must be found.' In a practical context, Kering's ESG Roadshow presentation showcases strategic milestones to improve its CSR impact (Kering, 2021). This implies that ethical factors 'have lasting implications on a company's public image, the emotions it evokes, and its relationships with consumers, employees, investors and other stakeholders' (Atwal and Kaiser, 2020).

Digital luxury

The pandemic accelerated the adoption of digital luxury. The forced closure of physical stores compelled luxury consumers to purchase goods through online channels. For example, survey data released by Ruder Finn and the Consumer Search Group reported that 55 per cent of respondents in mainland China claimed they started using online channels more often to purchase luxury goods after Covid-19 began (Ruder Finn Group, 2021).

Consumers are now more familiar with making luxury purchases online. Indeed, online is set to become the single biggest channel for personal luxury goods. According to Bain & Co (2021), online is set to constitute 28–30 per cent of the global market in 2025.

China is at the forefront of digital luxury in which social selling has become the norm for many categories, including hard luxury, which has traditionally trailed other categories, notably beauty and fashion. For instance, Blancpain launched a WeChat pop-up boutique sale where 81 pieces of the Fifty Fathoms Limited Edition sold out instantly. Likewise, Vacheron Constantin is one of an increasing number of high-end watch brands to open a store on Tmall Luxury Pavilion.

The growing favourable reception of online sales is also changing purchase behaviour for jewellery. According to De Beers (2021), diamond jewellery sales on the Tmall, Taobao and JD platforms increased in the first quarter of 2021 by 49 per cent year on year. Indeed, there appears to be no limit to how far online sales will grow. Livestreaming is the new digital sales platform that luxury brands cannot ignore. According to Bain & Co (2022), jewellery accounted for 20 per cent of livestream sales revenues.

However, digital luxury is not just about a transactional relationship. According to McKinsey & Co (2018), nearly 80 per cent of luxury sales today are 'digitally influenced', which is consistent with the growth in digital channel usage. It can be observed that the pandemic will have reinforced the significance of so-called digital touchpoints as people spend more time digitally engaged. Indeed, there is evidence to suggest that the stickiness of digitalization is permanent. For example, 77 per cent of mobile gamers from the United States and 68 per cent from the UK who spent more time on mobile games since the Covid-19 outbreak reported that they were very or somewhat likely going to continue playing mobile games at the same rate once the pandemic has ended (Statista, 2022).

As a result, luxury brands are investing in developing digital content to target gaming communities. For example, labels including Prada, Balenciaga and Louis Vuitton have launched in-game skins. Indeed, the democratization of digital luxury is a continual consequence of digitally connected consumers. The growing consumer acceptance of the virtual world (see Chapter 8) is a call for luxury brands to leverage digital touchpoints and 'step out of their current comfort zones and plan their digital strategies for the future' (Wang, 2022, p 477). For example, Porsche uses the digital brand ambassador or virtual influencer Ayayi to engage with a younger Chinese demographic cohort.

There appear to be no boundaries to how digital has accelerated to become not only a channel to reach a global audience but also a platform for creative expression. During the pandemic, TikTok hosted livestream runway shows for brands including Saint Laurent and Louis Vuitton. Fast-forward to March 2022, and brands including Etro and Dolce & Gabbana participated in Metaverse Fashion Week, 'a chance for brands to decelerate and, instead, prioritize meaningful collaborations and unique creative outputs without physical constraint' and 'a means of monetizing a digital space and generating new profit' (Ryder, 2022).

Destination China

The Chinese luxury consumer was renowned for extravagant shopping excursions to international luxury retail destinations such as Paris, Milan and New York. This was generally attributed to consumers being able to take advantage of price savings on authentic purchases but also to access the latest collections. Indeed, there was also the status and even thrill of purchasing luxury brands abroad.

Strict international travel restrictions resulting from the pandemic dramatically shifted the shopping experience from overseas to closer to home. In essence, the pandemic was a catalyst that has established a burgeoning Chinese domestic luxury market. According to BCG-Altagamma data, Chinese consumers made only 14 per cent of all luxury purchases abroad in 2020 compared to 56 per cent in 2019 (BCG, 2021).

As a result, luxury brands are reallocating resources to pursue the domestic Chinese luxury consumer. For example, 2021 saw the opening of two new Breguet boutiques in China, at Beijing's Wang Fu Central and in Nanjing Road in Shanghai. According to Bain & Co, 55 per cent of all new luxury store openings in 2021 were in mainland China compared to 14 per cent in North America and Europe (Savills, 2022).

Moreover, luxury brands are taking advantage of the development of designated duty-free zones such as on the island province of Hainan to expand their retail footprint. For example, Van Cleef & Arpels opened a flagship store in Sanya. The island province's offshore duty-free stores generated revenues of US $9.47 billion in 2021, an 84 per cent increase versus 2020 (Retail in Asia, 2022). Luxury duty-free may just be the beginning of alternative luxury retail destinations in China, even when travelling restrictions are relaxed. A June 2021 McKinsey survey reported that 62 per cent of respondents planned to return to Hainan for duty-free shopping, and 41 per cent planned to spend more during their next trip (McKinsey & Co, 2021b).

Moreover, the growing importance of domestic luxury demand has also accelerated the need for luxury brands to develop branding content for the Chinese market. For example, Burberry's art and culture programme 'Burberry Generation' has hosted numerous exhibitions that showcase young Chinese creative talent. Indeed, there has been a greater emphasis on brands collaborating with Chinese designers. For example, Estée Lauder partnered with SHUSHU/TONG to launch a limited-edition beauty gift box to celebrate the Qixi Festival and Glenfiddich partnered with digital designer Stephanie Fung to launch a limited-edition NFT fashion collection.

Well-being

The Covid-19 pandemic has led consumers to reassess personal values. Strict lockdowns reinforced the fragility of psychological well-being and it is an experience that many will not forget lightly as they reassess their real-life needs. For example, a city-wide lockdown in Shanghai in 2022 had dramatic consequences. Younger generations in urban China, notably Gen Zs and Millennials who have been brought up in times of relative abundance, experienced shortages of essentials for the very first time in their lives.

Indeed, levels of stress remained consistently high throughout the pandemic. According to NielsenIQ's Future Pulse Survey (Q2 2021), 35 per cent of global consumers state that Covid has had a negative impact on their mental health and 23 per cent believe it has negatively impacted their physical health (Nielsen, 2021). These pressures appear to be more acute among younger age cohorts. According to January 2021 global survey data reported by Deloitte (2021), 46 per cent of Gen Zs and 41 per cent of Millennials said that they feel stressed all or most of the time.

Consequently, there has been an increased awareness of physical and mental well-being. As stressed by Nielsen (2021), 'Health and wellness is THE single most powerful consumer force of 2021.' A McKinsey Future of Wellness 2020 study found that 74.1 per cent, 66.6 per cent, 51.3 per cent and 48.2 per cent of Brazilian, Chinese, UK and US respondents respectively said they had increased their prioritization of wellness compared to two to three years previously (McKinsey & Co, 2021c). The market success of Peloton (see case study) during consecutive lockdowns is testimony to how consumers were striving to embrace healthier lifestyles as part of the $1.5 trillion global wellness market (McKinsey & Co, 2021c).

This consumer trend is challenging luxury brands to integrate well-being into the brand proposition. Inspiration can be drawn from a broad range of initiatives. 'Peace on Purpose' is a partnership between the UN Foundation and Lululemon that provides a series of mindfulness tools. An expanding range of wellness experiences is being offered within the travel and hospitality sector such as at Belmond and Six Senses Hotels Resorts Spas. Indeed, Sephora's launch of the label Clean + Planet Positive recognizes the growing consumer sensitivity towards health and well-being that also touches on environmental wellness.

However, an interesting development is how brands that are not strictly wellness oriented are leveraging associations with self-care. Madhappy, an LA-based lifestyle brand launched in 2017, is positioned, according to its website, to make the world a more optimistic place. The brand, which has received funding from LVMH Luxury Ventures, is not just about style but has built a community that is dedicated 'towards making a real impact in the mental health space' and 'working every day to de-stigmatize mental health and create more conversation around it' (Madhappy, 2022). Its micro-website, The Local Optimist provides wide-ranging content including stories, interviews, podcasts and playlists that cover subjects such as climate anxiety, burnout, sleep stress and eating disorders.

The pandemic has permanently changed many facets of luxury consumer behaviour and 'encouraged companies to become less risk-averse and experiment with new business ideas' (Lojacono and Ru Yun Pan, 2021, p 249). For example, the widespread use of grocery and restaurant delivery services during the pandemic has impacted customer expectations of customer service. Sephora's introduction of a one-hour delivery service for many of its stores in China demonstrates that many of these trends are likely to 'stick'. In a similar vein, as more people choose to work from home, luxury fashion brands such as Zegna have placed a greater focus on functional leisurewear collections as opposed to formalwear. As societies return to a degree of normalcy, consumer trends will continue to evolve but many will be deeply rooted in the pandemic. Luxury executives must look back in order to plan for the future.

CASE STUDY   Getting Peloton back into shape

Peloton was founded by John Foley, Graham Stanton, Hisao Kushi, Tom Cortese and Yony Feng in 2012 with the goal to bring a high-tech fitness system into consumers' homes as defined by its mission statement:

> Peloton uses technology and design to connect the world through fitness, empowering people to be the best version of themselves anywhere, anytime (Peloton, 2022a).

Peloton is officially available in the United States, Canada, Australia, the UK and Germany and was positioned at its launch as a high-end luxury brand as defined by its price positioning and slick brand communications.

The brand enjoys high brand awareness and the indoor exercise bike has become synonymous with the Peloton brand. A Peloton bike monthly membership fee enables customers to access a range of services such as live and on-demand classes. Customers can also connect to other members. Real-time data from every class includes key performance metrics such as heart rate, resistance, cadence and output.

There is also the option to access the Peloton app that is included as part of the all-access membership, or that can be bought separately. The app gives members access to live and on-demand classes for a range of activities such as running, walking and building strength. Peloton's 'Artist Series' has added entertainment appeal such as 'Peloton x Beyoncé Artist Series'.

Peloton went public at $29 per share in September 2019. Investors were impressed and convinced that Peloton was a game-changer in the high-growth fitness category. Its share price increased by 396 per cent in calendar year 2020 and the company was valued at $50 billion in January 2021 (CNN Business, 2022).

The outbreak of the Covid-19 pandemic in 2020 resulted in lockdowns around the world. As a result, gyms were closed for business and the Peloton bike became a 'must have' to exercise at home. As noted by Peloton CFO Jill Woodworth, 'The recent spikes in Covid cases and newly imposed lockdowns… have had a significant positive impact on sales' (Thomas, 2020). Peloton's 2020 revenue generated through the sale of its fitness products and through subscription fees for membership to its digital interactive platform was $1.8 billion – doubled compared to 2019 (Bhattacharya, 2022).

Following the easing of lockdown restrictions, the company's financial performance dramatically changed direction. The company lost $815 million in the first half of 2022 – more than in the preceding five years combined. Financial data revealed that the gross margin total decreased from 42 per cent in 2019 to 25 per cent in Q2 of 2022 (Kohan, 2022). Peloton's stock market value has virtually crashed since it reached an all-time high $151.72 on December 1 2020. The share price has fallen by over 50 per cent in 2022 and is now (June 2022) trading at below the $10 dollar mark (Yahoo Finance, 2022).

In addition, a series of PR mishaps had a negative impact on brand image and stock value (Solis, 2021). A 30-second 2019 Christmas advert titled 'The Gift that Gives Back' was widely criticized as being sexist, which caused a massive backlash, especially on social media. In May 2021, Peloton had to recall its treadmills in the United States over safety concerns after the death of a child and dozens of other injuries. In December 2021, there was the on-screen death of the *Sex and the City* character Mr Big, while riding a Peloton.

Peloton has introduced measures to help rebuild its market position. The company decreased its price to win over new consumers as outlined in the Q1 2022 Shareholder Letter, 'We continue to believe price remains a barrier to purchase for many consumers and this is our latest step to improve the accessibility of our platform' (Peloton, 2022b). Peloton Bike costs $1,195 (previously $1,495) and the latest upgrade, Peloton Bike+ $1,995 (previously $2,495).

Further, the company announced a series of restructuring measures to reduce costs with the objective to improve the bottom line. This included winding down the development of its Peloton Output Park manufacturing plant in Ohio (US) and a significant reduction in their workforce (Peloton, 2022c).

However, Peloton is facing increasingly competitive pressures. A growing list of competitors such as Lululemon's Mirror are offering similar home gym and fitness solutions and the growing popularity of fitness apps provide personalized fitness routines.

In February 2022, Barry McCarthy replaced co-founder John Foley as CEO (Peloton, 2022d). The global wellness market remains a big and growing market and is estimated to be worth more than $1.5 trillion (McKinsey & Co, 2021c). Peloton is the world's largest interactive fitness platform with more than 6.6 million members. However, a quick search of resale sites such as eBay questions if Peloton can leverage this market opportunity.

If a turnaround is not imminent, Peloton could be an acquisition target for the likes of Amazon or Nike (Olsen, 2022). Can Peloton get the company up to speed and customers back on track?

Questions

- Critically assess Peloton's strategy to return to growth and profitability.
- What advice would you provide to Barry McCarthy on the direction Peloton has the greatest opportunity for success?

Summary

Covid-19 presented a range of global challenges for the luxury industry. The pandemic has significantly impacted consumer behaviour and accelerated key trends. Many of these changes will be lasting and will transform how luxury brands deliver a luxury experience. This disruption will also put pressure on brands to create new business practices that are coherent with evolving consumer values. A new set of competencies will be critical for companies to develop a luxury ecosystem that will shape the future of luxury business. A failure for luxury companies to adapt to this 'new normal' could mean an uncertain future.

Key Takeaways

- The pandemic has demonstrated that luxury brands need to scan the environment to anticipate future consumer behaviour patterns such as a heightened interest in well-being.
- Brand purpose will redefine the luxury brand's identity.
- Luxury brands need to digitalize all relevant brand touchpoints.
- Luxury brands need to commit greater resources to meet domestic market demand in mainland China.
- The case of Peloton demonstrates that companies need to develop and execute an effective post-pandemic strategy.

References

Atwal, G and Kaiser, M (2020) Coronawashing: How Can Firms Establish Moral Authenticity?, *The European Business Review*, available at: https://www.europeanbusinessreview.com/coronawashing-how-can-firms-establish-moral-authenticity/

Bain & Company (2021) After another big year, online luxury sales approach a milestone, https://www.bain.com/insights/online-luxury-sales-approach-a-milestone-snap-chart/ (archived at https://perma.cc/5YKZ-4PDM)

Bain & Company (2022) A brilliant recovery shapes up: The global diamond industry 2021–22, https://www.bain.com/insights/a-brilliant-recovery-shapes-up-the-global-diamond-industry-2021-to-22/ (archived at https://perma.cc/9BVF-4QBN)

BCG (2020) The Pandemic Is Heightening Environmental Awareness, available at: https://www.bcg.com/de-de/publications/2020/pandemic-is-heightening-environmental-awareness

BCG (2021) True-Luxury Global Consumer Insights, https://web-assets.bcg.com/f2/f1/002816bc4aca91276243c72ee57d/bcgxaltagamma-true-luxury-global-consumer-insight-2021.pdf (archived at https://perma.cc/2JB9-3C5W)

Bhattacharya, A (2022) Peloton has gone from sprinting to sputtering to the finish line, available at: https://qz.com/2114746/peloton-hires-mckinsey-to-review-its-cost-structure/ (archived at https://perma.cc/2JB9-3C5W)

Black, S (2022) Digital luxury: Towards a sustainable future? In P-Y Donzé, V Pouillard and J Roberts (eds) *The Oxford Handbook of Luxury Business*, Oxford University Press

CNN Business (2022) Advanced Chart, available at: https://money.cnn.com/quote/chart/chart.html?symb=PTON (archived at https://perma.cc/L2TF-2YET)

De Beers (2021) 2021 Diamond Insight Report, https://www.debeersgroup.com/reports/insights/the-diamond-insight-report-2021 (archived at https://perma.cc/L2TF-2YET)

Deloitte (2021) The Deloitte Global 2021 Millennial and GenZ Survey, https://www2.deloitte.com/global/en/pages/about-deloitte/articles/millennialsurvey.html (archived at https://perma.cc/2N2T-2PTV)

Edelman (2017) Earned Brand 2017, https://www.edelman.com/research/earned-brand-2017 (archived at https://perma.cc/MHF4-HM4A)

Edelman (2020) Edelman Trust Barometer 2020, https://www.edelman.com/sites/g/files/aatuss191/files/2020-03/2020%20Edelman%20Trust%20Barometer%20Brands%20and%20the%20Coronavirus.pdf (archived at https://perma.cc/92UM-Z775)

HSBC (2021) Future Consumer and the Four C's, https://www.gbm.hsbc.com/insights/global-research/future-consumer (archived at https://perma.cc/7CJD-EDBW)

Kering (2021) Kering ESG Roadshow December 2021, https://www.kering.com/assets/front/documents/KERING%20-%20ESG%20Presentation%20December%202021%2007122021.pdf (archived at https://perma.cc/H7HY-LR4S)

Kohan, S E (2022) A Bumpy Ride For Peloton With Profits Down
$815 Million, available at: www.forbes.com/sites/shelleykohan/2022/02/09/
a-bumpy-ride-for-peloton-with-profits-down-815-million/?sh=
44245eeb473d (archived at https://perma.cc/N5RD-DDNQ)

Lojacono, G and Ru Yun Pan, L (2021) *Resilience of Luxury Companies
in Times of Change*, De Gruyter

Madhappy (2022) Our Mission, https://www.madhappy.com/pages/about
(archived at https://perma.cc/N5RD-DDNQ)

Maignan, I and Ferrell, O C (2000) Measuring corporate citizenship in
two countries: The case of the United States and France, *Journal of
Business Ethics*, **23** (2), pp 283–97

McKinsey & Co (2018) The age of digital Darwinism, https://www.
mckinsey.com/~/media/mckinsey/industries/retail/our%20insights/
luxury%20in%20the%20age%20of%20digital%20darwinism/the-age-
of-digital-darwinism.ashx (archived at https://perma.cc/XC7A-PANL)

McKinsey & Co (2020) Survey: Consumer sentiment on sustainability in
fashion, https://www.mckinsey.com/industries/retail/our-insights/
survey-consumer-sentiment-on-sustainability-in-fashion (archived at
https://perma.cc/2RX5-E8K6)

McKinsey & Co (2021a) Welcome to luxury fashion resale: Discerning
customers beckon to brands, https://www.mckinsey.com/industries/
retail/our-insights/welcome-to-luxury-fashion-resale-discerning-
customers-beckon-to-brands# (archived at https://perma.cc/8J8V-UGLY)

McKinsey & Co (2021b) Hainan's $40 billion prize: The new battleground
for global luxury, https://www.mckinsey.com/cn/our-insights/our-
insights/hainans-40-billion-prize-the-new-battleground-for-global-
luxury (archived at https://perma.cc/LNK7-UUHR)

McKinsey & Co (2021c) Feeling good: The future of the $1.5 trillion
wellness market, https://www.mckinsey.com/industries/consumer-
packaged-goods/our-insights/feeling-good-the-future-of-the-1-5-trillion-
wellness-market (archived at https://perma.cc/H6LC-JNDX)

Nielsen (2021) How consumers are looking at their physical and mental
health, https://nielseniq.com/global/en/insights/analysis/2021/how-
consumers-are-looking-at-their-physical-and-mental-well-being-in-2021/
(archived at https://perma.cc/8YYU-RKSB)

Olsen, C (2022) Amazon reportedly circling exercise bike maker Peloton
as company falters, available at: https://www.theguardian.com/
business/2022/feb/04/peloton-amazon-potential-acquisition-deal

Peloton (2022a) The Peloton Story, available at: https://www.onepeloton.
com/company (archived at https://perma.cc/B9VX-K8YR)

Peloton (2022b) Peloton Q1 2022 Shareholder Letter, available at: https://investor.onepeloton.com/static-files/4e16bcc7-dd3b-40ec-acb6-840e691b40ee

Peloton (2022c) PELOTON ANNOUNCES COMPREHENSIVE PROGRAM TO REDUCE COSTS AND DRIVE GROWTH, PROFITABILITY, AND FREE CASH FLOW, available at: https://investor.onepeloton.com/news-releases/news-release-details/peloton-announces-comprehensive-program-reduce-costs-and-drive

Peloton (2022d) PELOTON ANNOUNCES LEADERSHIP TRANSITIONS TO POSITION PELOTON FOR SUSTAINABLE GROWTH, PROFITABILITY, AND LONG-TERM SUCCESS, available at: https://investor.onepeloton.com/news-releases/news-release-details/peloton-announces-leadership-transitions-position-peloton/

Pies, I, Hielscher, S and Beckmann, M (2009) Moral commitments and the societal role of business: An ordonomic approach to corporate citizenship, *Business Ethics Quarterly*, **19** (3), pp 375–401

Rambourg, E (2020) *Future Luxe*, Figure 1 Publishing

Retail in Asia (2022) Hainan sets US$15.8 billion duty free goal for 2022, https://retailinasia.com/in-markets/hainan-sets-us15-8-billion-duty-free-goal-for-2022/ (archived at https://perma.cc/BRV6-3BDG)

Ruder Finn Group (2021) Ruder Finn and Consumer Search Group jointly announce the 2021 China Luxury Forecast, https://www.ruderfinnasia.com/en/news/ruder-finn-consumer-search-group-jointly-announce-2021-china-luxury-forecast/ (archived at https://perma.cc/JUE3-W877)

Ryder, B (2022) Metaverse Fashion Week Is Officially Here, available at: https://jingdaily.com/metaverse-fashion-week-recap/

Savills (2022) Refocus on China, https://www.savills.ag/research_articles/261115/327226-0/refocus-on-china (archived at https://perma.cc/7TVB-D4KE)

Solis, B (2021) And Just Like That, Peloton Fires Back Following Public Relations Crisis, available at: https://www.forbes.com/sites/briansolis/2021/12/13/and-just-like-that-fast-advertising-saves-the-day-for-peloton-following-public-relations-crisis/?sh=3dd1f74a5b2e

Statista (2022) Sustained increase in mobile gaming time post-COVID-19 according to mobile gamers in the United States and Great Britain as of April 2021, https://www.statista.com/statistics/1237584/mobile-gaming-predictions-us-gb-gamers/ (archived at https://perma.cc/849F-9JAU)

The Local Optimist, https://www.localoptimist.com/ (archived at https://perma.cc/GN2C-BDYH)

The RealReal (2022) The RealReal announces Vision 2025 financial targets at Investor Day 2022, https://investor.therealreal.com/news-releases/news-release-details/realreal-announces-vision-2025-financial-targets-investor-day/ (archived at https://perma.cc/RV5G-FDWP)

Thomas, L (2020) Peloton says recent spike in Covid-19 cases, lockdowns are boosting sales, available at: https://www.cnbc.com/2020/11/05/peloton-says-recent-spike-in-covid-19-cases-lockdowns-boosting-sales.html (archived at https://perma.cc/MW9N-65EV)

ThredUp (2021) 2021 Resale Report, https://www.thredup.com/resale/#size-and-impact (archived at https://perma.cc/JD55-WNAQ)

Wang, Q (2022) Luxury in China. In P-Y Donzé, V Pouillard and J Roberts (eds) *The Oxford Handbook of Luxury Business*, Oxford University Press, Oxford

Yahoo Finance (2022) Peloton Interactive, Inc., available at: (PTON) https://finance.yahoo.com/quote/PTON/ (archived at https://perma.cc/3Y9Y-RQ9R)

The environmental and social impact of luxury: consumer concerns and practices

04

YAN SUN
RACHEL WANG

LEARNING OBJECTIVES

- To understand the key environmental and social challenges faced by luxury businesses.
- To understand sustainability at product, process and supply chain levels with examples from different luxury businesses.
- To understand and critically contemplate the debate on the 'bright' and 'dark' sides of luxury businesses.
- To understand and critically contemplate the paradox of luxury: sustainability versus extravagance.

Introduction

This chapter explores the environmental and social impact of luxury business from the perspective of consumer concerns and the current practices adopted by luxury businesses in addressing these concerns. It starts by explaining how the environmental and social impacts of luxury businesses have been exacerbated by globalization and the growing awareness of sustainability by consumers. It then explains the focus on the environmental and social impact of luxury businesses at the three levels of product, process and supply chain, followed by discussions on the dark side and hidden issues in relation to luxury businesses. Five case studies from luxury hospitality, luxury automotive, fine dining, superyachts and private jets are then presented to further the understanding of the environmental and social challenges encountered by luxury businesses, especially beyond the mainstream luxury businesses, such as luxury fashion, luxury goods and luxury jewellery.

Globalization, sustainability and luxury businesses

With the latest information technology and the use of highly advanced supply chains, 'go global' has become the winning route for business. According to the BBC (2022), 'Globalisation is the process by which the world is becoming increasingly interconnected as a result of massively increased trade and cultural exchange.' For instance, a company or brand expands to a new market (outside the country of origin) and business operates in more than one country. Capital, goods and services move around freely without geographic limits. Successful brands, including non-luxury and luxury, such as McDonald's, Coco-Cola, Gucci and Dior, are recognized by billions of consumers worldwide.

In the late 20th and early 21st centuries, while our world has moved at a dramatic pace to become interconnected through trade and exchange, negative influences have cast a shadow in the form of environmental and social issues (Liu et al, 2017). Integration of social and environmental protection has become one of the biggest challenges for international corporations (Gualandris et al, 2015). However, with its focus on unique, valuable and rare materials, luxury is claimed to create a dream for customers and consumers instead of reflecting on environmental and ethical concerns (Yang et al, 2017). Thinking of 'creating a dream' or a 'dream coming true', perhaps monetary cost and sustainability concerns would not be the first things popping into an individual's mind.

Nevertheless, the luxury sector inevitably faces social and environmental challenges in a globalized market. As for the social challenges, for example, in 2019, some major global hotel brands, including some luxury hotel brands, were accused of profiting from sex trafficking. Lawyers claimed in a landmark case that women and children were held captive, abused and sold for sex in their guest rooms across the United States (Hodal, 2019). In 2022, holiday cruise giant MSC was accused of using Cuban workers as 'slaves', for which a lot of evidence has been presented to the International Criminal Court, including, but not limited to, the confiscation of the workers' property, banning them from returning to Cuba for eight years and keeping them away from their young children (De Filippis, 2022). Regarding environmental challenges, luxury gastronomy, for example, has been known for its abundance, use of rare species and disregard for seasonality (Batat and De Kerviler, 2019), which consequently raises consumers' concerns about environmental impacts such as animal welfare, damage to the ecological system and the high carbon footprint incurred in the supply chain.

The luxury sector, traditionally representing premium quality, craftsmanship and exclusivity, has begun to show increased concern about sustainability and responsibility. A number of recent trends in the global luxury market, such as changing social norms in new markets and among new consumers, have led luxury brands to serious consideration of sustainability (Winston, 2016). Taking rare materials as an example, limited access to certain types of material ideally presents 'exclusivity and rarity', which are two main characteristics defining luxury. Therefore, it is critical for luxury brands to make their products stand out among competitors on the market by using raw materials of premium quality and with limited access. If we look at luxury leather, Italy is the global leader in the leather tanning industry, contributing nearly 15 per cent of luxury leather products worldwide even during the Covid-19 pandemic (Conseil National du Cuir, 2020). However, the luxury sector has to reconsider the serious social and environmental impact related to leather material. There is a relatively large carbon footprint as a result of animal agriculture, which is also the greatest threat to waterways. In addition, tanneries are one of the most heavily polluting industries worldwide, due to the large number and variety of chemicals used in the process, which present risks to the health of workers and to the natural environment (PETA, 2022).

Moreover, in the initial decades of the 21st century, more and more headline stories have appeared on various media channels criticizing the luxury industry in terms of violation of social and environmental responsibility (O'Flaherty, 2017). For example, following up on the notorious Volkswagen emissions scandal, the US environmental regulators reported that the same tampered software devices used by Volkswagen to cheat air pollution tests were also used in its diesel luxury line, which includes Porsche and Audi (Autogyaan, 2015). In 2017, the luxury cruise brands owned by Carnival Corporation and PLC emitted, in European seas alone, 10 times more disease-causing sulphur oxide than all of Europe's 260+ million passenger vehicles (Transport and Environment, 2019).

Following a series of failures of product sustainability in the luxury sector and the circulation of these headline stories in the public domain, consumers tend to perceive that luxury businesses are only about pleasure and extravagance and question the compatibility of luxury and sustainability. At the same time, more and more researchers and practitioners have begun to explore whether luxury is compatible with sustainability and whether sustainable practices can be naturally integrated while enhancing the uniqueness, pleasure and joy of luxury experiences.

Sustainability at the product, process and supply chain levels

Alongside the increasing concerns from consumers, practitioners and researchers about the social and environmental impact of the luxury sector, we have witnessed the arrival of many formal mandates that regulate governmental and organizational practices, exemplified by the Sustainable Development Goals (SDG) in the UN 'Agenda 2030' (D'Alessandro and Besada, 2019). Responding to increased regulations in recent years, the luxury sector has been adopting environmentally friendly and sustainable practices at the product design, manufacture and distribution stages (Karaosman et al, 2020), meaning that the environmental and social impact of an organization can be categorized at three levels: product, process and supply chain.

At the product level, product sustainability aims at the provision of both economic benefits to companies and social and environmental benefits to society, meaning to achieve balanced contributions of products to the triple bottom line of people, planet and prosperity (Dyllick and Rost, 2017). For instance, the use of certified organic materials is an emerging trend at the product level. The cases presented in this chapter demonstrate a great number of approaches taken by different luxury businesses to address sustainability issues at the product level. From a business perspective, product sustainability not only addresses negative environmental and social impacts, but also meets changing consumer and public demand. According to Deloitte (2021), Millennials and Generation Z expect businesses to be 'awake' to the use of non-sustainable raw materials in products, which has an influence on customers' choice of brand. As a result, businesses can differentiate their products and become more competitive.

At the process level, according to the typology from the UN's environmental programme, sustainable process integration focuses on emission reduction/pollution prevention, energy and material efficiency such as water consumption and energy management, and material and fuel substitution and recycling technologies in the production or service process (Fu et al, 2017). Sustainable approaches can be integrated in the preparation, production, and after-production stages throughout the process. For instance, in the largest emerging market, China, many luxury brands have joined the Clean by Design programme, which helps businesses to improve operational efficiency and tackle environmental issues by reducing waste and emissions in the production process (GMA, 2021). Fu et al (2017) pointed out that the adoption of sustainable processes has the potential to greatly reduce energy consumption and pollution emissions and improve recycling, considering that one-third of global energy consumption and pollution emissions are attributed to production or service processes.

However, outsourcing makes it extremely challenging to monitor the production process, because the manufacturing site is thousands of miles away from the headquarters of the luxury business. For instance, silk production in Italy is mostly outsourced to Asia nowadays because of the lower costs brought by globalization (Karaosman et al, 2020). Therefore, luxury businesses need to take further steps and work along with their suppliers to keep the process transparent, which leads to sustainability issues at the supply chain level.

At the supply chain level, an early study defined sustainable supply chain management, from a broad view, as:

> [The] management of material, information and capital flows as
> well as cooperation among companies along the supply chain while
> taking goals from all three dimensions of sustainable development, i.e.
> economic, environmental and social, into account that are derived from
> customer and stakeholder requirements (Seuring and Muller, 2008,
> p 1700).

While sustainability from a supply chain perspective can be defined as:

> [The] ability to achieve needs of an individual company and its network
> through the coordination of activities to improve economic performance
> by conserving and enhancing resources usage efficiency, reducing the
> risk of human health and safety, and improving human capabilities and
> human well-being (Santiteerakul et al, 2015, p 223).

Both the broad and narrow understanding of sustainable supply chain management suggest that, for multinational corporations, a complex and powerful supply chain network is the lifeline to keep the business flowing 24/7 across borders without geographic limits. However, a supply chain network includes various levels of suppliers covering different areas, which brings a lot of extra work for businesses in terms of resource allocation and staff training. As pointed out by Villena and Gioia (2020), companies tend to focus on their top-tier suppliers, but the real risks come lower down.

Even if companies are willing to work with all suppliers, there are still a lot of challenges, such as that companies do not directly deal with all firms in their supply chain. For instance, subcontracting is a common practice in many industries, including but not limited to hospitality, travel, automotive manufacturing, shipment manufacturing, and fashion and apparel production. Those businesses place large volumes of orders in short periods of time, and workers' health and safety can be compromised by subcontractors in various locations. Companies are not aware of worsening situations in overseas suppliers until an accident suddenly makes the headlines.

Take the example of organic farming, which is part of the supply chain for luxury food service and fine dining. When converting a farm to organic principles, there are many environmental merits, such as increasing biodiversity, reducing energy consumption, improving the health of farmworkers and livestock and minimizing the agricultural chemicals entering the food supply (Parker, 2021). However, taking an example from the United States, according to the audit report of the National Organic Program by the United States Department of Agriculture (USDA), the purported organic products are neither safer, healthier, tastier nor better for the environment, and may not even be organic in the first place. Consumers have collectively spent hundreds of billions of dollars purchasing premium-priced organic food products based on false or misleading perceptions about comparative product food safety, nutrition and health attributes (Lightsey, 2021).

Besides, there are also direct negative environmental impacts of a global supply chain. Taking rare materials as an example again, in order to derive materials of top quality, a global supply chain is needed to source and distribute these rare materials all over the world by breaking geographical limits. Inevitably, keeping items flowing in the supply chain leads to enormous energy consumption and carbon emissions. According to McKinsey (2016), 'the typical consumer company's supply chain creates far greater social and environmental costs than its own operations, accounting for more than 80 per cent of greenhouse gas emissions and more than 90 per cent of the impact on air, land, water, biodiversity, and geological resources.'

Luxury businesses are learning to manage the social and environmental impact and, hopefully, more businesses will actively get involved in sustainable supply chain management.

Luxury, environmental and social issues

Luxury usually represents non-essential and unnecessary purchases, relating to overproduction and resource exploitation (Voyer and Beckham, 2014; Franco et al, 2019). For example, luxury fashion has been frequently criticized for unethical operations and environmental damage, exemplified by the burning of unsold apparel (Harris et al, 2016; Franco et al, 2019; McKinsey & Company, 2019). The luxury travel and tourism sector is criticized for its generation of plastic waste, the environmental and social issues brought by over-tourism and the environmental impact of large cruise ships or private jets (Osburg et al, 2020).

Perceptions of luxury consumption vary in different markets and consumer groups worldwide. On the one hand, consumers tend to associate luxury businesses with high quality and virtue. Luxury businesses also often act as incubators for innovations and technology advancement (Osburg et al, 2020), while the elite luxury consumers frequently cast the trickle-down effect on those less affluent (Athwal et al, 2019). For example, Joy et al (2012) found that 'luxury brands are perceived by consumers as highly aspirational and free of environmental and labour exploitation'. In the UK, customers feel that luxury goods are prestigious and not necessarily related to a negative impact on the environment and society (Moraes et al, 2017). McKinsey & Company (2019) suggest that consumers pay little attention to business ethics in the luxury sector because they assume that the high price tag is a guarantee of ethical practices.

On the other hand, more hidden facts about luxury businesses have been revealed in recent years. For instance, in the production of leather goods, the tanning process uses a large amount of polluting substances and chemicals, and the residuals are directly emitted into the environment, including rivers and land (Pati et al, 2014; De Klerk et al, 2019; Jung et al, 2016). Livestock farming also has a direct impact on global warming (Crowley, 2018). Another example of 'environmentally unfriendly action' is 'to get rid of unwanted and unsold products (in perfect condition)'. Destruction of inventory is a common practice in the business world, but it has only received consumers' attention in recent years. This practice is being taken as a serious environmental offence and leads to angry reactions from consumers (Khomami, 2018; Matthams, 2019). If we set aside ethical and sustainability concerns, 'getting rid of unwanted/unsold goods' is designed to avoid promotional sales (a common practice of non-luxury brands) and stock drawbacks to maintain the exclusivity and value of the brand (Park et al, 2021). This practice is reasonable to some extent in terms of brand management and cost control, but it is not popular with consumers and societies.

Growing environmental awareness can be seen among consumers, particularly the young generation, who are challenging the luxury sector from various perspectives. However, opinions on luxury and luxury consumption vary among young consumers across markets. For instance, Millennials in South Korea showed negative perceptions of eco-friendly materials used in luxury products (Han et al, 2017); young consumers in the United States shared positive views on goods made from recycled materials (Rolling and Sadachar, 2018); young female consumers in South Africa chose genuine leather goods because of durability and quality (De Klerk et al, 2019); and mixed opinions on leather substitutes were found among the young generation in France and Saudi Arabia (Dekhili et al, 2019).

If a product (luxury or non-luxury) is seen as unethical or environmentally irresponsible, and these concerns are fuelled by the press and broader media, particularly social media, a headline story could trigger a PR crisis and rapidly put the brand at risk from actions such as negative online campaigns, brand boycotts, and anti-consumption protests (Yuksel et al, 2020). This negative coverage could seriously damage customer loyalty, overall esteem of the brand and business, and the value of the brand. Meanwhile, the negative perception of the brand makes customers reconsider luxury purchases for fear of getting involved in sensitive issues (Muncy and Iyer, 2021). Consequently, these issues drive both luxury businesses and authorities to find an alternative or substitute. For example, genuine leather is replaced by emerging leather substitutes which are mainly plant-based and fungus-based textures, including cactus-based material, fruit skin, or a combination of coconut, hemp, vegetable oil etc (Western, 2018; Petter, 2019; Farra, 2020). 'Lab-grown leather material' is the latest development in leather substitutes seen on the market (Keech et al, 2020).

Moreover, the sustainability concerns from some luxury businesses go beyond a mere environmental problem. For example, sustainability in food service and luxury gastronomy is greatly shaped by social and economic concerns (Vidergar et al, 2020), which affect a wide range of activities involved in food production and consumption, including, but not limited to, energy use, control of pests and diseases, overcoming soil fertility constraints, solving water problems, biodiversity, farm size, food manufacture, processing and packaging, food distribution, wholesaling, retail and transport, food storage and preparation, and disposal and recycling of food and packaging waste (Gössling and Hall, 2022). It is becoming increasingly clear that the negative impacts of the modern, industrialized food system are wide-ranging. A sustainable chef in the luxury dining scene needs to respond to customers' desires for good food and positive sensory and dining experiences while minimizing the use of natural resources and toxic materials as well as waste, pollutants and emissions, and do this in a manner that seeks to maximize staff and community social and economic well-being and environmental and public health throughout the life cycle of the foodservice so as not to jeopardize the needs of the future (Gössling and Hall, 2022).

Compared to mass-produced goods, the luxury sector targets a niche market and serves a small group of consumers. However, luxury brands are not immune to social change and consumption trends. It is widely acknowledged that 'natural resources are finite and should be reserved for future generations' (Henckens et al, 2016). Besides the changes taking place in living standards for individuals, the 'green mindset' has led to mutations in consumer behaviour and consumption patterns (Rosen, 2012; Shao, 2019). From traditional business models to common practices, luxury brands have been searching for solutions to balance 'enjoyment brought by luxury' and 'sustainability'.

The dark side of the luxury business

With a rich history, luxury has many definitions, reflecting various characteristics under different time periods. Strongly influenced by cultural, social and individual contexts, 'luxury' as a term usually has a subjective definition (Berry, 1994). Nowadays, luxury is defined as 'rare, refined and expensive products and services of high quality, as well as associated with a rich, comfortable and sumptuous lifestyle' (Roberts, 2019).

Even during the Covid-19 pandemic, the sales of the overall luxury market reached €1.1 trillion in 2021, which was 10 per cent below 2019 (Financial Times, 2022). As estimated by Bain & Co (2021), the personal luxury goods market will reach €360–380 billion by 2025 with an encouraging growth of 6–8 per cent annually. On the other hand, 18 per cent of the population (11.7 million) in the UK live in poverty, including 4.3 million children (UK Parliament, 2021). The moral dilemma of luxury consumption has attracted massive attention and prompted many headline stories around issues such as social inequality; for instance, the richest 1 per cent own more wealth than the rest of the world population combined (BBC, 2016).

Luxury is associated with prosperity, and the demand greatly encourages productivity and creativity (Roberts, 2019). However, we cannot turn a blind eye to the negative outcomes brought by luxury businesses and luxury consumption.

First, marketing activities, including luxury campaigns, create false needs and desires for people who cannot afford a luxury lifestyle and put ordinary consumers at risk of debt and misery to satisfy these urges (Armitage and Roberts, 2014).

Second, the hunger for luxury stimulates criminal behaviour, according to Cook (2017). For example, luxury businesses in the UK and United States have become a target of crime in the past few years, while spending on security services among the super-rich has increased dramatically (Cox, 2016).

Third, luxury lifestyles and personal wealth significantly influence individuals' behaviour, encouraging traits such as impatience, intolerance and aggressiveness. Freeland (2013) suggested that people from the upper class behave more unethically than individuals from lower social classes. For the super-rich, it is a common practice to take advantage of legal services advising on how to pay less tax, using tax avoidance and evasion. Arguably, tax avoidance is against social morals, even if it is allowed from a legal perspective, because it reduces the fiscal resources available to serve our communities. With access to the best financial and legal services, the super-rich actively seek various methods to minimize their tax liability and maximize their personal wealth (Hopkins and Bengtsson, 2017; Obermaier and Obermayer, 2017).

Fourth, inequity and unbalanced development are accelerated because the best resources are taken by the luxury sector to serve a small number of wealthy consumers (Roberts, 2019). Luxury itself is not negative, but it is not for everyone on the market. Luxury used to be exclusive to certain social ranks, such as royal families in Europe. Nowadays, luxury is becoming more and more accessible. A lowered entry level makes it possible for ordinary people to join the 'club' and have a taste of luxury. However, the easier access to luxury (or so-called affordable luxury) makes bubbling experiences for a larger population. Unfortunately, the perception of luxury and luxury consumption become misleading and confusing for consumers who do not have a privileged background.

Finally, the luxury sector has been repeatedly accused of environmental degradation and relevant issues have been brought into question. For instance, gold mining is socially and environmentally damaging, with local labour being exploited and water resources polluted by chemicals (Naylor, 2011; BBC, 2020).

Luxury is part of human culture, and also a fast-growing economic sector with an increasing number of employees worldwide. The above concerns are unlikely to eliminate the luxury sector. A new global economic structure is emerging in the post-pandemic period, with dramatic changes taking place in household income, social status and consumption behaviours. The luxury sector will step into a more exciting and challenging era and encounter a diversity of customers and consumption patterns in global markets.

Case studies

The rest of this chapter presents five case studies of luxury businesses from different sectors: luxury hospitality, fine dining, superyachts, luxury automotive and private jets. These case studies depict the environmental and social challenges faced by these luxury businesses and how they are addressing these challenges. Discussion questions are also provided at the end of each case study.

LUXURY HOTEL CASE   Kempinski Hotel

Case description

Kempinski is one of Europe's oldest luxury hotel groups, dating back to 1897. It has a growing collection of luxury hotels around the world in Europe, the Middle East, Africa, Asia and the Americas.

According to Kempinski (2022), the company are aware of their responsibility towards the environment, putting their ecological footprint at the core of their business model in order to create a sustainable yet luxurious guest experience. Their mission is to deliver uncompromising luxury while ensuring a minimal environmental and social impact.

Recognizing the areas in hotel operations that have a high impact on energy and water consumption and waste management, multiple technologies to optimize those areas have been implemented in Kempinski hotels.

First, they have partnered with EarthCheck (https://earthcheck.org/), which runs a sustainability certification programme for the hospitality industry. The economic concerns addressed in the EarthCheck programme include employment conditions, support for the local economy, use of fair trade goods and services, and recognition of the seasonality of revenue streams, which all contribute to the economic and social health of the region

(Kempinski, 2022). The participating hotels aim to create luxury guest experiences while closely monitoring and reporting the environmental and social impact of their operations, including energy and water consumption, carbon footprint, waste generation and community engagement. As of the end of 2021, 14 of their hotels hold EarthCheck Silver Certification, six hotels are benchmarked Bronze, and one is awarded Gold Certification.

Second, their chefs share their passion for food by utilizing local flavours and delivering culinary experiences in harmony with the environment, working with local producers to serve products from the local area. They use sustainable food sourcing practices, promote animal welfare in food procurement and take thorough assessments of their food supplies.

Third, their principle of 'protecting the environment without compromising on quality' is not limited to choosing food suppliers but applies to all vendors. According to Kempinski (2022), in order to create a sustainable supply chain, they work with certified providers of laundry products and services that manage water and energy consumption responsibly and minimize the impact on the environment from the use of chemicals. They reduce the use of plastic and reinforce recycling practices where a sustainable alternative is not available. For example, they have taken a stand to eliminate single-use plastic from all hotel amenities, and since 2020, they have removed plastic straws, cocktail sticks, stirrers, combs, toothbrushes and plastic packaging for all bathroom items such as hygiene sets, emery boards, cotton buds, cotton pads, etc, and replaced them with sustainable alternatives, such as paper-wrap amenities or wooden material, where possible. They expect to avoid 48 tonnes of plastic use over a one-year period from their European, Middle Eastern and African hotels (Kempinski, 2022). They also collaborate with Clean the World (https://cleantheworld.org/), an organization that collects and recycles soap bars and bottled toiletries discarded by the hospitality industry.

Last but not least, they help to tackle infectious diseases for the benefit of local communities in the countries where they operate. Kempinski is one of the founders of the BE Health Association (http://behealth.com/), which facilitates the prevention, detection and treatment of diseases.

Questions for discussion

1   What challenges are luxury hotels facing in creating a luxury guest experience that is sustainable and respectful to the environment?

2   Are these challenges unique to luxury hotels or generic to all categories of hotel? If they differ, which challenges are unique to luxury hotels and which challenges are generic to all categories of hotels?

3 What practices have been adopted by Kempinski in order to address the environmental and social impact of luxury hotels?

4 How well do you think that Kempinski is addressing the environmental and social impact of luxury hotels?

5 What else could be done by Kempinski to address the environmental and social impact of luxury hotels?

6 According to Kempinski, its mission is 'to deliver uncompromising luxury while ensuring a minimal environmental and social impact'. To what extent do you think Kempinski achieves their mission statement?

7 Are you aware of other practices adopted by the luxury hospitality industry to address the environmental and social impact caused by luxury hospitality? What are these practices? How are these practices different from Kempinski's?

8 Which socially and environmentally responsible practices undertaken by luxury hotels are transferable to other luxury businesses?

9 How do you think that the socially and environmentally responsible practices undertaken by luxury hotels compare to those adopted by their counterparts in the service sector, e.g. luxury retail or luxury travel?

SOURCE Adapted from the Kempinski website: www.kempinski.com/en/hotels/about-us/sustainability/our-sustainability-approach/

LUXURY AUTOMOBILE CASE   Bentley 'BEYOND 100' strategy

Case description

Bentley Motors Limited, founded in 1919, is a British manufacturer and marketer of luxury cars and SUVs, and a subsidiary of the Volkswagen Group since 1998. In 2020, Bentley launched the 'Beyond 100' manifesto, which outlines its intention to become the most sustainable luxury automotive brand in the world.

Along with 'Beyond 100', Bentley (2022) have announced their commitment to the electrification of their product lines, reducing the environmental impact of their factory, achieving end-to-end carbon neutrality and climate positivity of their operations, and extending their sustainable commitments to their suppliers and global retailer networks.

In order to achieve these manifesto commitments, Bentley operate their luxury automotive business with sustainable methods using new technologies, materials, fuels and skills.

The core of their manifesto is electrification and emission-free vehicles, which commits Bentley to launch a new electric model each year from 2025. Their latest steps forward include the launches of the new Flying Spur Hybrid and Bentayga Hybrid (Bentley, 2022). The Flying Spur Hybrid can travel at motorway speeds using just electric power, and can accelerate from zero to 60 mph in just 4.1 seconds. The Bentayga Hybrid combines an electric motor with a 3.0 litre petrol engine, and can drive on electric power alone for up to 25 miles.

Bentley are also conscious of the potential damage to the environment from electric vehicles. For example, their RaRE project (Rare-earth Recycling for E-machines) explores how discarded magnetic material can be used to make new, recyclable magnets; OCTOPUS (Optimized Components, Test and simulatiOn toolkits for Powertrains that integrate Ultra high-speed motor Solutions) aims to create a fully integrated e-axle without any rare-earth magnets (Bentley, 2022).

For leather handling, Bentley is a fully approved corporate member of the Leather Working Group (https://www.leatherworkinggroup.com/) which audits leather manufacturers against clear best practice benchmarks and stringent audit standards that are independently monitored (Bentley, 2022). Bentley is working towards ensuring all of its leather is sourced from suppliers and tanneries that have successfully completed the Leather Working Group audit process, with the end goal of each one achieving the Leather Working Group's gold standard award.

Going beyond the product level, Bentley have also adopted sustainable approaches to their manufacturing process. They began building one of the UK's largest arrays of solar panels in the early 2010s. Following a second phase, more solar panels are in place on the factory's carport, providing up to 40 per cent of the factory's electricity needs, and the additional gas and electricity purchase is certified green. In 2019, their site in Crewe was certified carbon neutral to PAS 2060 by the Carbon Trust (https://www. carbontrust.com/) (Bentley, 2022).

Other ways are sought to reduce their carbon footprint in the process. According to Bentley (2022), hydrotreated vegetable oil (HVO) fuel has provided an ultra-low-emission alternative for in-house logistics vehicles, making the factory the first luxury automotive plant to run all in-house operations on renewable fuels or green electricity. The fuel itself, known as Green D+, cuts tailpipe CO_2 emissions by over 86 per cent while reducing nitrous oxide by up to 30 per cent and particulates by up to 80 per cent, in comparison to conventional fuel.

Another project, dubbed Power Down, explores the energy savings made by small changes to the way they work, such as switching off screens, fans, lights and chargers at the end of every day.

A number of actions have also been taken to improve recycling. For example, the amount of factory waste going to landfills has fallen by more than 99 per cent, to just 3.57 kg per vehicle in 2021 (Bentley, 2022). In their paint shop, reverse osmosis treatment units are used to ensure the water they use is pure enough to give every car a peerless finish. For every three litres of water used this way, only one litre goes into the paint. The amount of water used in building cars has fallen by 55.9 per cent to 9.31 cubic metres per vehicle since the early 2010s. Recycling systems are installed to capture the wastewater and put it to use elsewhere on the factory site, alongside rainwater collection from roofs.

Initiatives have been taken to improve biodiversity across their Crewe site. According to Bentley (2022), they have installed a green wall at the factory, which contains over 2,600 locally grown plants, spanning 28 different species of ferns, grasses and evergreens. All year round, an automated system irrigates them with exactly the right amount of hydration. The wall is predicted to produce around 40 kg of oxygen in a year, helping to filter out toxins and dust. 30,000 British Apis Mellifera honeybees were introduced to the factory site, where 1,000 wildflowers have also been planted. Each hive is capable of producing 15 kg of honey, which also helps the local ecosystem.

Besides the product and process level, considerations were also made to the supply chain level, by extending their commitment to their brand partners. For example, Bentley (2022) is in partnership with the Scotch whisky distiller, The Macallan. The two businesses are working together to promote the use of sustainable materials and develop a community of artisan suppliers. The partnership will build on research already undertaken by both brands, covering responsible sourcing and packaging, working with sustainable suppliers and creating an environmentally friendly whisky-making process (Bentley, 2022).

Questions for discussion

1 What challenges are luxury automobile businesses encountering in creating luxury cars that are sustainable and respectful to the environment?

2   Are these challenges unique to luxury cars or generic to all automotive manufacturers? If they differ, which challenges are unique to luxury cars and which challenges are generic to all categories of cars?

3   What practices have been adopted by Bentley in order to address the environmental and social impact of luxury cars?

4   How well do you think that Bentley is addressing the environmental and social impact of luxury cars?

5   What else could be done by Bentley to address the environmental and social impact of luxury cars?

6   According to their 'Beyond 100' manifesto, Bentley's mission is 'to become the most sustainable luxury automotive brand in the world'. To what extent do you think Bentley achieve their mission statement?

7   Are you aware of other practices adopted by the luxury automotive industry to address the environmental and social impact of luxury cars? What are these practices? How are these practices different from Bentley's?

8   Which socially and environmentally responsible practices undertaken by luxury automotive are transferable to other luxury businesses?

9   How do you think that the social and environmentally responsible practices undertaken by the luxury automotive industry compare to those adopted by other luxury transport industries, e.g. luxury aircraft or luxury yachts?

SOURCE   Adapted from the Bentley website: www.bentleymotors.com/en/world-of-bentley/beyond-100.html

LUXURY YACHT CASE   Oceanco superyachts

The superyacht industry is challenged with a more direct impact on the ocean and marine environment compared to other industries, especially considering increasing awareness around the environmental impact of diesel-powered yachts.

Oceanco, founded in 1987, is a young yacht builder in the Netherlands, building customized full-displacement yachts in the 80-metre+ range. Their goal is to build the most exciting superyachts possible, to achieve zero impact on the environment and to create a better world for future generations.

Oceanco (2022) aim to be leaders in yacht building that is sustainable and driving positive change. Beyond building yachts with green technologies and efficiency, their ambition is to more than halve their impact on the environment by 2030, including the aims of 100 per cent electricity usage to be supplied by renewable energy sources, zero waste production during the build process and to be 100 per cent waste-free or circular across the entire supply chain.

In order to achieve these goals, they have engaged with various initiatives that promote environmental stewardship and conservation, such as experimenting with energy transition for the industry, exploring alternative fuels, advancing battery systems and fuel cells, and selecting or creating new materials to be used on board.

One of their major innovations is the hybrid yacht, which adopts energy propulsion with zero fossil fuels, using solar power and kite sails and converters that instantly create renewable electric energy (Oceanco, 2022). The hybrid propulsion system has two shaft lines, each with a controllable pitch propeller. In normal sailing mode, the propellers are set to minimize drag and prevent the shafts from turning. In the other mode, the pitch of the propellers is altered to create a lifting force as the water passes over them, which enables some of the kinetic energy to be stored and used on board. At the same time, the lifting force rotates the shafts, which are connected to a permanent magnet electric propulsion motor (EPM), converting the wind energy that is moving the yacht through the water into electrical energy. When the system reaches its full potential, it is possible to achieve a fully zero-emission transatlantic crossing where both propulsion and on-board services are powered by the wind alone. There are also material innovations, such as using carbon fibre or aluminium instead of steel, which saves fuel due to decreased weight.

As pointed out by long-standing superyacht builders Benetti (Reynolds, 2020), the complete life cycle of a green yacht must be considered to ensure the many parts of the yachts can be easily dismantled and recycled when taken out of service. Beyond new-build yachts, Oceanco is committed to working with operational yachts to ensure they stay at the top of their game, whether the yacht was originally created by Oceanco or another builder. The Oceanco dedicated life cycle support team provides routine maintenance, refit planning, complex upgrades, rebuilds and conversions. Their ambition is to respect, preserve and renew existing superyachts, giving them a new lease of life that is aligned with the current and the future (Oceanco, 2022).

Sustainability mandates are presenting significant challenges for superyacht builders. For example, several government edicts are implementing tighter emissions laws in certain ports in Europe and North America (Reynolds, 2020). There are zones that limit emissions; mandates have been put in place for shipbuilders to reduce nitric-oxide emissions from large vessels. The International Maritime Organization (IMO) (https://www.imo.org/) has been working to prevent pollution and regulate ships to be greener.

However, a long-term strategy is yet to emerge for the superyacht industry to make further improvements in sustainability to address the environmental challenges they are encountering in the ocean and marine environment (Reynolds, 2020). These challenges include but are not limited to reducing fuel consumption, promulgating the creation of marine reserves, providing solutions to overfishing, carbon offsetting, eliminating plastic and using materials that focus on the circular economy.

Supplementary reading: 'Yachting trade shows & luxury events: How sustainable are we?' https://medium.com/@accessriviera

Questions for discussion

1   What challenges are superyacht businesses facing in creating luxury vessels that are sustainable and respectful to the environment?

2   Are these challenges unique to superyachts or generic to shipbuilding? If they differ, which challenges are unique to the superyacht and which challenges are generic to all shipbuilders?

3   What practices have been adopted by Oceanco in order to address the environmental and social impact of superyachts?

4   How well do you think Oceanco is addressing the environmental and social impact of superyachts?

5   What else could be done by Oceanco to address the environmental and social impact of superyachts?

6   Oceanco's ambition is 'to build the most exciting superyachts possible, to achieve zero impact on the environment, and to create a better world for future generations'. To what extent do you think Oceanco achieves its mission statement?

7   Are you aware of other practices adopted by the superyacht industry to address their environmental and social impact? What are these practices? How are these practices different from Oceanco's?

8   Which socially and environmentally responsible practices undertaken by superyacht builders are transferable to other luxury businesses?

9   How do you think that the social and environmentally responsible practices undertaken by superyacht builders compare to those adopted by other marine industries, such as shipping and fishing?

SOURCE   Adapted from the Oceanco website: www.oceancoyacht.com/approach/

LUXURY DINING CASE   The clover rating by Michelin Guide

The Michelin Guide is renowned for its prestigious rating of the world's best restaurants and has become one of the most respected fine dining handbooks globally (Campbell, 2020). However, with the growing awareness of sustainability and environmental impact, the guide has been criticized for the perfectionism it demands, which may encourage the wasteful use of produce. The sustainability issue is not entirely new for the Michelin Guide. In 2019, it started a 'soft' introduction to 'sustainability' criteria by handing out specific 'Sustainability Awards' to recognize chefs across several destinations (Lee, 2020). In January 2020, a new symbol, in the form of a green four-leaved clover, was added to the guide. The clover symbol, also called a 'sustainable gastronomy selection', recognizes sustainable gastronomy and celebrates restaurants that are taking responsibility for the conservation of resources and the protection of biodiversity (Campbell, 2020). A switch to renewable energy is also taken into account.

According to Gwendal Poullennec, the international director of the Guide, the ambition of this initiative is 'to help uncover the most dedicated chefs, who are fully invested in sustainable gastronomy and, therefore, a sustainable society' (Miller, 2020) and 'to amplify the scope of the good and ingenious practices of chefs by putting them in the spotlight. The ideas and methods developed by these chefs can help raise awareness of an entire sector to its customers and the general population' (Lee, 2020). In 2020, 50 restaurants in France and 27 in Scandinavia were named 'industry role models' and awarded the green clover (Miller, 2020).

One example that stood out in the 2020 Michelin Guide was the permaculture gardens at three-starred restaurant Mirazur, in the South of France. According to Mauro Colagreco, the owner and chef of Mirazur, they have always worked with sustainability (Jordan, 2020). In his interview with Jordan (2020), Mirazur explained that:

> The first thing in my kitchen was no waste. We use the whole product to create dishes, sauces, broths, and more. When we cannot use the product anymore, we put it in the compost for the garden, and give it back to the earth. Cultivating our organic garden with permaculture is also important for us, to respect nature and to create biodiversity.

They grow a large variety of herbs and many citrus trees. The vegetable garden is only a few hundred yards from the restaurant, and they collect fresh herbs, vegetables, fruits and flowers daily. To Mirazur, respecting nature is respecting their client – their body and soul (Jordan, 2020). Another thing that they started in 2018 was the Plastic Free certification (https://www.plasticfreecertification.org/), meaning that there is no more single-use plastic in Mirazur's kitchen. They also asked their suppliers to follow the plastic-free approach.

Other examples highlighted by the 2020 Michelin Guide are two-starred chef David Toutain's collaboration with environmentally friendly producers and craftsmen, and chef Bertrand Grébaut's bio-waste recycling scheme at his one-star-rated restaurant Septime, both in Paris (Michelin, 2022).

However, Copenhagen-based chef Christian Puglisi has condemned and criticized the green clover. According to Fine Dining Lovers (2020), Puglisi, the chef of one-starred restaurant Relae, investigated the criteria used by the Michelin Guide to award the new green clover for sustainable gastronomy and claimed that it amounts to 'greenwashing' because the Guide's criteria simply involve asking over the phone whether a restaurant's operations are sustainable. Chef Puglisi further commented:

> I was excited to hear that Michelin's guide had wanted to take sustainability seriously. After decades of making chefs trim fish and meat into exact squares and perfect rolls, it was about time for some redemption. It is disrespectful towards the ones in this industry taking the current issues seriously. It is hurting the credibility of our restaurant scene to announce leaders to be setting the standard for the rest of the world to follow. (Fine Dining Lovers, 2020)

Chef Puglisi claimed that he is committed to sustainable practices in his restaurant, something he takes very seriously and which involves a lot of work and sacrifice. Food sustainability is a serious issue, and if the green clover by the Michelin Guide is nothing more than 'greenwashing', it undermines the efforts of chefs who make a real difference.

Although there is no single definition of environmentally friendly eating, it is usually regarded as something that leads to one or all of the following:

- a reduction in the throughput of resources (e.g., energy, water and other resources);
- the conservation of biodiversity; and/or
- reduced production of waste and/or greenhouse gas emissions (Vanhonacker et al, 2013; Gössling and Hall, 2022).

Moreover, there is no single definition of a sustainable fine dining operation (Kim and Hall, 2020). Consideration of environmentally friendly eating means that attention is given not only to food preparation and waste reduction but also to the supply chain (Pirani and Arafat, 2016; Wang et al, 2017). Different countries and regions have different emphases on strategies and practices (National Restaurant Association, 2018; Raab et al, 2018; Higgins-Desbiolles et al, 2019). What is perceived as environmentally friendly eating and the relative environmental impact of food services can vary between different locations and businesses, and sustainability behaviours and priorities can differ between businesses.

Questions for discussion

1 What challenges are fine dining establishments facing in creating a luxury dining experience that is sustainable and respectful to the environment?

2 Are these challenges unique to fine dining or generic to food service? If they differ, which challenges are unique to fine dining and which challenges are generic to all food service?

3 What practices have been adopted by fine dining businesses in order to address the environmental and social impact of fine dining?

4 How well do you think the green clover introduced by the Michelin Guide is addressing the environmental and social impact of fine dining?

5 What else could be done by the Guide to address the environmental and social impact of fine dining?

6 The green clover initiative introduced by the Michelin Guide is 'to help uncover the most dedicated chefs, who are fully invested in sustainable gastronomy and, therefore, sustainable society'. To what extent do you think the Guide achieves its goal?

7   Are you aware of other practices adopted by luxury dining businesses to address their environmental and social impact? What are these practices? How are these practices different from the examples promoted by the Michelin Guide in 2020?

8   What do you think about Copenhagen-based chef Christian Puglisi's claim about the green clover?

SOURCE Adapted from 'Michelin star restaurants go green with new clover rating': www.euronews.com/green/2020/06/09/michelin-star-restaurants-go-green-with-new-clover-rating

LUXURY AIR TRAVEL CASE   The debate about private jets

The ongoing Covid-19 pandemic has exacerbated the concerns around health and safety in air travel due to the confined and narrow spaces in commercial air flight, while travelling by private jet is estimated to be relatively popular among those who can afford it. Trying to catch this trend, Costco's $17,499 Wheels Up membership programme grants customers access to 365 days of flying in Wheels Up's private planes, even for last-minute bookings (Rosenberg, 2020). This option could be convenient and extremely popular among wealthy shoppers, especially compared to the reduced number of routes offered by airlines and the tightened restrictions on air travel.

However, private jets are often used as a metaphor for excess, extravagance, unsustainability and even criminality when contemplating sustainable aviation for commercial purposes (Gollan, 2019). Some of the primary criticisms of private jet use are: 1) the amount of fuel burnt and 2) the CO_2 emission per passenger is a lot higher than that of a commercial jet (Coffey, 2019), which questions the efficiency and the average personal carbon footprint of private jet travel. A 2019 study revealed that private jet travel in the UK alone contributes approximately 1 million tonnes of CO_2 emissions annually, which is about the same amount created by 450,000 cars in the same period (Rosenberg, 2020). A similar study from the Common Wealth think tank revealed that there were 128,000 private jet flights between the UK and the EU in 2018, and private jet passengers account for 10 times as many greenhouse gas emissions as commercial travellers and 150 times more than train travellers (Rosenberg, 2020). As a result, Common Wealth is pushing for a private jet ban across the UK by 2025, hoping that consumers will seek out more sustainable means of travel, and that companies will invest in more sustainable means of flying.

Despite the criticism, the private aviation industry has flourished and the debate has gone beyond the rumination on fuel usage and CO_2. Gollan (2019) noted that more than a dozen studies had been conducted on private jet users since 2007. According to him, these studies discovered that back in 2007, on average, the occupants of a private jet spent $69,000 at their destination, excluding airport services, such as fuel, landing fees and catering. In today's dollars, accounting for inflation, that means each private jet arrival brings over $85,000 into the local economy. In the United States, travel on those private jets brings over $215 billion into the economy annually as well as over 1 million jobs. As Gollan (2019) argues, private jets often create access to places with little or no scheduled airline service, driving economic growth in less accessible local areas. 80 per cent of private aircraft are flown into airports in small towns and communities and a single private aircraft can bring a community as much as $2.5 million, suggesting that fewer private flights would equate to fewer jobs in these areas (Gollan, 2019). Private jets are also often on the front lines of bringing in supplies after natural disasters. For example, after the Haiti earthquake, there were 715 flights rescuing over 3,800 people and bringing more than 1.4 million pounds of critical supplies to the island (Gollan, 2019).

As passengers are more aware of the environmental and sustainable concerns, the private aviation sector has progressed with some green solutions, such as sustainable fuel alternatives. For example, Gulfstream Aerospace has been testing sustainable fuels since the early 2010s. In 2019, 23 of 58 private jets that were displayed at a business aviation trade show in Geneva arrived powered by such fuels (Gollan, 2019). The industry's US trade group, the National Business Aviation Association (NBAA), has said 'the industry would continue its goal of increasing fuel efficiency 2 per cent per year between 2020 and 2030' and has pledged 'to achieve net-zero CO_2 emissions by 2050' (NBAA, 2021). Victor, a private jet charter company, has announced plans to 'define a new sustainable future for private aviation', going beyond carbon neutral (Coffey, 2019). The company launched a carbon reduction programme called 'beyond offset', which guarantees to offset passengers' carbon footprint on every flight by no less than 200 per cent. The idea is for the net effect to go beyond carbon neutral and become carbon negative. Offsetting means calculating emissions per flight and then purchasing equivalent 'credits' from projects that prevent or remove the emissions of an equivalent amount of greenhouse gases elsewhere (Coffey, 2019). Another green solution unique to private aviation is the fractional ownership of private jets and private charters, which, it's claimed, was leading the sharing economy before it was called the sharing economy (Gollan, 2019). The fractional model enables up to 16 different people to share a single jet.

Gollan (2019) extended the debate and stated that private jet travel can actually be beneficial to the overall ecosystem. For example, while flying times are similar, shorter flights using private terminals often cut total travel time by half. Using more convenient airports also makes the journey quicker and cuts emissions on the ground. Most private flights use different airports where they can taxi on and off the runway faster, burning less fuel than sitting in a long line waiting to get airborne. However, it is not just about the amount of carbon a journey produces, but the efficiency, meaning the number of passengers, and what they are responsible for (Coffey, 2019).

Questions for discussion

1 What challenges are private jet businesses facing in creating a luxury flying experience that is sustainable and respectful to the environment?

2 Are these challenges unique to private aviation or generic to luxury transportation? If they differ, which challenges are unique to private aviation and which challenges are generic to luxury transportation?

3 What practices have been adopted by private jet businesses in order to address the environmental and social impact of their flights?

4 How well do you think the practices introduced by the private aviation sector are addressing their environmental and social impact?

5 What else could be done by private aviation to address their environmental and social impact?

6 Both Gollan and Coffey argued that private jets could be 'greener' than they are perceived by the general public. Would you agree or disagree with them and why?

7 Are you aware of other practices taken by the private aviation sector in addressing their environmental and social impact? What are these practices? How are these practices different from the current practices adopted by other means of luxury transportation?

8 Taking Costco's $17,499 Wheels Up membership programme as an example, what would be the potential environmental and social impacts of this programme?

SOURCE Adapted from 'Private jet travel is greener than you think': www.forbes.com/sites/ douggollan/2019/08/22/private-jet-travel-is-greener-than-you-think/?sh=3caae4426745 and 'How bad are private jets for the environment?': www.independent.co.uk/travel/news-and-advice/ private-jets-environment-carbon-footprint-climate-change-harry-meghan-markle-a9071391.html

Chapter summary

This chapter discusses the environmental and social concerns of luxury business raised by consumers and exemplifies the current practices adopted by a wide range of luxury businesses, from luxury travel, tourism and hospitality sectors. Both the consumers' concerns and the sustainable approaches undertaken by luxury businesses reinforce the long-standing paradox of sustainability versus extravagance about luxury businesses, and the debate on the 'bright' and 'dark' sides of luxury businesses. Given the doubts on whether luxury and sustainability are compatible from consumers, practitioners and researchers, there is a long way to go for luxury businesses to address these concerns at the product, process and supply chain levels, in order to achieve balances between their economic and societal benefits and contribute to the triple bottom-line of people, planet and prosperity.

References

Armitage, J and Roberts, J (2014) Luxury new media: Euphoria in unhappiness, *Luxury: History, Culture, Consumption*, **1**, pp 113–32

Athwal, N, Wells, V, Carrigan, M and Henninger, C (2019) Sustainable luxury marketing: A synthesis and research agenda, *International Journal of Management Reviews*, **21**, pp 405–26

Autogyaan (2015) Volkswagen emission scandal now hit luxury cars Porsche, Audi, 3 November, https://www.autogyaan.com/15458/ emission-scandal-porsche-audi/ (archived at https://perma.cc/JN2A-WTFL)

Bain & Co (2021) Luxury market rebounds in 2021, set to return to historic growth trajectory, https://www.bain.com/about/media-center/press-releases/2021/luxury-report-2021/ (archived at https://perma.cc/UV87-P8QZ)

Batat, W and De Kerviler, G (2019) How can the art of living (art e vivre) make the French luxury industry unique and competitive? *Marché & Organisations*, **37** (1): 15

BBC (2016) Oxfam says wealth of richest 1% equal to other 99%, https://www.bbc.co.uk/news/business-35339475 (archived at https://perma.cc/ZV4K-KJDB)

BBC (2020) Why it's getting harder to mine gold, *BBC Future*, 27 October, https://www.bbc.com/future/article/20201026-why-its-getting-harder-to-mine-gold (archived at https://perma.cc/KQV5-GGMW)

BBC (2022) Globalisation, https://www.bbc.co.uk/bitesize/guides/zxpn2p3/revision/1 (archived at https://perma.cc/KWT2-72QB)

Bentley (2022) Beyond100: Bentley's path to sustainability, https://www.bentleymotors.com/en/world-of-bentley/beyond-100.html (archived at https://perma.cc/ZBB4-WZRA)

Berry, C J (1994) *The Idea of Luxury: A conceptual and historical investigation*, Cambridge University Press, Cambridge, MA

Campbell, M (2020) Michelin star restaurants go green with new clover rating, *Euronews*, 9 June, https://www.euronews.com/green/2020/06/09/michelin-star-restaurants-go-green-with-new-clover-rating (archived at https://perma.cc/DNL2-5D8Z)

Coffey, H (2019) How bad are private jets for the environment?, *The Independent*, 20 August, https://www.independent.co.uk/travel/news-and-advice/private-jets-environment-carbon-footprint-climate-change-harry-meghan-markle-a9071391.html (archived at https://perma.cc/R8TT-YWJT)

Conseil National du Cuir (2020) World trade in the leather industry, https://conseilnationalducuir.org/en/press/releases/2020-02-20 (archived at https://perma.cc/992W-HGBN)

Cook, G (2017) Luxury retail's war with organised crime, *The Business of Fashion*, 24 November, https://www.businessoffashion.com/articles/retail/luxury-retails-war-with-organised-crime/ (archived at https://perma.cc/L8AJ-NHM3)

Cox, H (2016) Safe as houses: how the super-rich make their homes super-secure, *Financial Times*, 7 September, https://www.ft.com/content/069be746-6f92-11e6-a0c9-1365ce54b926 (archived at https://perma.cc/E7R3-8YWQ)

Crowley, H (2018) Raw materials & luxury fashion, https://ugc.futurelearn.com/uploads/files/39/1f/391fadd3-5ade-401a-bbc4-5524ee402adf/Raw_Materials_and_Luxury_Fashion_Factsheet.pdf (archived at https://perma.cc/3YBV-WUVG)

D'Alessandro, C and Besada, H (2019) Advancing the 2030 agenda for sustainable development, in T Shaw, L Mahrenbach, R Modi and Y Xu (eds) *The Palgrave Handbook of Contemporary International Political Economy*, Palgrave Macmillan, London

De Filippis, A (2022) Holiday cruise giant MSC using Cuban workers as 'slaves', says NGO, *Euronews*, 27 January, https://www.euronews.com/my-europe/2022/01/26/holiday-cruise-giant-msc-using-cuban-workers-as-slaves-says-ngo (archived at https://perma.cc/2TK6-DADZ)

Dekhili, S, Achabou, M A and Alharbi, F (2019) Could sustainability improve the promotion of luxury products? *European Business Review*, **31** (4), pp 488–511, http://doi.org/10.1108/EBR-04-2018-0083 (archived at https://perma.cc/CER5-CXC5)

De Klerk, H, Kearns, M and Redwood, M (2019) Controversial fashion, ethical concerns and environmentally significant behaviour: The case of the leather industry, *International Journal of Retail and Distribution Management*, **47** (1), pp 19–38, http://doi.org/10.1108/IJRDM-05-2017-0106 (archived at https://perma.cc/QR26-9G79)

Deloitte (2021) Global Power of Luxury Goods 2020 – The new age of fashion and luxury, https://www2.deloitte.com/content/dam/Deloitte/at/Documents/consumer-business/at-global-powers-luxury-goods-2020.pdf (archived at https://perma.cc/99X8-TLHB)

Dyllick, T and Rost, Z (2017) Towards true product sustainability, *Journal of Cleaner Production*, **162**, pp 346–60

Farra, E (2020) Leather's carbon footprint is immense, but this plant-based alternative could be the way forward, *Vogue*, 5 February, https://www.vogue.com/article/reishi-launch-vegan-sustainable-faux-leather-alternative (archived at https://perma.cc/SQ5V-WR2S)

Financial Times (2022) What 2022 holds in store for luxury, 6 January, https://www.ft.com/content/2beb415c-156c-4b8b-8384-101a0b13a3d8 (archived at https://perma.cc/G3F6-Q8LT)

Fine Dining Lovers (2020) Copenhagen Chef slams Michelin Guide's Green Clover as "greenwashing", https://www.finedininglovers.com/article/chef-puglisi-slams-michelin-green-clover (archived at https://perma.cc/GRD7-G84N)

Franco, J, Hussain, D and McColl, R (2019) Luxury fashion and sustainability: Looking good together, *Journal of Business Strategy*, **41** (4), pp 55–61, http://doi.org/10.1108/JBS-05-2019-0089 (archived at https://perma.cc/R5P4-FCM8)

Freeland, C (2013) *Plutocrats: The rise of the new global super-rich and the fall of everyone else*, Penguin Books, London

Fu, Y, Kok, R, Dankbaar, B, Ligthart, P and van Riel, A (2017) Factors affecting sustainable process technology adoption: a systematic literature review, *Journal of Cleaner Production*, **205** (20), pp 226–51

GMA (2021) China Luxury Market Guide, 8 April, https://marketingtochina.com/china-luxury-market-guide/ (archived at https://perma.cc/8XXD-WH6W)

Gollan, D (2019) Private jet travel is greener than you think, *Forbes*, 22 August, https://www.forbes.com/sites/douggollan/2019/08/22/private-jet-travel-is-greener-than-you-think/?sh=64a3a23b6745 (archived at https://perma.cc/9PL7-4R95)

Gössling, S and Hall, M (2022) *The Sustainable Chef: The environment in culinary arts, restaurants, and hospitality*, Routledge, New York, NY

Gualandris, J, Klassen, R D, Vachon, S and Kalchschmidt, M (2015) Sustainable evaluation and verification in supply chains: Aligning and leveraging accountability to stakeholders, *Journal of Operations Management*, **38**, pp 1–13

Han, J, Seo, Y and Ko, E (2017) Staging luxury experiences for understanding sustainable fashion consumption: A balance theory application, *Journal of Business Research*, **74**, pp 162–67. http://doi.org/10.1016/j.jbusres.2016.10.029 (archived at https://perma.cc/5RDL-BY83)

Harris, F, Roby, H and Dibb, S (2016) Sustainable clothing: Challenges, barriers and interventions for encouraging more sustainable consumer behaviour, *International Journal of Consumer Studies*, **40** (3), pp 309–18, http://doi.org/10.1111/ijcs.12257 (archived at https://perma.cc/HYG5-K2WQ)

Henckens, M L C M, Van Lerland, E C, Driessen, P P J and Worrell, E (2016) Mineral resources: Geological scarcity, market price trends, and future generations, *Resources Policy*, **49**, pp 102–11

Higgins-Desbiolles, F, Moskwa, E and Wijesinghe, G (2019) How sustainable is sustainable hospitality research? A review of sustainable restaurant literature from 1991 to 2015, *Current Issues in Tourism*, **22** (13), pp 1551–80

Hodal, K (2019) Major global hotel brands accused of profiting from sex trafficking, *The Guardian*, 11 December, https://www.theguardian.com/global-development/2019/dec/11/major-global-hotel-brands-accused-of-profiting-from-sex-trafficking (archived at https://perma.cc/K7YP-Y95Q)

Hopkins, N and Bengtsson, H (2017) What are the Paradise papers and what do they tell us? *The Guardian*, 5 November, https://www.theguardian.com/news/2017/nov/05/what-are-the-paradise-papers-and-what-do-they-tell-us (archived at https://perma.cc/5MCU-WBJT)

Jordan, E (2020) How Mirazur feeds sustainability in the hills of Menton, *Whitewall*, 15 July, https://whitewall.art/lifestyle/how-mirazur-is-feeding-sustainability-in-the-hills-of-menton (archived at https://perma.cc/L3SJ-R7HU)

Joy, A, Sherry, J Jr, Venkatesh, A, Wang, J and Chan, R (2012) Fast fashion, sustainability, and the ethical appeal of luxury brands, *Fashion Theory – Journal of Dress Body and Culture*, **16** (3), pp 273–95, http://doi.org/10.2752/175174112X13340749707123 (archived at https://perma.cc/2ULM- BQXC)

Jung, H, Kim, H and Oh, K (2016) Green leather for ethical consumers in China and Korea: Facilitating ethical consumption with value–belief–attitude logic, *Journal of Business Ethics*, **135** (3), pp 483–502, http://doi.org/10.1007/s10551-014-2475-2 (archived at https://perma.cc/XDX2-6TJZ)

Karaosman, H, Perry, P, Brun, A and Morales-Alonso, G (2020) Behind the runway: extending sustainability in luxury fashion supply chains, *Journal of Business Research*, **117**, pp 652–63

Keech, J, Morrin, M and Podoshen, J S (2020) The effects of materialism on consumer evaluation of sustainable synthetic (lab-grown) products, *Journal of Consumer Marketing*, **37** (5), pp 579–90, http://doi.org/10.1108/JCM-09-2018-2876 (archived at https://perma.cc/KG7T-JWQ4)

Kempinski (2022) Our sustainability approach, https://www.kempinski.com/en/hotels/about-us/sustainability/our-sustainability-approach/ (archived at https://perma.cc/Y7L7-LWH4)

Khomami, N (2018) Burberry destroys £28m of stock to guard against counterfeits, *The Guardian*, 19 July, https://www.theguardian.com/fashion/2018/jul/19/burberry-destroys-28m-stock-guard-against-counterfeits (archived at https://perma.cc/J2XM-YHFB)

Kim, M and Hall, C (2020) Can sustainable restaurant practices enhance customer loyalty? The roles of value theory and environmental concerns, *Journal of Hospitality and Tourism Management*, **43**, pp 127–38

Lee, D (2020) What's the deal with Michelin's new Green Clovers? *Fine Dining Lovers*, 31 January, https://www.finedininglovers.com/article/michelin-guide-green-clovers (archived at https://perma.cc/7RMS-98MW)

Lightsey, D (2021) Farm fraud: Consumers spend billions on food that might not be organic, *Genetic Literacy Project*, 18 February https://geneticliteracyproject.org/2021/02/18/farm-fraud-consumers-have-spent-billions-on-organic-food-that-might-not-be-organic/ (archived at https://perma.cc/BRJ6-TMSE)

Liu, Y, Zhu, Q and Seuring, S (2017) Linking capabilities to green operations strategies: the moderating role of corporate environmental proactivity, *International Journal of Production Economics*, **187**, pp 182–95

Matthams, K (2019) France moves to ban the destruction of unsold luxury goods in favour of recycling, *Forbes*, 6 June, https://www.forbes.com/sites/katematthams/2019/06/06/france-moves-to-ban-the-destruction-of-unsold-luxury-goods-in-favor-of-recycling/ (archived at https://perma.cc/BV6B-ZQMA)

McKinsey (2016) Starting at the source: Sustainability in supply chains, 11 November, https://www.mckinsey.com/business-functions/sustainability/our-insights/starting-at-the-source-sustainability-in-supply-chains (archived at https://perma.cc/QLU6-7RY6)

McKinsey & Company (2019) The state of fashion 2019, https://www.mckinsey.com/~/media/mckinsey/industries/retail/our%20insights/the%20state%20of%20fashion%202019%20a%20year%20of%20awakening/the-state-of-fashion-2019-final.pdf (archived at https://perma.cc/7G9D-UXYN)

Michelin (2022) Michelin debuts new sustainable gastronomy icon, https://guide.michelin.com/hk/en/article/news-and-views/michelin-new-sustainable-gastronomy-icon (archived at https://perma.cc/3ZL5-Z4E9)

Miller, I (2020) A sustainability scandal is taking the shine off Michelin stars, *Wired*, 16 March, https://www.wired.co.uk/article/michelin-stars-greenwashing (archived at https://perma.cc/U4YK-SUPH)

Moraes, C, Carrigan, M, Bosangit, C, Ferreira, C and McGrath, M (2017) Understanding ethical luxury consumption through practice theories: A study of fine jewellery purchases, *Journal of Business Ethics*, **145** (3), pp 525–43, http://doi.org/10.1007/s10551-015-2893-9 (archived at https://perma.cc/SQ76-N2SD)

Muncy, J A and Iyer, R (2021) Anti-consumer ethics: What consumers will not do for ethical reasons, *Strategic Change*, **30** (1), pp 59–65

National Business Aviation Association (NBAA) (2021) Business aviation pledges net-zero carbon by 2050 and increasing fuel efficiency as part of renewed climate commitments, https://nbaa.org/press-releases/business-aviation-pledges-net-zero-carbon-by-2050-and-increasing-fuel-efficiency-as-part-of-renewed-climate-commitments/ (archived at https://perma.cc/8BT5-7QKT)

National Restaurant Association (2018) The state of restaurant sustainability 2018, https://furtherwithfood.org/wp-content/uploads/2018/02/Sustainability_FINAL_pdf.pdf (archived at https://perma.cc/TA3G-43RZ)

Naylor, R T (2011) *Crass Struggle: Greed, glitz, and gluttony in a wanna-have world*, McGill-Queen's University Press, Montreal and Kingston

Obermaier, F and Obermayer, B (2017) *The Panama Papers: Breaking the story of how the rich and powerful hide their money*, Simon and Schuster, London

Oceanco (2022) Approach: what if 'different' is in our DNA? https://www.oceancoyacht.com/approach/ (archived at https://perma.cc/Y8SD-M62H)

O'Flaherty, M (2017) The eco has landed: Sustainability gets stylish, *Financial Times*, 9 March, https://www.ft.com/content/cabf4d6a-0359-11e7-aa5b-6bb07f5c8e12 (archived at https://perma.cc/DYJ7-K38F)

Osburg, V, Davies, I, Yoganathan, V and McLeay, F (2020) Perspectives, opportunities and tensions in ethical and sustainable luxury: introduction to the thematic symposium, *Journal of Business Ethics*, **169**, pp 201–10

Park, C L, Nunes, M F and Paiva, E L (2021) (Mis)managing overstock in luxury: Burning inventory and brand trust to the ground, *Journal of Consumer Behaviour*, **20**, pp 1664–74

Parker, I (2021) The great organic-food fraud, *The New Yorker*, 15 November, https://www.newyorker.com/magazine/2021/11/15/the-great-organic-food-fraud (archived at https://perma.cc/4R3G-CWEY)

Pati, A, Chaudhary, R and Subramani, S (2014) A review on management of chrome-tanned leather shavings: A holistic paradigm to combat the environmental issues, *Environmental Science and Pollution Research*, **21** (19), pp 11266–82, http://doi.org/10.1007/s11356-014-3055-9 (archived at https://perma.cc/9PB2-CYBQ)

PETA (2022) Environmental hazards of leather, https://www.peta.org/issues/animals-used-for-clothing/leather-industry/leather-environmental-hazards/ (archived at https://perma.cc/GDP7-XUBU)

Petter, O (2019) Is 'vegan leather' really more sustainable than the real thing? *The Independent*, 1 November, https://www.independent.co.uk/life-style/fashion/vegan-leather-real-fake-pvc-sustainable-sustainability-fashion-ethics-a9060911.html (archived at https://perma.cc/2KYJ-64QY)

Pirani, S and Arafat, H (2016) Reduction of food waste generation in the hospitality industry, *Journal of Cleaner Production*, **132**, pp 129–45

Raab, C, Baloglu, S and Chen, Y (2018) Restaurant managers' adoption of sustainable practices: An application of institutional theory and theory of planned behavior, *Journal of Foodservice Business Research*, **21** (2), pp 154–71

Reynolds, E (2020) The rise of sustainable yachting, *Luxury Tribune*, 25 December, https://www.luxurytribune.com/en/the-rise-of-sustainable-yachting (archived at https://perma.cc/2DXG-FNEL)

Roberts, J (2019) Luxury international business: a critical review and agenda for research, *Critical Perspectives on International Business*, **15** (2/3) pp 219–38

Rolling, V and Sadachar, A (2018) Are sustainable luxury goods a paradox for millennials? *Social Responsibility Journal*, **14** (4), pp 802–15, http://doi.org/10.1108/SRJ-07-2017-0120 (archived at https://perma.cc/W4SF-P4VY)

Rosen, M A (2012) Engineering sustainability: A technical approach to sustainability, *Sustainability*, **4** (9), pp 2270–92

Rosenberg, I (2020) Costco is now renting out private jets – here's how that will impact the environment, *Greenmatters*, 19 November, https://www.greenmatters.com/p/environmental-impact-private-jet (archived at https://perma.cc/66NE-R55Z)

Santiteerakul, S, Sekhari, A, Bouras, A and Sopadang, A (2015) Sustainability performance measurement framework for supply chain management, *International Journal of Product Development*, **20** (3), pp 221–38

Seuring, S and Muller, M (2008) From a literature review to a conceptual framework for sustainable supply chain management, *Journal of Cleaner Production*, **16**, pp 1699–1710

Shao, J (2019) Sustainability consumption in China: New trends and research interests, *Business Strategy and the Environment*, **28** (8), pp 1507–17

Transport and Environment (2019) One corporation to pollute them all: Luxury cruise air emissions in Europe, https://www.transportenvironment.org/wp-content/uploads/2021/07/One-Corporation-to-Pollute-Them-All_English.pdf (archived at https://perma.cc/S2XN-N8Y3)

UK Parliament (2021) Poverty in the UK: Statistics, https://commonslibrary.parliament.uk/research-briefings/sn07096/ (archived at https://perma.cc/GW6H-SBEU)

Vanhonacker, F, Van Loo, E J, Gellynck, X and Verbeke, W (2013) Flemish consumer attitudes towards more sustainable food choices, *Appetite*, **62**, pp 7–16

Vidergar, P, Perc, M and Lukman, R K (2020) A survey of the life cycle assessment of food supply chains, *Journal of Cleaner Production*, **286**, p 125506

Villena, V and Gioia, D (2020) A more sustainable supply chain, *Harvard Business Review*, https://hbr.org/2020/03/a-more-sustainable-supply-chain (archived at https://perma.cc/NMP3-VV6H)

Voyer, B G and Beckham, D (2014) Can sustainability be luxurious? A mixed-method investigation of implicit and explicit attitudes towards sustainable luxury consumption, *Advances in Consumer Research*, **42**, pp 245–50, https://www.acrwebsite.org/volumes/1017922/volumes/v42/NA-42 (archived at https://perma.cc/U8ZX-6C8W)

Wang, L E, Liu, G, Liu, X, Liu, Y, Gao, J, Zhou, B and Cheng, S (2017) The weight of unfinished plate: A survey based characterization of restaurant food waste in Chinese cities, *Waste Management*, **66**, pp 3–12

Western, B (2018) Bolt threads launches its first mylo leather product with a stylish tote bag, *Forbes*, 8 September, https://www.forbes.com/sites/westernbonime/2018/09/08/bolt-threads-launches-its-first-retail-product-with-the-mylo-driver-bag/#44eba2cc680c (archived at https://perma.cc/6MMF-G79H)

Winston, A (2016) Luxury brands can no longer ignore sustainability, *Harvard Business Review*, 8 February, https://hbr.org/2016/02/luxury-brands-can-no-longer-ignore-sustainability (archived at https://perma.cc/9UG7-7FUC)

Yang, Y, Han, H and Lee, P (2017) An exploratory study of the mechanism of sustainable value creation in the luxury fashion industry, *Sustainability*, **9**, pp 1–16

Yuksel, U, Thai, N T and Lee, M S (2020) Boycott then! No, boycott this! Do choice overload and small-agent rationalization inhibit the signing of anti-consumption petitions? *Psychology & Marketing*, **37** (2), pp 340–54

PART TWO
Managing luxury brands today

Sustainable luxury and circular economy

05

YAN SUN
ELEONORA CATTANEO

LEARNING OBJECTIVES

- To understand sustainability from both academic and industrial perspectives.
- To discuss sustainable practices adopted by various brands on the market.
- To explore circular economy and relevant business models operated in sectors.
- To investigate how the circular model fits within the luxury sector overall.
- To identify potential issues related to circular economy and their impact on the luxury market and brands.

An overview of sustainability and luxury

According to Dean (2018), sustainable luxury encompasses design, production and consumption practices that are environmentally or ethically conscious (or both). Moreover, a comprehensive approach to sustainability should also strive to correct historically unethical practices within the luxury industry, including cruelty to animals, environmental damage and exploitation of the workforce (Lundblad and Davies, 2016). Seidman (2007, p 58) proposed that 'sustainability is about much more than our relationship with the environment; it's about our relationship with ourselves, our communities, and our institutions'. Corporate objectives now aim for 'the creation of resilient organizations through integrated economic, social and environmental systems' (Hockerts and Wüstenhagen, 2010).

Traditionally, luxury and sustainability have not been considered a good fit (Low, 2010). Some academic studies show that sustainable luxury products were perceived to be of lower quality than their traditionally manufactured counterparts (Kapferer and Michaut, 2014; Torelli et al, 2012). Several studies have described luxury as the polar opposite of sustainability: superfluous, ostentatious and of no utilitarian use (Guercini and Ranfagni, 2013; Beckham and Voyer, 2014; Torelli et al, 2012). Consumers placed the luxury industry last in a list of product categories linked with a sustainable agenda, below both the financial and petrochemical sectors, according to a survey published by Salon (2014). Luxury brands often confirmed negative perceptions with their actions: Burberry destroyed unsold products worth millions of dollars as recently as 2018 (Paton, 2018) and Dior scored zero in Fashion Revolution's Transparency Index, a ranking of companies according to the extent to which they disclose their social and environmental policies, practices and impact (Rivera, 2017).

There has been a slow change in direction as luxury consumers increasingly demand 'convincing answers to questions of environmental and social responsibility' (Bendell and Kleanthous, 2007). The luxury industry has also faced growing demand, resulting in a scarcity of resources, thereby driving the need for conservation (Öymen Kale and Öztürk, 2016; Depeyre et al, 2018). Being behind the curve on sustainability was not a desirable position, although perhaps it has also been the result of a larger trend that has emerged in the last two decades, namely the accessibility of luxury goods for the 'happy many' rather than the 'privileged few' (Moraes et al,

2017). Luxury consumers' growing concern for the environmental and societal impact of their purchases has encouraged many brands to develop more sustainable business practices (Li and Leonas, 2019; Athwal et al, 2019), albeit later than might have been expected, considering that luxury tends to be market-driving rather than market-driven and often acts as a model for the industry.

There is now wide consensus among academics and practitioners that ethical and sustainable business practices will ultimately ensure a luxury brand's long-term success (De Angelis et al, 2017; Arrigo, 2018; D'Arpizio et al, 2021).

The academic perspective

Luxury consumers' perceptions of sustainable products and practices have been researched more extensively since 2010 (Griskevicius et al, 2010; Cervellon and Shammas, 2013; Hennings et al, 2013). Luxury brand values are linked to status and feeding one's ego (Cervellon and Shammas, 2013), whereas concern for issues related to the environment or ethical business practices is seen to represent altruism (Griskevicius et al, 2010). Several studies have shown that luxury consumers do not actively look for sustainable products, assuming that the 'luxury' component excludes unsustainable practices (Davies et al, 2012; Janssen et al, 2015; Moraes et al, 2017). By focusing on heritage and quality, luxury brands distance themselves from images of pollution, scarce resources and global warming (Joy et al, 2012). It can also be argued that luxury is inherently sustainable since it has 'lasting worth' and durability (Kapferer and Michaut, 2014).

However, the same studies also show that there are consumers who wish to communicate an ethical identity through their luxury purchases (Davies et al, 2012). Cervellon and Shammas (2013) found that some consumers actually want social responsibility to be expressed through their choices of specific luxury products. Hennings et al (2013) suggested that consumers are increasingly evaluating brands that cause social or environmental damage as no longer best in class. It should also be noted that there is a new generation of consumers driving luxury sales. Millennials and Generation Z are forecast to account for 40 per cent of the global personal luxury goods market by 2035 according to Bain & Co, contributing 130 per cent of market growth between 2021 and 2025. This cohort demand sustainable practices, messaging and products aligned with the image they wish to broadcast on social media where, as they 'perceive themselves as brands', they wish to position their identity accordingly. Generation Z have been described as the 'intentional' (as opposed to aspirational) consumer generation as they ponder every purchase and carefully consider whether a particular brand fits with their values (Danziger, 2022). Almost 60 per cent of Millennials express concern over climate change and over 70 per cent are willing to pay more for sustainably made goods (Passport, 2020). The use of recycled materials in luxury manufacture is well received by Millennials (Rolling and Sadachar, 2018). It should also be noted, however, that luxury buyers are not prepared to compromise on quality or design in favour of a sustainable product. A study by Sun et al (2022) showed that perceived aesthetics influence the purchase intention of vegan leather luxury, and buyers will not accept these sustainable products if they do not also exhibit high quality and design excellence, as with any luxury purchase. Luxury buyers also show a preference for sustainable products when their design is perceived to be consistent with the brand identity as opposed to mimicking born-sustainable brands (De Angelis et al, 2017). The brand's unique identity is also important, as ethical and sustainable initiatives appear to be more successful when they are communicated in association with inconspicuous, as opposed to conspicuous, luxury brands (Janssen et al, 2015).

Interestingly, the younger generations' preferences appear to influence older generations, who are also moving to a more sustainable approach with their luxury buying behaviour (Scalefast, 2021). Another accelerator has been the Covid-19 pandemic, which required lockdowns that drove many luxury consumers to reassess their values (Connell, 2021) and begin to examine the environmental and social footprints of brands.

The industry perspective

The luxury industry includes multiple product and service categories, from fashion and accessories to jewellery, cars, hospitality and many more. Sustainability is relevant to every category, with many issues common to all.

Environmental damage

Gold mining uses large quantities of hazardous chemicals such as mercury and sodium cyanide. Producers often use a technique which creates high quantities of mercury vapour emissions as well as liquid and solid toxic waste. Korte and Coulston (1998) estimated that a minimum of 1 kilogram of mercury is emitted for every kilogram of gold produced with the 'amalgamation' technique often used in Brazil, and therefore thousands of tonnes of mercury have been discharged from local manufacturers into the forest and urban environments in Latin America.

The traditional leather tanning process used by most of the leather industry is among the most toxic in all of the fashion supply chain; the chemicals used to tan the leather are not biodegradable, and contaminate soil and rivers if not treated. Vegetable tanning, which uses natural agents, takes longer to complete and is more expensive than standard tanning.

Ethical and provenance issues

Diamond mining has a history of causing conflict due to the financial incentives involved. Diamonds have often supplied additional motivation and funding for African conflicts, resulting in the deaths of millions of people. Millions more have become refugees (Bendell and Kleanthous, 2007). Angola, the Democratic Republic of Congo (DRC), Liberia and Sierra Leone are still recovering from conflicts of this nature. Diamonds trafficked out of some war-torn regions are still being used for money laundering, tax fraud and organized crime, according to Global Witness (2022), a human rights charity.

'Jewellery, Swiss watches, and other compact but costly commodities are often used as a parallel currency by criminals since they can readily be resold and are difficult to trace' (Bendell and Kleanthous, 2007). As a result, the EU has added sellers of high-value products, valued at €15,000 (£10,400) or more, to the list of organizations that must implement measures to avoid assisting money launderers in moving funds.

As reported by the Business & Human Rights Resource Centre (2021), KnowTheChain, an organization that reports on employment issues, published an Apparel and Footwear Benchmark Report (2021) ranking some of the world's major fashion companies on a scale of 0 to 100 in terms of their efforts to fight forced labour, with 100 representing the best practices. Luxury apparel brands scored particularly poorly, averaging 31/100. Italian luxury fashion house Prada's score was just 5/100, while peers such as the French luxury goods corporate Kering managed 41/100 and the German upper premium brand Hugo Boss 49/100.

Excessive consumption

The United Nations Emissions Gap Report (United Nations, 2020) estimates that 10 per cent of the world's population emits almost half of the world's carbon pollution. The wealthiest 1 per cent globally, around 70 million people, account for 15 per cent of global emissions, which is more than the 3.5 billion people in the lowest 50 per cent income bracket. According to Oswald et al (2020), households in the top 10 per cent of income earners consume roughly 45 per cent of all energy for land transportation and around 75 per cent of all energy for aviation, compared to 10 per cent and 5 per cent for the lowest 50 per cent of households, respectively. Similarly, Ivanova and Wood (2020) show that transportation accounts for a considerable portion of the emissions of the highest-emitting European Union households.

Luxury travel and tourism, with its focus on private travel, exotic resorts in hard-to-reach destinations and excessive consumption of resources, accompanied by unthinking disposal of items which could be reused, has long been a target for appeals to develop more sustainable practices. Luxury travellers consume four times more water per day than the typical European and more than other types of travel, according to the Travel Foundation, an independent charity which advocates climate-positive tourism (Robertson, 2017).

Sustainable practice

Stella McCartney pioneered a cruelty-free, ethical approach when she founded her fashion brand in 2001. In more recent years, a growing number of luxury brands such as Gucci, Versace and Michael Kors have stopped using animal fur in favour of synthetics. Starting with the Fall/Winter collection 2022, the 13 Kering group fashion brands will no longer employ animal fur in any product and the group has also introduced metal-free tanning in its directly owned tanneries.

Unlike faux fur, leather alternatives have yet to gain traction in luxury fashion; vegan leather makes up just 2 per cent of women's leather goods produced by luxury brands, led (again) by Stella McCartney. In 2021, Prada launched a collection of handbags and other accessories, Prada Re-Nylon, using regenerated fibre, but all of their other collections are leather based. The niche luxury brand von Holzhausen uses plant-based leather made from bamboo, and the brand So Long Marianne won the Best Ethical Luxury Brand award 2021 with their PETA (People for the Ethical Treatment of Animals) certified vegan leather products (Sun et al, 2022). Veja launched a biodegradable, vegan version of its popular V-10 sneaker using leather-like corn starch waste in 2021, and sales of niche brands using vegan leather, including Nanushka and Awake, are increasing rapidly (Cattaneo, 2022).

Luxury retail is also a showcase for sustainable practice: Prada and Saint Laurent, for example, have obtained the Leadership in Energy and Environmental Design (LEED) Platinum Certification for a number of their global flagship stores designed with low-energy lighting, minimal water consumption and better indoor air quality. All of LVMH's logistics centres have implemented standards to ensure optimal working conditions for employees and their corporate offices have been modified to comply with LEED standards. Bottega Veneta's headquarters are equipped with 12,960 square feet of solar panels, a water recycling system and limited external lighting, all of which significantly reduce their environmental footprint. Arrigo (2018) found that in-store interactions at these locations are very effective, as the atmosphere of a luxury flagship provides an immersive experience for the customer. The brand can use verbal and non-verbal communications to promote sustainable development values to customers directly.

Sustainability is also relevant beyond personal luxury and is being embraced across industries (Cattaneo, 2022). Six Senses resorts started to reduce disposable plastic use in the 1990s, offering their own-brand water in glass bottles, and more recently eliminating plastic straws and disposable food and beverage containers from all properties in 2016. Their stated objective is to be plastic-free by the end of 2022 and they were one of the first signatories of the Global Tourism Plastics Initiative, led by the UN Environment Programme and UN World Tourism Organization, in collaboration with the Ellen MacArthur Foundation. New York-based brand Stefano Navi has developed a line of sustainable jewellery using certified lab-grown diamonds and recycled gold, while London-based Vashi abides by the Kimberley Process, meaning all of their diamonds are conflict-free, while the metal is all 100 per cent recycled and the business model is built around minimizing waste and carbon footprint.

Sustainability watchdog Positive Luxury was established in 2011 with the aim of engaging brands in environmental projects (Positive Luxury, 2022). It created the Butterfly Mark as an accredited certification for brands that meet specific sustainability standards, and has a community of over 150 global members, from Dior Couture to Krug and IWC. The Butterfly Mark certification is built around an ESG+ framework (Environmental, Social, Governance and Innovation). Each brand is given 'positive actions' according to its activity, turnover, and the location of its operations and supply chain.

The Fashion Pact, a worldwide federation of luxury brands, launched in 2019 (The Fashion Pact, 2020) with the commitment to act across three pillars of environmental urgency: addressing global warming, restoring biodiversity and protecting the oceans (Farra,

2019). The signatories represented one-third of the fashion industry in 2022 and have made a commitment to implement science-based targets for climate, to achieve net-zero carbon impact by 2050, generating new revenue and long-term competitive advantage.

An overview of circular economy

Circular economy (CE) has been drawing significant attention from both governments and businesses around the world since 2010 (Shivarov, 2020). Strongly promoted in political circles and by industrial groups, circular economy seems to provide a path to sustainable development by changing the mode of economic activities. Increasingly, academic researchers and industrial practitioners are showing interest in 'circulating materials' in the global economy. The conventional view of economic activity focused on a process of 'take, make and dispose' (Whalen and Whalen, 2020) is falling out of favour.

What is circular economy (CE)?

The ideas behind circular economy first emerged around the 1970s, representing a transition from 'resource extraction, manufacturing, consumption and disposal of products' to 'materials circulating' within the economy (Stahel, 2019). One widely used definition was proposed by the Ellen MacArthur Foundation: 'Circular economy is an industrial economy that is restorative or regenerative by intention and design' (Ellen MacArthur Foundation, 2013, p 14). Another definition, focusing on practical business approaches, takes circular economy as a blanket term covering relevant activities in production (e.g. reduce, reuse and recycle materials), distribution and consumption processes (Blomsma and Brennan, 2017). Similarly, Korhonen et al (2018) suggest that circular economy is a cluster concept accommodating various attributes across sectors and drawing interest from the whole of society.

Inevitably, many more different definitions are found in existing literature. The argument on the definition of circular economy is ongoing and the concept is open to modification from different perspectives. Kirchherr et al (2017) reviewed 114 definitions of circular economy and indicated 'CE is most frequently depicted as a combination of reduce, reuse and recycle activities, whereas it is oftentimes not highlighted that CE necessitates a systemic shift.' This definition clearly emphasizes a systemic change, which reduces the demand for raw materials and makes room to reuse and recycle products (Sharma et al, 2021; Kuo and Chang, 2021). Furthermore, this definition inspires both individuals and organizations to explore possibilities to respond to challenges at economic and social levels.

Clearly, circular economy is related to CSR and sustainability. The key themes under circular economy lie in: usage of secondary raw materials (Schreck and Wagner, 2017); reuse and recycling of products (Grohens et al, 2013); life cycle extension (Tukker, 2015); the minimization of waste (Wang et al, 2015); industrial symbiosis (Homrich et al, 2018); and renewal of materials (Ghisellini et al, 2016). As one of the popular notions promoted by the European Union (EU) in the past five years, circular economy is suggested as an approach towards the circular economic model, which is expected to reduce the damage caused by climate change (European Commission, 2015; 2020).

In the following sections, we will discuss relevant business models, circular luxury, and critiques of circular economy and industrial practice. Examples and cases are included for further discussion. A few questions are proposed to encourage further exploration in this area.

Circular economy business model

In the first decades of the 21st century, increasing numbers of researchers and practitioners have turned their attention to the circular economy, for instance, calling attention to the state of the planet, emphasizing the importance of ecological systems and promoting ways to live in harmony with our environment. Related to other burning issues, such as climate change and sustainability, circular economy has captured headlines and become a top story across various media channels. However, confused, frustrated and overwhelmed individuals (even organizations) find it extremely challenging to understand circular economy and related business models.

A critical review of literature and cases conducted by Whalen and Whalen (2020) summarized three types of Circular Business Models (CBMs): pay-per-use, product life extension and resource value extension.

Pay-per-use

As this phrase suggests, with pay-per-use a consumer enjoys the benefits of a product without owning the product. Clearly, this is not a new business model. From formal-wear rental to car hire, consumers across markets are already familiar with this consumption model. Taking one step further towards circular economy, companies not only focus on how to maximize the usage of current products, but also consider how to design and manufacture future products that are long-lasting and possibly can be reprocessed into new products.

'Product as a service' is the approach adopted by many companies across several sectors, including Signify (which was called Philips Lighting before 2019). Inspired by a client who wanted to buy light and lighting as a service (intangible), rather than a product (tangible), the concept of 'Pay Per Lux' was born, and Philips' innovative solution is to provide the exact amount of light to serve professional clients and individual consumers (no more, no less). According to the CEO of Philips, 'the conventional model of customer ownership of the product is replaced by customer access to the product, Paying for Performance' (Philips, 2013). This innovative business model allows customers to have the best lighting solution without owning the hardware. The National Union of Students (NUS) is one of the customers in the UK embracing the 'Pay Per Lux' solution and 'cradle-to-cradle' lighting successfully delivered by Philips (McManan-Smith, 2014; Philips, 2014).

Following the success of the pay-per-use model, another business opportunity emerged. Platforms, particularly digital platforms using information to match consumers' demand with products/services on the market, rapidly became part of our daily life. For example, Uber is a US provider of mobility as a service. 'Get in the driver's seat and get paid' is made possible on this platform, which has the largest network in the world of active riders (Uber, 2022). Sharing platforms have been introduced to more and more sectors and markets, e.g. a rental service for designer handbags and accessories. With a low cost (as a rental fee, compared to the purchase price of the product), consumers enjoy the benefits of the rental product and the convenience of switching to different items as they like (e.g. using a different handbag every day/week).

Product life extension

Terms we use every day, such as reuse, repair, refill and recondition, are brought together under the concept of product life extension. The purpose is to better benefit the whole of society through extending the lifespan of products and minimizing product disposal. Across industries, hands-on approaches are taken to an organizational level by engaging in repair, refurbishment or remanufacture (Kiorboe et al, 2015).

Nudie Jeans, a Swedish brand, has led the way in extending product life for more than 20 years (Nudie Jeans, 2021). Specializing in denim jeans, the company successfully created its brand identity by using 'Earth-loving materials' and providing 'free repair forever'. According to Nudie Jeans (2021), organic fair-trade and recycled cotton is used, and the production remains transparent. Further approaches towards product life extension include a free repair service, reselling second-hand products and recycling worn-out items. 'You decide how far they go' (Nudie Jeans, 2017) is the challenge presented by Nudie Jeans to its customers: the lifespan of a pair of Nudie Jeans is in the hands of the individual customer.

Some companies engage in the process of extending product life from a unique perspective, by facilitating products moving from one owner to another. For instance, eBay, a multinational e-commerce corporation, became the world's online marketplace by facilitating consumer-to-consumer (C2C) and business-to-consumer (B2C) sales through its website since 1995 (eBay, 2022). According to eBay's (2020) Recommence Report, 72 per cent of US eBay sellers said that buying pre-owned products has become more common in recent years, and 81 per cent of Gen Z felt that buying pre-owned goods had become more common in 2020. 39 per cent of German sellers surveyed said that they sell pre-owned items because of the positive environmental impact. In 2020–2021, 720,000 metric tonnes of carbon emissions were conserved through people selling their pre-owned electronics and apparel on eBay.

In November 2021, 'eBay Refurbished' was officially launched online, introducing a new destination for like-new (nearly new) products (eBay, 2021), and refurbished items from top brands like Apple, Samsung and Dyson are available to purchase with warranties (of varying durations). This approach is clearly reflected and greatly supported by new shopping behaviours observed in the United States in recent years. According to Yahoo Finance (2021), about '62 per cent of respondents are considering buying refurbished electronics, and 84 per cent are open to receiving refurbished gifts this holiday season'. In addition to better value brought by like-new products, 66 per cent of Americans believe this is a way to shop sustainably and this growing trend was led by Millennials in 2020, 64 per cent of whom have bought a refurbished item (eBay, 2021).

O2, a telecommunication services provider in the UK, also offers a 'Like New' deal, for example on the Apple iPhone 11, and resells pre-owned gadgets and recycles unwanted items (O2, 2021). The decline in household incomes caused by the Covid-19 pandemic encouraged consumers to switch to pre-owned products instead of brand-new items, which could be considered a new opportunity for the circular economy from a different perspective.

Resource value extension

The development of renewable inputs, recycled materials and resource recovery from a business and environmental perspective is termed resource value extension (Lacy and Rutqvist, 2015; Whalen and Whalen, 2020).

Targeting two of the biggest challenges to our planet's environment – plastics and animal agriculture – Ecovative, a materials company, uses mycelium to grow substitute materials to serve various industries (Ecovative, 2022a). For instance, mushroom-derived materials are used as sustainable alternatives to replace plastics and polystyrene foams for packaging. Also, mushroom-based vegan leather has become a substitute for genuine leather and can be used in the fashion industry. According to Ecovative (2022b), 'half the meat sold by 2040 will come from non-animal sources', and as a partnership with MyForest Food, MyBacon was a big success when it first launched in November 2020. Ecovative reflects the development of renewable inputs and their industrial applications.

Uniqlo, a Japanese casualwear designer, manufacturer and retailer, is encouraging customers to switch to a more sustainable consumption model. Re-Uniqlo aims to recycle used garments and turn them into brand new clothing and, working alongside non-governmental organizations (NGOs), wearable used clothing is distributed to vulnerable groups and people in need worldwide (Uniqlo, 2022). One of the largest manufacturers of solar panels, Trina Solar in China, continues to develop its entire manufacturing and operation process through technological innovation, encompassing recycling, energy saving and emission reduction (Arias, 2018; Trina Solar, 2022).

Kroger, the largest supermarket chain in the United States, has unveiled a clean energy production system which converts tonnes of food waste into biogas energy to help to power one of its distribution centres (Lacy and Rutqvist, 2015, p 58). Interface, a global manufacturer of commercial flooring, started its journey towards environmental sustainability in 1994, through recovering discarded nylon fishing nets to produce modular carpet (Lacy and Rutqvist, 2015, p 57). In 2018, all products manufactured by Interface, including luxury vinyl tiles, achieved carbon neutrality across the entire product life cycle (Interface, 2022).

Too good to be true?

At first sight, the business models addressed above look hugely attractive, offering benefits for business, consumers and society. Is it too good to be true? A review of studies on the circular economy highlighted two challenging findings: 'the peculiar finding focuses on profits and growth while little attention is given to ecological sustainability; the disconcerting finding suggests circular business models may further destabilize our ecological system if without broader changes driven by public policy' (Whalen and Whalen, 2020, p 632).

CBMs are usually presented to companies and enterprises with a promise of profits and business growth, as well as environmental and ecological benefits. In other words, CBMs are identified as paths to link business success and environment protection by increasing production efficiency, seeking new revenue growth and extending resource value. However, firms are microeconomic entities, whereas our ecological problems are much more macroeconomic (Whalen and Whalen, 2020). A circular economy cannot be achieved by corporations on the global market, since it requires great collaboration from citizens across countries. Problems that the circular economy is aiming to tackle appear as environmental challenges, but are intertwined with issues of inequality, migration and democracy (Goodwin, 2015; Narberhaus and von Mitschke-Collande, 2017). For instance, if small business could survive from the venture capital on the market, small business owners might become advocates of equality and resource efficiency. Recycling, reuse and renewal of materials and resources is the right thing to do to support environmental recovery; however, it cannot be the heal-all solution.

Circular model and luxury

In the last decade, the luxury industry has been growing dramatically across continents; from mature markets to emerging markets, 'new' consumers rapidly join 'old' consumers to enjoy luxury products and services. When the entire business world was badly hit by the Covid-19 pandemic overnight, luxury industry was one of the few sectors seeing a clear bounce back and steadily catching up in the year following the start of the pandemic.

Like all other sectors, luxury industry is facing challenges and trying to adapt to changes brought by a dynamic environment. Factors including the latest technological developments, post-pandemic impact and the perceived preferences of future consumers are driving fast-paced change in the luxury sector. Luxury brands have attracted a lot of criticism in recent years and have become quite unpopular in terms of sustainability and environmental protection (Lee et al, 2018). Ethical dilemmas and burning issues such as pollution, animal rights, resource waste and cheap labour have made a lot of headline stories about the luxury sector and put luxury brands into a difficult situation.

Growing demand, particularly from emerging markets and new consumers, is bringing exciting opportunities to global luxury brands; however, at the same time, this puts the luxury industry under pressure to respond to a scarcity of resources (Kunz et al, 2020). Among luxury categories, the fashion and textiles industry is recognized as the second most polluting manufacturing sector (Ku, 2018). Luxury brands are also criticized and blamed for 'nonreusable materials' and 'use of endangered animal skins' (Jain, 2019). Inevitably, sustainable practices are receiving serious consideration by luxury brands and various attempts at sustainable operations in luxury are increasingly observed.

Is sustainable luxury (SL) the solution to support brands and save our environment? Previous studies have explained that sustainable goals cannot be achieved by luxury brands alone, but also need collaborative support from business partners (Karaosman et al, 2018; Shashi et al, 2020a; 2020b). It is no wonder that circular economy approaches are now promoted by both academics and practitioners.

Geissdoerfer et al (2018) define circular economy as 'a regenerative system in which resource input and waste, emission and energy leakage are minimised by slowing, closing and narrowing material and energy loops'. This can be achieved through 'long-lasting design, maintenance, repair, reuse, remanufacturing, refurbishing and recycling' (Fraccascia et al, 2021).

For instance, Stella McCartney, a luxury brand and an advocate of sustainability, announced that 'Our goal is to create a business that is restorative and regenerative by design, striving to incorporate as many circular materials as possible into our collections', including recycled fabric used in various products since 2011 and the latest movement to use biodegradable materials from 2020 (Stella McCartney, 2022).

Furthermore, two typical strategies – upcycling and recycling – are proposed to help the luxury sector switch to circular economy (Adiguzel and Donato, 2021). Distinguished from 'recycling', 'upcycling' refers to re-using scrapped items or materials to create new products without the process of 'downgrading', which involves energy consumption and material recreation (Kamleitner et al, 2019; Park and Lin, 2020).

In 2018, high-end fashion brand Burberry was caught destroying unsold goods, including clothes, accessories and perfume worth £28.6 million (BBC, 2018). In response, Burberry explained that 'the energy generated from burning unwanted goods was captured, this operation is made environmentally friendly' (BBC, 2018). However, Burberry is not the only company combatting excess stock. Getting rid of unwanted goods is a dirty secret of the fashion industry, re-framed as 'part of the business process'.

In contrast to mass producers of goods, discounting or lowering the price is not a wise move for the luxury sector. The reason is obvi-ous: discounts devalue the luxury brand, disturb the luxury market and damage luxury consumers' confidence. From a luxury business perspective, getting rid of unwanted goods is considered necessary to protect brands from falling into the hands of unauthorized sellers and counterfeiters.

As the luxury industry's guilty secret, getting rid of unsold prod-ucts is a normal practice across brands. Richemont 'admitted taking back and destroying $560 million of top-end timepieces by Cartier, Piaget and Vacheron Constantin in two years, rather than have them appear on the resale market'. Fortunately, luxury watches can be dismantled, components can be reused, gemstones can be removed and embedded in other products. France was the first country to take this issue to the national level by passing an anti-waste law in 2019 to prohibit luxury brands from destroying unsold items (Matthams, 2019).

Can luxury and sustainability co-exist?

There are various definitions of luxury from the existing literature. The following characteristics are widely used and agreed to define luxury: excellent quality, high price, scarcity, uniqueness, craftman-ship and heritage (Ko et al, 2016). In other words, luxury products and services aim to provide the best (*best of the best*) product and top (*top of the top*) experience to customers by using the best available materials and most coveted resources. Enormous effort goes into achieving the status of *best of the best* and *top of the top*, which can lead to sourcing raw materials and adding labour resources without worrying too much about the cost, because luxury is not necessity and typical luxury consumers are not price sensitive. Therefore, 'conflict and contradiction' are found in the existing literature in terms of 'luxury and sustainability' even while sustainable products are leading radical change in the luxury industry (Achabou and Dekhili, 2013; Kapferer and Michaut-Denizeau, 2020).

Do younger generations have different preferences?

Environmental concern keeps increasing among young generations, particularly Millennials and Gen Z consumers, who are currently contributing 85 per cent of global luxury sales growth (Luxe Digital, 2022). Obviously, young, affluent generations are the target consumer groups for global high-end brands. Luxury brands need to embrace this change to bond with future consumers who believe that they can make environmental and social impact in line with their personal values through their purchase decisions. According to Nielsen (2015), 73 per cent of Millennials are willing to spend more on a product that comes from a sustainable brand and, compared to older generations, young consumers are much more socially conscious.

Is 'upcycling' a viable solution?

Even with consumers showing some interest in sustainable products, the extent of the adoption of green consumption practices and willingness to purchase circular products remain unknown. The latest research suggests that product image and product safety have a significant impact on purchase decision among consumers in general (Calvo-Porral and Levy-Mangin, 2020). However, similar questions are under-researched in the luxury context, such as purchase intention, consumption behaviour and consumer perceptions towards luxury.

A few brands, including luxury and non-luxury operations, have launched recycled and upcycled products (e.g. Stella McCartney and Dior). Recycling refers to the process of converting waste materials into new materials, and downgrading normally takes place. A recycling symbol, usually with a number ranging from 1 to 7 within a triangle, can be found on plastic bottles. This symbol offers relevant information regarding the toxic chemicals used in the plastic, e.g. 'how bio-degradable the plastic is, how likely the plastic is to leach, and ultimately the safety of the plastic' (The Berkey, 2022). For instance, a plastic bottle (Plastic #1) which contained bottled water can be recycled and re-produced materials (plastics) are used to manufacture new plastic (Plastic #6). The material is downgraded from Plastic #1 to Plastic #6 through the recycling process.

Although the idea of recycling has been popular in the past decade, not all consumers feel comfortable with recycling and recycled products. Two barriers, 'contamination, and disgust perception' inhibit consumers from accepting recycled products which will be in close contact with skin, such as clothes (Meng and Leary, 2019). A recent study cast some light on this question with a further interpretation: the perceived value of recycled products is positively associated with green self-identity, which suggests a higher behavioural intention among consumers (Confente et al, 2020).

Compared to recycling, upcycling seems more attractive because: (1) the lifespan of materials is extended without energy-consuming degradation of materials; and (2) repurposed products reflect creativity and originality (Adiguzel and Donato, 2021). Upcycling encourages the use of repurposed products by successfully combining sustainability (circular materials) and luxury (uniqueness through creativity). In the latest literature, a storytelling approach is suggested to link the product's past identity to the repurposed product, with a proven effect on purchase intention (Kamleitner et al, 2019). Storytelling is also applied by luxury brands to present the unique heritage and history of the product design. The link to the past makes consumers feel special because of the unique story behind the product.

To create a successful upcycled product without breaking down the original materials requires a lot of skill, demonstrating creative influence, aesthetic quality and excellent craftsmanship, in line with the characteristics of luxury (Bridgens et al, 2018). Compared to pre-owned (second-hand) luxury products, upcycling positively affects consumers' purchase intention, which is explained by novelty perception (Adiguzel and Donato, 2021).

Critiques of circular economy

In the five years to 2022, circular economy has not only made a strong appearance globally but also become a key principle for policy making across continents, including China, Africa, the EU and the United States (Corvellec et al, 2021). The circular economy builds an ideal circle to reduce resource use and environmental impact from economic activities. In consequence, circular business models contribute to sustainability and ecological systems by reducing cost, increasing revenues, lowering risks and bringing new opportunities for industries and sectors worldwide (Lazarevic and Valve, 2017; Ellen MacArthur Foundation, 2020).

However, the notions of circular economy are widely questioned from various perspectives, and critiques of circular economy and related models appear in different academic fields. In summary:

1 **Over a hundred definitions exist** and terms mean different things to different people and stakeholders (Kirchherr et al, 2017), with conceptual fragmentation and lack of paradigmatic strength leading to further confusion (Blomsma and Brennan, 2017; Inigo and Blok, 2019).

2 **A neglect of established knowledge** and an over-simplified understanding of consumption and consumers inhibits its development (Casson and Welch, 2021).

3 **Limited implementation** of the concept of circular economy and unknown practicalities at various levels, such as the policy level, the organizational level and individual level inhibit its expansion (Inigo and Blok, 2019; Geissdoerfer et al, 2018; Kirchherr et al, 2018).

4 **It is presented as a solution to sustainability while underestimating the challenges**, for instance the short-term and long-term environmental impacts remain unknown (Murray et al, 2017; Akerman et al, 2020).

These issues inevitably cause a lot of misunderstanding in society and leave a paradox for all stakeholders to consider. With growing interest in circular economy and relevant business models, these questions should be better answered and more clearly justified.

Following the critiques from academic fields above, dilemmas caused by circular economy in the real business world are presented as follows:

1 **Potential societal problems.** According to the San Francisco County Transportation Authority, ride-sharing and carpooling platforms (such as Uber) have contributed to local traffic congestion, which increased 180 per cent in major cities in the United States in 2017–18 (Said, 2017; Road Show, 2021; MIT News, 2021; Bloomberg, 2021).

2 **Rental and relax.** Product rental might not be very helpful in expanding the product lifespan because individuals use a rental product in a less careful way, compared to goods they own (Tukker, 2004). 'Less careful usage' leads to frequent product replacement, which works against circular economy. Although the pay-per-use business model potentially offers a profit margin, very little environmental gain is generated from this process.

3 **Consumers may make more purchases using saved money.** With the money saved from product rental or other types of circular activities, individuals can make more purchases. This is not what circular economy promotes. When fuel efficiency improved on family cars, people saved money on fuels. However, this 'saving' encouraged people to drive more and others even purchased a new car with a more powerful engine because they could afford it (Zink and Geyer, 2017).

Most of the literature and studies on circular economy focus on redesigning relevant systems from the ecological perspective. It has been unclear how the concept of circular economy will lead to great social impact, and important moral and ethical issues are missing from the construct (Murray et al, 2017).

Chapter summary

This chapter focuses on sustainable luxury and circular economy. Starting with an overview of sustainability and luxury, we looked into sustainability from both academic and industrial perspectives.

Through a few examples, we explored sustainable practices adopted by different businesses on the market.

Following the discussion of sustainability, we explored circular economy from various angles, and shared relevant business models. Furthermore, we took a closer look at the luxury sector and investigated how circular economy is developing in the context of international luxury.

Finally, we identified a few potential issues related to circular economy for luxury brands and explained how these would impact businesses. A case study, including discussion questions, is provided below for independent study and class activities.

CASE STUDY   Is 'lab-grown' a credible alternative to the mined diamond?

Unlike faux fur or vegan leather, lab-grown diamonds share identical chemical and physical properties with naturally formed diamonds – pure carbon crystallized in an isotropic 3D form. Lab-grown diamond production has been rising consistently in recent years, with 6–7 million carats produced in 2020 alone, although it is still marginal compared to mined diamonds, which reached 111 million carats in 2021 (Bain, 2021). Exploitation and a persistent lack of transparency have plagued the mined diamond industry, with reform efforts yielding mixed results, and the lab-grown diamond industry promotes a cleaner diamond option (in every aspect).

Lab-grown diamonds are marketed particularly to environmentally conscious younger consumers, with brands such as Pandora and De Beers selling them alongside mined ones. The market for lab-grown diamonds is expected to reach a value of $5.2 billion in 2023, according to diamond industry analyst Paul Zimnisky (2019).

There are very different positions on the environmental footprint of synthetic diamonds. One report on the topic, commissioned by the Diamond Producers Association (representing seven of the world's largest diamond miners, including De Beers, Alrosa and Rio Tinto), suggests that the greenhouse gas emissions produced mining natural diamonds are three times lower than those created when growing diamonds in a lab.

A study by Martin (2010) compared emissions from a diamond mine to the process used by a manufacturer of the synthetic alternative, using miles per

Figure 5.1 Survey results

Do you consider natural diamonds or lab-grown diamonds more sustainable in regard to the following factors?

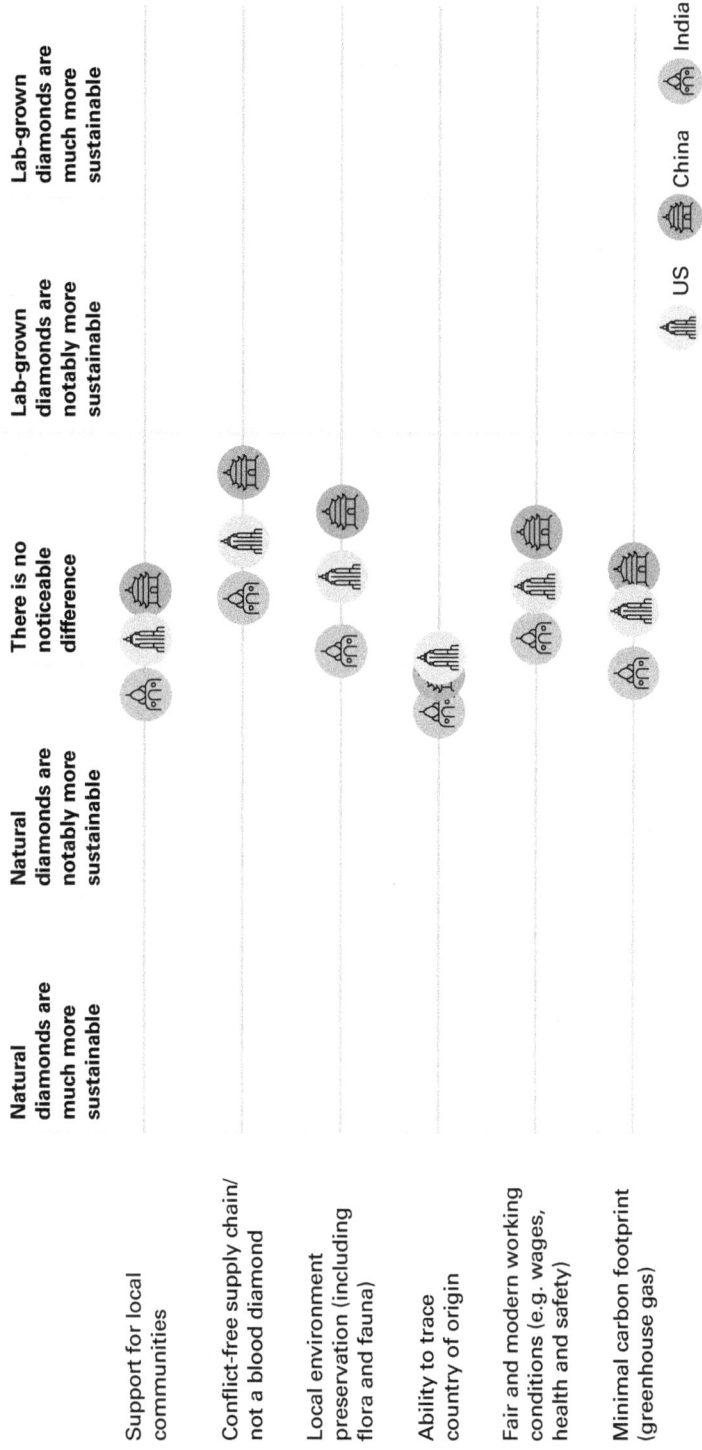

	Natural diamonds are much more sustainable	Natural diamonds are notably more sustainable	There is no noticeable difference	Lab-grown diamonds are notably more sustainable	Lab-grown diamonds are much more sustainable

Support for local communities

Conflict-free supply chain/ not a blood diamond

Local environment preservation (including flora and fauna)

Ability to trace country of origin

Fair and modern working conditions (e.g. wages, health and safety)

Minimal carbon footprint (greenhouse gas)

US China India

SOURCE Reproduced with permission of Bain (2021)

Figure 5.2 Word clouds generated from survey results in the US, India and China

What comes to your mind when you think about lab-grown diamonds?

US

India

China

SOURCE Reproduced with permission of Bain (2021)

gallon as a metric. The outcome was that if the annual production of the mine was switched to synthetic diamonds, 483 million miles worth of auto emissions could be saved. The calculation was based on translating the energy usage data into the average greenhouse gas emissions from the energy source of the mine.

According to Bain & Company's 2020–2021 global diamond report, 50–60 per cent of lab-grown diamonds are produced using high-pressure, high-temperature technology,[1] rather than the cleaner chemical vapour deposition technique.[2] Many lab-grown diamond brands still do not share their factories or origins.

Millennials and Gen Z are the main purchasers of diamonds for engagement rings, with nearly 70 per cent considering buying a lab-grown alternative. A study conducted by marketing firm MVI in 2019 found that 80 per cent of consumers surveyed were aware of lab-made diamonds, compared with less than 10 per cent in 2012. However, the reasons for considering a synthetic diamond are not particularly focused on their perceived sustainability, according to Bain's research in three key markets: China, India and the United States.

A key driver for purchase for some consumers is that lab-grown diamonds can be up to 40 per cent less expensive than natural diamonds. However, this also dilutes their perceived value, as Bain's research found.

Brand also affects the perception of lab-grown diamonds: MVI research showed that Brilliant Earth and DIAMA by Swarovski enjoyed the most recognition among Millennials and Gen Z consumers. De Beers also offers a lab-grown range, under the brand LightBox, with a range of fashion jewellery such as earrings and necklaces. Engagement rings with natural stones are kept separate under the Forevermark brand.

Discussion questions

1 Are lab-grown diamonds sustainable?

2 What are the barriers to the adoption of lab-grown diamonds?

3 How should brands position lab-grown diamonds?

4 Develop a communication proposal for a lab-grown diamond ring.

Notes

1 To grow an HPHT diamond, a small diamond seed is placed in carbon and exposed to extreme heat and pressure, replicating the way diamonds are naturally grown underground by the earth. The diamond seed is exposed to temperatures of over 2,000 degrees Fahrenheit and pressure of about 1.5 million PSI (pounds per square inch). The carbon melts and forms a diamond around the seed. It is then cooled and the diamond is formed.

2 The CVD method places a diamond seed in a vacuum chamber. This chamber becomes filled with carbon-rich gases and is heated to nearly 1,500 degrees Fahrenheit. The gas turns into plasma from these extremely high temperatures, causing the release of carbon pieces. These carbon pieces become layered onto the diamond seed, which grows the diamond.

References

Achabou, M A and Dekhili, S (2013) Luxury and sustainable development: Is there a match? *Journal of Business Research,* **66** (10), pp 1896–1903

Adiguzel, F and Donato, C (2021) Proud to be sustainable: Upcycled versus recycled luxury products, *Journal of Business Research*, **130**, pp 137–46

Akerman, M, Humalisto, N and Pitzen, S (2020) Material politics in the circular economy: The complicated journey from manure surplus to resource, *Geoforum*, **116**, pp 73–80

Arias, J (2018) Solar energy, energy storage and virtual power plants in Japan, EU-Japan Centre for Industrial Cooperation, www.eu-japan.eu/sites/default/files/publications/docs/min18_1_arias_solarenergy-energystorageandvirtualpowerplantsinjapan.pdf (archived at https://perma.cc/253Z-2DV3)

Arrigo, E (2018) The flagship stores as sustainability communication channels for luxury fashion retailers, *Journal of Retailing and Consumer Services*, **44**, pp 170–77

Athwal, N, Wells, V K, Carrigan, M and Henninger, C E (2019) Sustainable luxury marketing: A synthesis and research agenda, *International Journal of Management Reviews*, **21** (4), pp 405–26, http://doi.org/10.1111/ijmr.12195 (archived at https://perma.cc/2PY6-B5EA)

Bain (2021) Brilliant Under Pressure: The Global Diamond Industry 2020–21, www.bain.com/insights/global-diamond-industry-2020-21/ (archived at https://perma.cc/NRA4-GXTV)

BBC (2018) Burberry burns bags, clothes and perfume worth millions, https://www.bbc.co.uk/news/business-44885983 (archived at https://perma.cc/2XCJ-2ZEN)

Beckham, D and Voyer, B G (2014) *Can Sustainability be Luxurious? A mixed-method investigation of implicit and explicit attitudes towards sustainable luxury consumption*, ACR North American Advances

Bendell, J and Kleanthous, A (2007) *Deeper Luxury,* WWF-UK, Godalming

Blomsma, F and Brennan, G (2017) The emergence of circular economy: A new framing around prolonging resource productivity, *Journal of Industrial Ecology*, **21** (3), pp 603–14

Bloomberg (2021) How much traffic do Uber and Lyft cause? www.bloomberg.com/news/articles/2019-08-05/uber-and-lyft-admit-they-re-making-traffic-worse (archived at https://perma.cc/MLV4-USX4)

Bridgens, B, Powell, M, Farmer, G, Walsh, C, Reed, E, Royapoor, M and Heidrich, O (2018) Creative upcycling: Reconnecting people, materials, and place through making, *Journal of Cleaner Production*, **189**, pp 145–54

Business & Human Rights Resource Centre (2021) 2021 KnowTheChain Apparel & Footwear Benchmark, www.business-humanrights.org/en/from-us/briefings/2021-knowthechain-apparel-footwear-benchmark/ (archived at https://perma.cc/S3SF-PAYT)

Calvo-Porral, C and Levy-Mangin, J P (2020) The circular economy business model: Examining consumers' acceptance of recycled goods, *Administrative Science*, **10** (2), p 28

Casson, C and Welch, D (2021) Histories and futures of circular economy. In R B Swain and S Sweet (eds) *Sustainable Consumption and Production, Volume II: Circular economy and beyond* (pp 35–54), Springer International Publishing

Cattaneo, E (2022) Sustainable Luxury. In S Studente (ed) *Contemporary Issues in Luxury Brand Management,* Routledge

Cervellon, M C and Shammas, L (2013) The value of sustainable luxury in mature markets: A customer-based approach, *Journal of Corporate Communications*, **55**, pp 90–101

Confente, I, Scarpi, D and Russo, I (2020) Marketing a new generation of bio-plastics products for a circular economy: The role of green self-identity, self-congruity, and perceived value, *Journal of Business Research*, **112**, pp 431–39

Connell, R (2021) The luxury consumer, sustainability and social responsibility: It's complicated, *Sustainable Brands*, https://sustainablebrands.com/read/walking-the-talk/the-luxury-consumer-sustainability-and-social-responsibility-it-s-complicated (archived at https://perma.cc/MP33-SG9L)

Corvellec, H, Stowell, A F and Johansson, N (2021) Critiques of the circular economy, *Journal of Industrial Ecology*, **26** (2), pp 421–32

Danziger, P (2022) Luxury's got a new change agent: Gen Z, *The Robin Report*, www.therobinreport.com/luxurys-got-a-new-change-agent-gen-z/ (archived at https://perma.cc/5TSU-29UT)

D'Arpizio, C, Levato, F, Gault, C, de Montgolfier, J and Jaroudi, L (2021) From surging recovery to elegant advance: The evolving future of luxury, Bain & Co, www.bain.com/insights/from-surging-recovery-to-elegant-advance-the-evolving-future-of-luxury/ (archived at https://perma.cc/PA4N-4XCU)

Davies, I A, Lee, Z and Ahonkai, I (2012) Do consumers care about ethical luxury? *Journal of Business Ethics*, **106**, pp 37–51

Dean, A (2018) Everything is wrong: A search for order in the ethnometaphysical chaos of sustainable luxury fashion, *The Fashion Studies Journal*, www.fashionstudiesjournal.org/longform/2018/2/25/everything-is-wrong-a-search-for-order-in-the-ethnometaphysical-chaos-of-sustainable-luxury-fashion-4h33n (archived at https://perma.cc/4N8G-GJZT)

De Angelis, M, Adıgüzel, F and Amatulli, C (2017) The role of design similarity in consumers' evaluation of new green products: An investigation of luxury fashion brands, *Journal of Cleaner Production*, **141**, pp 1515–27

Depeyre, C, Rigaud, E and Seraidarian, F (2018) Coopetition in the French luxury industry: Five cases of brand-building by suppliers of luxury brands, *Journal of Brand Management*, **25** (5), pp 463–73

eBay (2020) Recommence Report, https://static.ebayinc.com/assets/Uploads/Documents/eBay-Recommerce-Report-2020.pdf (archived at https://perma.cc/H7Z9-J8FH)

eBay (2021) eBay launches 'Refurbished' offering, www.ebayinc.com/stories/news/ebay-launches-refurbished-offering/ (archived at https://perma.cc/ZD3W-FH5N)

eBay (2022) Our company, www.ebay.co.uk/ (archived at https://perma.cc/2KJ4-ABD8)

Ecovative (2022a) Food 2022, https://ecovative.com/food (archived at https://perma.cc/ZYX9-2ARS)

Ecovative (2022b) Why 2022, https://ecovative.com/why (archived at https://perma.cc/UW9P-5N5Z)

Ellen MacArthur Foundation (2013) Towards the Circular economy vol. 1: An economic and business rationale for an accelerated transition, https://ellenmacarthurfoundation.org/towards-the-circular-economy-vol-1-an-economic-and-business-rationale-for-an (archived at https://perma.cc/RK2S-J83J)

Ellen MacArthur Foundation (2020) Financing the Circular economy: Capturing the opportunity, https://ellenmacarthurfoundation.org/financing-the-circular-economy-capturing-the-opportunity (archived at https://perma.cc/A9C6-E9SE)

European Commission (2015) Closing the loop – An EU action plan for the circular economy COM/2015/0614, www.eea.europa.eu/policy-documents/com-2015-0614-final (archived at https://perma.cc/L8PZ-V6XK)

European Commission (2020) A new circular economy action plan: for a cleaner and more competitive Europe, https://ec.europa.eu/environment/strategy/circular-economy-action-plan_en (archived at https://perma.cc/FD58-8QKL)

Farra, E (2019) At the Copenhagen Fashion Summit, Kering's François-Henri Pinault shares a radical new vision of sustainability, www.vogue.com/article/francois-henri-pinault-kering-sustainability-vision (archived at https://perma.cc/VB7T-V4ZL)

Fraccascia, L, Giannoccaro, I, Agarwal, A and Hansen, E G (2021) Business models for the circular economy: Empirical advances and future directions, *Business Strategy and Environment*, **30** (6) pp 2741–44

Geissdoerfer, M, Morioka, S N, De Carvalho, M M and Evan, S (2018) Business models and supply chains for the circular economy, *Journal of Cleaner Production*, **190**, pp 712–21

Ghisellini, P, Cialani, C and Ulgiati, S (2016) A review on circular economy: The expected transition to a balanced interplay of environmental and economic systems, *Journal of Cleaner Production*, **114**, pp 11–32

Global Witness (2022) Conflict diamonds, www.globalwitness.org/en/campaigns/conflict-diamonds/ (archived at https://perma.cc/B5PQ-YJHK)

Goodwin, L (2015) How to bust the biggest myths about the circular economy, *The Guardian*, 12 March, www.theguardian.com/sustainable-business/2015/mar/12/circular-economy-myths-busted-reality-check (archived at https://perma.cc/E98V-MKJC)

Griskevicius, V, Tybur, J M and Van den Bergh, B (2010) Going green to be seen: Status, reputation and conspicuous conservation, *Journal of Personality and Social Psychology*, **98**, pp 343–55

Grohens, Y, Kishor Kumar, S, Boudenne, A and Weimin, Y (2013) *Recycling and Reuse of Materials and Their Products*, Taylor & Francis Group, New York, NY

Guercini, S and Ranfagni, S (2013) Sustainability and luxury: The Italian case of a supply chain based on native wools, Journal of Corporate Citizenship, **2013** (52), pp 76–89

Hennings, N, Wiedmann, K P, Klarmann, C and Behrens, S (2013) Sustainability as part of the luxury essence: Delivering value through social and environmental excellence, *Journal of Corporate Citizenship*, **52**, pp 25–35

Hockerts, K and Wüstenhagen, R (2010) Greening Goliaths versus Emerging Davids: Theorizing about the role of incumbents and new entrants in sustainable entrepreneurship, *Journal of Business Venturing*, **25** (5), pp 481–92

Homrich, A S, Galvao, G, Abadia, L G and Carvalho, M M (2018) The circular economy umbrella: Trends and gaps on integrating pathways, *Journal of Cleaner Production*, **175**, pp 525–43

Inigo, E A and Blok, V (2019) Strengthening the socio-ethical foundations of the circular economy: Lesson from responsible research and innovation, *Journal of Cleaner Production*, **233**, pp 280–91

Interface (2022) Carbon Neutral Floors, www.interface.com/GB/en-GB/sustainability/carbon-neutral-floors.html (archived at https://perma.cc/W8VW-GSJA)

Ivanova, D and Wood, R (2020) The unequal distribution of household carbon footprints in Europe and its link to sustainability, *Global Sustainability*, **3**, http://doi.org/10.1017/sus.2020.12 (archived at https://perma.cc/G2EQ-Y2QC)

Jain, S (2019) Factors affecting sustainable luxury purchase behaviour: A conceptual framework, *Journal of International Consumer Marketing*, **31** (2), pp 130–46

Janssen, C, Vanhamme, J and Leblanc, S (2015) Should luxury brands shout or whisper? The effects of brand prominence on consumer perceptions of responsible luxury, *Advances in Consumer Research*, **43**

Joy, A, Sherry, J F, Venkatesh, A, Wang, J and Chan, R (2012) Fast fashion, sustainability and the ethical appeal of luxury brands, *Fashion Theory*, **16**, pp 273–96

Kamleitner, B, Thurridl, C and Martin, B A S (2019) A Cinderella Story: How past identity salience boosts demand for repurposed products, *Journal of Marketing*, **83** (6), pp 76–92

Kapferer, J N and Michaut, A A (2014) Is luxury compatible with sustainability? Luxury consumers' viewpoint, *Journal of Brand Management*, **21**(1), pp 1–22

Kapferer, J N and Michaut-Denizeau, A (2020) Are Millennials really more sensitive to sustainable luxury? A cross-generational international comparison of sustainability consciousness when buying luxury, *Journal of Brand Management*, **26**, pp 35–47

Karaosman, H, Perry, P, Burn, A and Morales-Alonso, G (2018) Behind the runway: Extending sustainability in luxury fashion supply chains, *Journal of Business Research*, **117**, pp 652–63

Kiorboe, N, Sramkova, H and Krarup, M (2015) *Moving Towards a Circular Economy*, Nordic Council of Ministers, Copenhagen

Kirchherr, J, Piscicelli, L, Bour, R, Kostense-Smit, E, Muller, J, Huibrechtse-Truijens, A and Hekkert, M (2018) Barriers to the circular economy: Evidence from the European Union (EU), *Ecological Economics*, **150**, pp 264–72

Kirchherr, J, Reike, D and Hekkert, M (2017) Conceptualizing the circular economy: An analysis of 114 definitions, *Resource, Conservation and Recycling*, **127**, pp 221–32

KnowTheChain (2021) Apparel and Footwear Benchmark Report, https://knowthechain.org/wp-content/uploads/2021-KTC-AF-Benchmark-Report.pdf (archived at https://perma.cc/A4AF-E6UD)

Ko, E, Phau, L and Aiello, G (2016) Luxury brand strategies and customer experiences: contributions to theory and practice, *Journal of Business Research*, **69** (12), pp 5749–52

Korhonen, J, Nuur, C, Feldmann, A and Birkie, S E (2018) Circular economy as an essentially contested concept, *Journal of Cleaner Production*, **175**, pp 544–52

Korte, F and Coulston, F (1998) Commentary, some considerations on the impact on ecological chemical principles in practice with emphasis on gold mining and cyanide, *Ecotoxicology and Environmental Safety*, **41** (2), pp 119–29

Ku, K (2018) Wake up: The time for sustainability in the luxury industry is now, https://technode.com/2018/01/18/luxury-sustainability/ (archived at https://perma.cc/5KQQ-PKXZ)

Kunz, J, May, S and Schmidt, H J (2020) Sustainable luxury: current status and perspectives for future research, *Business Research*, pp 1–61

Kuo, L and Chang, B G (2021) The affecting factors of circular economy information and its impact on corporate economic sustainability-evidence from China, *Sustainable Production and Consumption*, 27, pp 986–97

Lacy, P and Rutqvist, J (2015) *Waste to Wealth: The circular economy advantage*, Palgrave Macmillan, Basingstoke

Lazarevic, D and Valve, H (2017) Narrating expectations for the circular economy: Towards a common and contested European transition, *Energy Research & Social Science*, 31, pp 60–69

Lee, S, Ha-Brookshire, J and Chow, P S (2018) The moral responsibility of corporate sustainability as perceived by fashion retail employees: a USA-China cross-cultural comparison study, *Business Strategy and the Environment*, 27 (8), pp 1462–75

Li, J and Leonas, K K (2019) Trends of sustainable development among luxury industry. In M Gardetti and S Muthu (eds) *Sustainable Luxury: Environmental footprints and eco-design of products and processes*, Springer, Singapore, https://doi.org/10.1007/978-981-13-0623-5_6 (archived at https://perma.cc/Y97R-CE9U)

Low, T (2010) Sustainable luxury: A case of strange bedfellows. Paper presented at the Tourism and Hospitality Research in Ireland Conference, www.shannoncollege.com/wp-content/uploads/2009/12/THRIC-2010-Full-Paper-T.-Low.pdf (archived at https://perma.cc/R2DR-3MQJ)

Lundblad, L and Davies, I A (2016) The values and motivations behind sustainable fashion consumption, *Journal of Consumer Behaviour*, 15 (2), pp 149–62

Luxe Digital (2022) Sustainable Luxury: Millennials buy into socially conscious brands, https://luxe.digital/business/digital-luxury-trends/millennials-buy-sustainable-luxury/ (archived at https://perma.cc/D5S6-SZNY)

Martin, A (2010) Q&A: Synthetic versus Mined Diamonds, *Stanford Alumni Magazine*

Matthams, K (2019) France moves to ban the destruction of unsold luxury goods in favor of recycling, www.forbes.com/sites/katematthams/2019/06/06/france-moves-to-ban-the-destruction-of-unsold-luxury-goods-in-favor-of-recycling/?sh=39efaa7b334e (archived at https://perma.cc/FCV8-9ZJQ)

McManan-Smith, T (2014) Philips delivers 'cradle-to-cradle' lighting, *The Energyst*, 3 February, https://theenergyst.com/philips-delivers-cradle-cradle-lighting/ (archived at https://perma.cc/PCX4-9N5Q)

Meng, M D and Leary, R B (2019) It might be ethical, but I won't buy it: Perceived contamination of, and disgust towards clothing made from recycled plastic bottles, *Psychology and Marketing*, **38** (2), pp 298–312

MIT News (2021) Study finds ride-sharing intensifies urban road congestion, 23 April, https://news.mit.edu/2021/ride-sharing-intensifies-urban-road-congestion-0423 (archived at https://perma.cc/Y577-QKKG)

Moraes, C, Carrigan, M, Bosangit, C, Ferreira, C and McGrath, M (2017) Understanding ethical performances in luxury consumption through practice theories: a study of fine jewellery purchases, *Journal of Business Ethics*, **145**, pp 525–43

Murray, A, Skene, K and Haynes, K (2017) The circular economy: An interdisciplinary exploration of the concept and application in a global context, *Journal of Business Ethics*, **140**, pp 369–80

MVI (2019) Lab-grown diamonds: recent consumer research and historical trends, www.paulzimnisky.com/home (archived at https://perma.cc/L99X-PL2C)

Narberhaus, M and von Mitschke-Collande, J (2017) Circular economy isn't a magical fix for our environmental woes, *The Guardian*, 14 July, www.theguardian.com/sustainable-business/2017/jul/14/circular-economy-not-magical-fix-environmental-woes-global-corporations (archived at https://perma.cc/5RFQ-6KM6)

Nielsen (2015) The sustainability imperative: New insights on consumer expectations, https://nielseniq.com/global/en/insights/analysis/2015/the-sustainability-imperative-2/ (archived at https://perma.cc/JSJ5-W3PD)

Nudie Jeans (2017) You decide how far they go, www.nudiejeans.com/blog/you-decide-how-far-they-go/ (archived at https://perma.cc/MD5U-6LWJ)

Nudie Jeans (2021) Nudie Jeans: Pioneering sustainable denim for 20 years, https://goodonyou.eco/nudie-jeans/ (archived at https://perma.cc/JL4J-Y555)

O2 (2021) Terms and conditions: Like New, www.o2.co.uk/termsandconditions/shop-purchasing-terms/like-new-terms-and-conditions (archived at https://perma.cc/9PYA-WKXJ)

Oswald, Y, Owen, A and Steinberger, J K (2020) Large inequality in international and intranational energy footprints between income groups and across consumption categories, *Nature Energy*, **5** (3), pp 231–39

Öymen Kale, G and Öztürk, G (2016) The importance of sustainability in luxury brand management, *Intermedia International E-journal*, **3** (4), pp 106–26

Park, H J and Lin, L M (2020) Exploring attitude-behaviour gap in sustainable consumption: comparison of recycled and upcycled fashion products, *Journal of Business Research*, **117**, pp 623–28

Passport (2020) Luxury Goods in the United Kingdom, www.euromonitor. com/luxury-goods-in-the-united-kingdom/report (archived at https:// perma.cc/R4ES-VL4S)

Paton, E (2018) Burberry, after provoking an uproar, will stop burning unsold merchandise, *The Seattle Times*, 6 September, www.seattletimes. com/business/burberry-after-provoking-an-uproar-will-stop-burning-unsold-merchandise/ (archived at https://perma.cc/R4ES-VL4S)

Philips (2013) Philips' transition from linear to circular economy, 13 December, www.engineeringsolutions.philips.com/news/philips-transition-linear-circular-economy/ (archived at https://perma.cc/2EVG-ZYWA)

Philips (2014) Lighting National Union of Students UK, www.lighting. philips.co.uk/cases/cases/education/national-union-of-students (archived at https://perma.cc/QWP6-4DBT)

Positive Luxury (2022) Shaping a sustainable future for luxury, www. positiveluxury.com/ (archived at https://perma.cc/HZ3Y-PFUF)

Rivera, L (2017) Fashion revolution: behind the scenes of a £2 trillion industry, *The Independent*, 24 April, www.independent.co.uk/life-style/ fashion/fashion-revolution-week-behind-the-scenes-of-a-ps2-trillion-industry-a7694831.html (archived at https://perma.cc/D2TB-M6QL)

Road Show (2021) Yet another study says Uber and Lyft are worse for traffic congestion, *CNET*, 4 February, www.cnet.com/roadshow/news/ uber-lyft-traffic-congestion-car-ownership-study/ (archived at https:// perma.cc/3T6S-9YP3)

Robertson, E (2017) Luxury travel 'doing more environmental damage than mass tourism', *Routes Online*, 25 September, www.routesonline. com/news/29/breaking-news/274970/luxury-travel-doing-more-environmental-damage-than-mass-tourism/ (archived at https://perma. cc/SX9V-XRBQ)

Rolling, V and Sadachar, A (2018) Are sustainable luxury goods a paradox for millennials?, *Social Responsibility Journal*, **14** (4), pp 802–15, http://doi.org/10.1108/SRJ-07-2017-0120 (archived at https://perma.cc/ S6AM-BQ2L)

Said, C (2017) Uber, Lyft Cars have heavy impact on SF streets, study finds, *SFGate*, 13 June, www.sfgate.com/business/article/Uber-Lyft-cars-have-heavy-impact-on-SF-streets-11214835.php (archived at https:// perma.cc/NKJ9-7ZDN)

Salon.com (2014) Sustainability survey, www.salon.com/about/salon_2014_year_end_survey (archived at https://perma.cc/5HS9-JGXA)

Scalefast (2021) What luxury DTC brands need to know about Millennial and Gen Z shoppers, www.scalefast.com/what-luxury-dtc-brands-need-to-know-about-millennial-and-gen-z-shoppers/ (archived at https://perma.cc/JM3D-EQ6Q)

Schreck, M and Wagner, J (2017) Incentivizing secondary raw materials markets for sustainable waste management, *Waste Management*, **67**, pp 354–59

Seidman, D (2007) *How We Do Anything Means Everything*, Wiley, Hoboken

Sharma, N K, Govindan, K, Lai, K K, Chen, W K and Kumar, V (2021) The transition from linear economy to circular economy for sustainability among SMEs: a study on prospects, impediments, and prerequisites, *Business Strategy and the Environment*, **30** (4), pp 1803–22

Shashi, P C, Cerchione, R and Ertz, M (2020a) Agile supply chain management: where did it come from and where will it go in the era of digital transformation? *Industrial Marketing Management*, **90**, pp 324–45

Shashi, P C, Cerchione, R and Ertz, M (2020b) Management supply chain resilience to pursue business and environmental strategies, *Business Strategy and the Environment*, **29** (3), pp 1215–46

Shivarov, A (2020) Circular economy: Limitations of the concept and application challenges, *Economic Science Series*, **9** (3), pp 144–52

Stahel, W (2019) *The Circular Economy: A user's guide*, Routledge, London

Stella McCartney (2022) Recycled nylon and polyester, www.stellamccartney.com/gb/en/sustainability/recycled-nylon-polyester.html (archived at https://perma.cc/X6V5-T6F5)

Sun, Y, Wang, R and Cattaneo, E (2022) What influences the purchase intentions of sustainable luxury among Millennials in the UK? *Strategic Change*, **31** (3), pp 323–36

The Berkey (2022) What numbers of plastic are safe for water bottles? The numbers behind water bottles, https://theberkey.com/blogs/water-filter/what-numbers-of-plastic-for-water-bottles-are-safe-for-you-the-numbers-behind-plastic-bottles (archived at https://perma.cc/6BQM-S6G7)

The Fashion Pact (2020) The Fashion Pact: First steps to transform our industry, https://thefashionpact.org/ (archived at https://perma.cc/E9YS-RAGX)

Torelli, C, Monga, A B and Kaikati, A M (2012) Doing poorly by doing good: Corporate social responsibility and brand concepts, *Journal of Consumer Research*, **38** (5), pp 948–63

Trina Solar (2022) Sustainability, www.trinasolar.com/us/our-company/sustainability (archived at https://perma.cc/9AST-CXFH)

Tukker, A (2004) Eight types of products service systems: Eight ways to sustainability? *Experiences from SusProNet, Business Strategy and Environment*, **13** (4), pp 246–60

Tukker, A (2015) Product services for a resource-efficient and circular economy – a review, *Journal of Cleaner Production*, **97**, pp 76–91

Uber (2022) Homepage, www.uber.com/gb/en/ (archived at https://perma.cc/MSE7-TG9T)

Uniqlo (2022) The power of clothing, www.uniqlo.com/uk/en/content/re-uniqlo.html (archived at https://perma.cc/2Z99-CFY3)

United Nations (2020) Environment Programme Emissions Gap Report, www.unep.org/emissions-gap-report-2020 (archived at https://perma.cc/6FK5-PL8L)

Wang, J, Li, Z and Tam, V W Y (2015) Identifying best design strategies for construction waste minimization, *Journal of Cleaner Production*, **92**, pp 237–47

Webb, B (2021) Are lab-grown diamonds really the sustainable future? *Vogue Business*, 17 June, www.voguebusiness.com/sustainability/are-lab-grown-diamonds-really-the-sustainable-future-pandora-de-beers (archived at https://perma.cc/LPX2-WFMG)

Whalen, C J and Whalen, K A (2020) Circular economy business models: A critical examination, *Journal of Economic Issues*, **54** (3), pp 628–43

Yahoo Finance (2021) eBay Launches 'Refurbished' Offering, 9 November, https://finance.yahoo.com/news/ebay-launches-refurbished-offering-140000062.html (archived at https://perma.cc/V9V4-WNRN)

Zimnisky, P (2019) Lab-grown diamonds: recent consumer research and historical trends, www.paulzimnisky.com/home (archived at https://perma.cc/L99X-PL2C)

Zink, T and Geyer, R (2017) Circular economy rebound, *Journal of Industrial Ecology*, **21** (3), pp 593–602

Advances in digital: new opportunities for luxury retail

06

NICOLETTA GIUSTI
TIZIANA TINI

> **LEARNING OBJECTIVES**
>
> - To understand the main reasons for the controversial relationship between luxury and digital.
> - To understand the historical development of luxury retail.
> - To understand the latest developments of the relationship.
> - To understand the main issues and opportunities related to the development of digital in luxury retail.

Luxury brands and the e-commerce revolution: a controversial love story

Luxury brands started populating the internet at the beginning of the 21st century, but the relationship they had with the internet remained quite limited and controversial for some time. Luxury carefully entertains (artificial) exclusivity and rarity and for a long time e-commerce, based on accessibility and low prices, was seen as antipodal and the collaborations were limited and careful. The evolution of everyday life, due to the banalization of digital facilities and to societal change, made the relationship possible and necessary, even if it did not lead to the always claimed and never happening 'end of brick and mortar', but to a tentative connection between the digital and physical experiences, better known as 'phygital'.

At the root of this – mutual – diffidence is the distance between the business models and related mentalities, as luxury is based on the creation of symbolic and economic value, following the Veblen effect, while e-commerce is based on the traditional economic trade-off between price and demand. Yet, luxury brands could endure the crisis of the Covid-19 pandemic, thanks to the growth of e-commerce, which literally doubled the market (D'Arpizio and Levato, 2021) due to a still tinkered and improvised, but very effective mix of home delivery, virtual visits, private sales and constant, multi-channel interaction with the customers.

E-commerce and multi-brand business models: the reasons for a controversial relationship between luxury and digital

Lauren Sherman of *Business of Fashion* sets the start of the relationship between luxury fashion design and digital as the creation of Yoox and Net-à-Porter (originally separate) in 2000. Indeed, the very first online store created for selling luxury was Luisaviaroma.com, the online version of an historical multi-brand from Florence, Italy.

Luisaviaroma.com was created in 1999. Until then, Luisaviaroma had been a traditional, yet creative, brick-and-mortar multi-brand store, founded in the 1920s in the city centre of the Renaissance's capital (Vogue, 2013). A few months later, at the beginning of the 2000s, Net-à-porter in London and Yoox in Milan opened their virtual doors. As underlined by the Pew Research Center regarding digital innovations, 'It's all just history repeating itself' (Vogels et al 2020). Once again, Florence played a central role for Italian fashion and in the global fashion system. The first time was on the 12th February 1951 at the 'Sala Bianca' of Palazzo Pitti, when a handful of US buyers, coming back from the Paris haute couture shows, were formally invited for the first time by Giovanni Battista Giorgini to discover Italian fashion (Giusti, 2009; Stanfill, 2021).

The multi-brand model led to Yoox pushing the boundaries of collaboration with brands to become the first provider of e-commerce platforms for luxury fashion design, developing the very first online flagship for a fashion luxury brand, Marni, in 2006. This role of infrastructure provider is still played by Yoox, with almost one-third of its business generated by managing 37 monobrand e-commerce websites for main brands at the time of its merger with Net-à-Porter in 2015 (Muret, 2015).

The main difference between the three founders, Luisaviaroma, Yoox and Net-à-Porter, is that Luisaviaroma was a brick and click and the other two were only online stores. Luisaviaroma.com was basically reproducing a whole brick-and-mortar concept store online, selling items they had in the physical store and marketing them following all the standards of luxury fashion design (Kapferer and Bastien, 2009). Yoox and Net-à-Porter were purely online players, with NAP daring to sell new collections online only, and Yoox basically being an online outlet, reselling previous seasons' collections. The role of the latter has probably been a strong influence in the initial diffidence of luxury brands towards e-commerce. While Luisaviaroma was developing a curated website, with content marketing (namely an online magazine, no longer published in 2022) and a strong accent on trends and aesthetic value, like in a brick-and-mortar concept store, Yoox in particular was following a more mainstream 'Amazon' model, with the accent on discounts and low prices and concentrating on the technical solutions, to better show the garment as a simple object. Two radically different approaches: the first true to luxury, where the accent is on aesthetic, and the second typical of commodities, where the accent is on the technical and material aspects.

These two different approaches had much to do with the speed of development of the relationship between digital and luxury. Luxury has a very 'blurred definition', but a common aspect of luxury goods is that they are indeed cultural products. Following the definition by Hirsch (1972), cultural products are 'nonmaterial goods directed at a public of consumers for whom they generally serve an esthetic or expressive, rather than a clearly utilitarian function' or, as put by Berry (1994), from a consumer culture perspective they are 'objects of desire that provide pleasure'. Where there is no pleasure, there is no desire and if luxury products are considered as simple 'technical objects' or commodities, whose main characteristics for desirability are low price and equivalence to any other good of the same kind, we are no longer in luxury. Considering luxury goods as commodities means depriving luxury of its most powerful asset: symbolic power (Bourdieu and Delsaut, 1975).

For this reason, in recent years luxury goods have been more and more subject to a process of 'decommoditization' (Riot et al, 2013) or 'artification' (Crane, 2019) when rarity and exclusivity were paradoxically endangered by success and big sales and by an ownership tightly in the hands of large conglomerates. Last but not least, apart from using strategies of artification and decommoditization, luxury plays much on the creation of value through the creation of memorable experiences, thereby playing, as it always has, a leading role in the so-called 'experience economy' (Pine and Gilmore, 1998).

To date, Chanel, always among the top five most valuable luxury brands in the world (Brand Finance, 2022), is not selling its ready-to-wear online; you can explore all the looks in every single detail, with the prices visible, but you will not be able to buy unless you go to a physical store and enjoy the experience. Louis Vuitton, by far the most valuable luxury brand in retail and 'the' retailer in luxury, as the most important retailer of the LVMH group – LVMH had 5,556 operating stores in 2021 (source: Statista) – had virtually no real B2C digital strategy and image – not to mention integration with retail – until the arrival of Virgil Abloh as Creative Director of Menswear in 2018. This reluctance was certainly due to the mutual lack of understanding between an industry that sells desire, meaning and experiences and operators selling goods and commodities at excellent prices.

The role of luxury wholesale retailers as innovators

The delay by luxury in developing a digital strategy and presence (Wetlaufer, 2001) is easy to understand in the light of our reflection on the very nature of the first providers of e-commerce for luxury (mainly in fashion), but surprising in the light of the role historically paid by wholesale retailers in developing innovation for the luxury industry.

It is worth highlighting that the first websites trading fashion on-line were 'multi-brand' stores, i.e. selling different brands on the same platform. Multi-brand stores – department stores but also small entrepreneurial brick-and-mortar independent shops – have indeed been at the heart of the development of luxury fashion design since the 18th century. Before the advent of big luxury groups in the later years of the 20th century and the diffusion of the 'Vuitton philosophy' (vertical integration starting from retail), distribution was almost all multi-brand. The first department stores were opened in London (Harding, Howell & Co in 1796) and Paris (Le Bon Marché in 1852), and in other main capital cities around the world. Department stores played a huge role in the development of ready-to-wear in the first 50 years of the 20th century (Giusti 2009), especially after the Second World War and the 'blessing' from Parisian haute couture. In particular, in the United States, department stores were ensuring the so-called 'trickle-down system' (Barber and Lobel, 1952) i.e. the diffusion, via sales of items, models of IP rights, of Paris fashion design within the world's largest market for luxury goods.

If department stores were the backbone of Paris-centred luxury fashion design, ensuring the transition from haute couture to ready-to-wear, the idea of selling several brands at a single point of sales was not limited to them. Smaller, independent 'boutiques' curated by entrepreneurs started emerging in Europe by the early 1950s, one of the first examples being the boutique of Emilio Pucci, in Capri. Pucci was also one of the first participating, with his own creations, in the first-ever show of Italian fashion design, at 'La Sala Bianca' of Palazzo Pitti in Florence in 1951 (Stanfill, 2021). Independent multi-brand stores have represented in Europe and in some of the main fashion capitals of the world one of the main vectors of innovation in luxury fashion design (Crane, 2000) and therefore for retail, thanks to their accessibility and their proximity to the field. Mary Quant, the British designer who popularized – their invention is controversial, as originally it was streetwear generated by a tax on cloth (Giusti, 2009) – miniskirts and hot pants, had her own multi-brand boutique called 'Bazaar' on King's Road; and speaking about London it is worth mentioning the iconic 'Biba', Barbara Hulanicki's 'style and retail phenomenon', which has a place of honour in the Victoria and Albert Museum (V&A, n.d.).

A common strategy for young, innovative designers between 1960 and the mid-1990s – before the advent of big conglomerates that raised entry barriers to the market (Crane, 1997) – was to present their own sketches to small independent multi-brand boutiques, which would ensure the first market test and financial support. Kenzo Takada, the first Japanese designer to become globally famous, started selling his drawings to several boutiques in Paris before opening his own store, called 'Jungle Jap' (Kawamura, 2004). Another famous name who started working for other brands and distributing initially through multi-brand stores, is Giorgio Armani (not to mention Gianni Versace) (Giusti, 2009).

In this huge network of luxury fashion design, independent multi-brand stores used to have a recognized role as talent scouts and, as we would say today, 'curators', acting as 'cultural entrepreneurs', i.e. not only 'people who use a novel combination of the available means of production' but also who 'build its own value through a personal charisma and using a cultural capital' (Aldrich, 2010). The importance of this role was widely recognized by the main gatekeepers of the system: *Women's Wear Daily* (now WWD), the most important newspaper in the field of luxury fashion design, used to have, at least twice a year, special articles collecting all the opinions of the buyers from the main wholesale retailers (Giusti and Colucci, 2013) and the Fashion designer Martin Margiela, in a monographic exhibition dedicated to his work and career in Paris.

The most successful cultural entrepreneurs in multi-brand retail gave birth to the so-called 'concept stores', the first examples of 'curated experiences' in luxury retail. The first one claiming this label was the famous 10 Corso Como, created by the sister of the former editor-in-chief of *Vogue Italia*, Franca Sozzani, Carla, in 1991, initially as an art gallery. Perhaps the most famous in the world and certainly the most renowned as 'innovative' was Colette, created in Paris in 1996. For the 21 years in which Colette was open, the store represented a creative hub, where not only customers from all over the world, but also professionals from the luxury world would go to breathe – ahead of time – 'the spirit of the time', which was extremely well represented in the brick-and-mortar experience of the store. Colette's layout and selection of products and brands certainly made a huge contribution to the decommoditization – and we could say 'luxuryfication' – of digital technologies. Colette, the place where it was not uncommon to meet Karl Lagerfeld, was one of the first to launch and sell watches and every kind of innovative digital object or media, as well as including non-traditional products like water, music, sneakers and t-shirts, frequently with the very first collaborations and co-branding experiences and every other object related to their 'playful and fresh' luxury concept. Colette was certainly not the first concept store, but for the huge influence it had in terms of trends, it is certainly thanks to two Parisian women, Sarah Andelman and her mother Colette Rousseaux, if luxury retail is now out of the closet of the leisure class with all the burden of heritage and tradition and closer to the new, upcoming classes and generations of digital natives.

It is certainly thanks to the path opened by concept stores in looking ahead and leading the trends, that luxury is one of the first and most advanced industries in the 'gaming economy', adopting gamification practices, platforms and opening the way to the Metaverse (Tini, 2022) as we will see at the end of this chapter.

In a more general way, independent retailers and concept stores have indicated to luxury the way to integrate not only new technologies and products, but also co-branding and collaborations, as well as art, culture and games and have, in short, developed the very idea of 'curatorship', perhaps the leading trend involving luxury brands in the first years of the 21st century.

Retail in transition: brick and mortar is dead, long live brick and click

In spite of the initial diffidence and the 'language' differences, luxury has long seen the digital world both as an investment and as a potential marketing and sales tool still with kind of mysterious and not yet understood instructions for use. The tycoon Bernard Arnault, head of the group LVMH, now the largest company in France in terms of market capitalization and by far the major luxury conglomerate in the world, started investing in digital in the mid-'90s (Wetlaufer, 2001). In 2001 Arnault's portfolio already counted a couple of portals – E-Luxury, which suspended sales in 2009, and Sephora. com, the latter with a brick-and-mortar correlate of points of sale – and a failure with the Swedish portal Boo.com, which went bankrupt in 2000. If Sephora.com, founded in 1999, in 2001 was just an experiment supposed to break even in 2002 (Wetlaufer, 2001), it is nowadays considered one of the most powerful and innovative brands of LVMH, representing one of the most successful examples of integration of 'bricks and clicks' i.e. of digital presence and physical points of sale. Other successive LVMH ventures were purely digital, like the famous 24 Sevres – still existing under the name 24S.com and fruit of the experience of Ian Rogers as CDO – or Clos19, dedicated to wine and spirit products only (Theodosi, 2017). For these two ventures, due to the lack of financial figures separate from the rest of the group (LVMH, 2022a and 2022b) it is unclear whether they are able to compete with the now tenors of luxury e-commerce, like YNAP and Farfetch.

Despite the language differences and the main underlying reciprocal diffidence, the courtship between digital and luxury has been long and, in the end, successful. The relationship was not passing just through investments and ventures, but, as the case of Ian Rogers, who passed from Apple to LVMH, shows, via managerial exchanges. Another famous example is Angela Ahrendts at Burberry from 2006 to 2013, then jumping to Apple, to be in charge of the Apple stores. Ahrendts' experience at Burberry – whose famous 'digitally enhanced' store on London's Regent's Street was for a long time a kind of luxury touristic attraction to be visited 'per se' – is perhaps a good indicator of the core of the question between luxury and digital: retail. Also very insightful is the fact that among the most famous transfers between luxury and digital and vice versa, we find Apple (see case study below) whose strategy, at least during the Steve Jobs era, was the strategy of a luxury company and whose physical points of sale represented for a long time the epitome of luxury experience in retail and CRM.

Perhaps it is not just a coincidence if the most successful experiences in digital for luxury are the ones focusing on the integration between digital and physical and not the simple online platforms; the need for human touch and memorable experiences is indeed still a consistent hurdle for an industry based on dreams and desire. Sephora is now one of the most profitable and innovative brands of LVMH and the double-digit growth of luxury e-commerce during the 2020–2021 pandemic was indeed due to a careful integration of digital and human, supported mainly by loyal customers and 'grands vendeurs' (star/best salespersons) who were keeping the bond, in spite of lockdowns and sanitary restrictions.

The image for the vertical growth of online shopping that literally spurred the luxury industry towards the future is not one of a single individual behind a computer or, more likely a mobile phone screen, clicking on luxury items as a solitary and punctual action, but one of a loyal or even new customer of a brand, looking for human contact and keeping the bond with her favourite client advisor or trying to keep or reconstruct an endangered identity, via a two-way shopping experience made up of messages, phone calls, remote shopping tours or private sales sessions and home delivery or individual appointments in-store (Giusti and Tini, 2021). Human touch remains one of the main pillars of the luxury experience.

CASE STUDY   Apple stores as Luxury Retail

On 15 May 2001 in a famous press conference at Tysons Corner, Virginia, a Steve Jobs very concerned about perpetuating Apple (Derrien, 2018; Vera, 2021), announced to journalists the opening of brick-and-mortar Apple retail.

This step followed the opening and immediate success of the online Apple store on 10 November 1997.

Notoriously a fan of the Japanese designer Issey Miyake, Jobs was systematically spending time in luxury boutiques when on holiday with his family (Schlender and Tetzeli, 2015). Apparently he was literally harassing the vendors with questions about sales, visual merchandising and other important points about the management of the stores.

Jobs was indeed very dissatisfied with the distribution of Apple products since his return to the company in 1997; computer stores used to be sorts of supermarkets, where sales were based only on technical aspects of the products and perpetual dumping. Let's mention also that until the arrival of Apple, computers used to be only black and design was not perceived as a main characteristic of the tech, especially from the point of view of sales. The experience of the Italian Olivetti, formerly a typewriter manufacturer, known for its collaborations with famous designers like Ettore Sottsass and Mario Bellini (Fuso, 2020; Olivetti, n.d.), was not initially integrated into a market dominated by US tech giants. It is perhaps not a coincidence that the first IBM laptop, the ThinkPad, making a change from other computers, was designed by a great designer, Richard Sapper (creator of the famous Brionvega radio and former apprentice to the famous designer Giò Ponti) and a Japanese design studio (Sapper, n.d.; Olivares, 2016).

Following the idea of the famous 1997 campaign 'Think Different', Apple launched the coloured iMac in 1999, consolidating the – disruptive at that time – idea of design as a major component of a tech product. After having opened the – immediately profitable – online store, finding the right place to sell Apple 'different' products was the next logical step forward.

The first Apple store (now simply 'Apple') opened at Tysons Corner on 19 May 2001 (Stein, 2021) soon afterwards in California, then all the others followed in major central locations of the cities in the world, like Fifth Avenue in New York and Via del Corso in Rome, following a location strategy not different from those of major luxury brands.

Apparently this strategy was not a simple coincidence. Bernard Arnault, who was opening the first renovated and integrated Louis Vuitton stores, designed by Peter Marino, is reported as having exchanges with Steve Jobs about the topic, and cross-fertilization between the two most successful examples of retail in the world was really happening (Vera, 2021).

Apple stores are conceived as sorts of hubs, where the customers can enjoy a holistic Apple experience of a unique mix of care for the customer, cool design and relational style. Last but perhaps least, in the stores you can find a technical solution for your device, you can buy the most recent technological wonders, but most of the time people also just hang out and spend some time in a familiar and pleasant environment, discovering something new and dreaming it (Giusti, 2022).

The store becomes, in this way, not just a simple 'point of sale', but a point of reference representing the entire universe of the brand, so intimate and familiar for loyal customers, possibly everywhere in the world.

That is why Apple stores, inspired by luxury stores and retail, became in a few years the benchmark of a luxury in-store experience and of the ideal type of brick-and-click strategy perhaps still unmatched by the official luxury brands.

Apple stores have been centred since the start on a full Apple experience, integrating online and offline, problem solving and sales, design and human relations. Unsurprisingly Steve Jobs is said to have consulted Bernard Arnault, who was launching in the same years the integrated Louis Vuitton retail, in collaboration with Peter Marino. Another detail of great importance is the presence of people who had worked in the Walt Disney Company – the great specialist of dreams – in the team that developed the Apple store (and vice versa) (Schlender and Tetzeli, 2015; Ryan 2010).

Location, design, customer experience, integration between physical and digital made Apple retail one of the best in the world and certainly made them – together with some product characteristics that we will explore later – for a long time perhaps the most advanced luxury stores in the world.

Luxury e-commerce websites, B2C, B2B, applications and 2DC: do we need a new classification for websites?

The first years of the 21st century have seen a continuous and extremely fast evolution in the digital industry; in terms of technology, we think about the number of websites but also the now prominent role played by mobile applications. This impressive technological acceleration driven by mass diffusion and consumption led not only to the expanding number of websites but also to a technological shift – from computers to mobile devices – leading to the prominent role played now by mobile applications. The classifications of Consumer-to-Consumer (C2C), Business-to-Consumer (B2C), Consumer-to-Business (C2B) and Business-to-Business (B2B) proposed by Dave Chaffey and PR Smith (2017) might be reviewed according to the state of the industry.

The question has risen with the predominance of what I suggest calling a 'mobile applications first approach' rather than the 'e-commerce first approach' we were used to. With the mobile applications first approach, the scope is to underline how younger fashion businesses start from application development rather than website development. More and more websites come after the mobile app.

The urgency of being attractive to the younger generations of customers pushed companies to prioritize mobile devices. The reason is not just due to the growth of mobile adoption, but also to the disruptive arrival of social networks. With Facebook first, then Twitter and Instagram, customers in the western world found new tools to enter into contact with brands or celebrities, with a proximity that was just unimaginable in the past. This 'new proximity' created by the range and intensity of digital relationships and interactions, has of course a strong reverse side to the coin, both for mental health and privacy. Among the (many) different issues generated, we can quote at least mental health, with FOMO (literally 'fear of missing out') and the growing concern about the amount of data and digital traces left online by users in their everyday online routine. FOMO, 'a pervasive apprehension that others might be having rewarding experiences from which one is absent' (Przybylski et al, 2013) can be considered a distinctive element of contemporary society.

Since the GDPR has been effective in Europe, from 25 May 2018, difficulties have arisen related to the use of third-party cookies and the surge of ad blockers. Until now there has been little global research (Tini, 2022) on the impact of ad blocking on engagement with the web. Data available is related to specific locations and does not give a full updated vision of the effect of its adoption by users; for example, by visiting the European Union website page about cookies it is clear how the matter is the source of debate within the European Community and keeps evolving in combination with the privacy regulations. The GDPR broke new ground in terms of consumer data protections, but it also caused businesses and users their fair share of frustration. Consumers are left with only slightly greater transparency – plus the burden of responsibility for understanding the data privacy ecosystem.

The effects of third-party cookies on the browsing experience are clear to all the fashion companies: fewer possibilities to use cookies leads to a poor user experience and decreased web engagement. Still, consumers don't want to let go of personalization. Despite their privacy concerns, 80 per cent of customers expect a tailored experience on the web (Lindecrantz et al, 2020).

With such changes, and the dismission of third-party cookies that allow businesses to track consumers across websites with little transparency for internet users, companies have focused on first-party cookies and developing a direct relationship with customers. How? As written previously, by focusing on application development, rather than a mobile version only (Ahuja et al, 2022).

This interest in applications leads us to a second step that supports the need for a new classification of e-commerce. For instance, when fashion e-commerce that traditionally was B2C started to adopt C2C marketing strategies or even integrating C2C platforms, allowing customers to give reviews on the products – how can we define those websites? The German company Zalando started proposing its own marketplace, allowing customers to sell past collections directly on its website. Asos started offering this option in 2010 (Fashion Network, 2010): are they still examples of B2C because we assume that the majority of their revenues come from B2C?

The acquisition of the website and printed magazine *Highsnobiety* by the pure player Zalando on 13 June 2022 underlines how content marketing is more relevant than ever and represents a strategic step for the German B2C e-commerce website. Shall we expect that e-commerce will become closer to the entertainment and content platforms, following the trend of brick-and-mortar stores integrating exhibition spaces or cafeterias?

Luxury and technological innovation: from TikTok to the Metaverse – the challenge of new platforms

As we have seen until now, luxury and innovation are two concepts tightly connected. It is more than just a claim on the LVMH corporate website. To quote Dior CEO Pietro Beccari's interview in the

Financial Times (March 2022): 'In consumer marketing you have to hammer the same message in different ways and incoherence is not allowed. Luxury brands are more complex, like a multi-faceted diamond, so some incoherence can even create desirability… You have to put chaos into your business.' Internet in the '90s, blogs and the rise of social networks in the 2000s, as well as augmented reality and the Metaverse in 2021–22 reshaped the strategies of luxury conglomerates and of the independent luxury companies.

Each technical innovation – as per NFTs – or each introduction of a new platform on the internet – Douyin/TikTok – represents both an opportunity and a risk for those companies that need to adjust or adapt their strategies to keep being relevant for the younger generations of customers, from Generation X to the Millennials, to Generation Z, without forgetting the involvement of Generation Alpha.

Advances in digital open new perspectives in terms of customer knowledge, personalization and experience. Digital is characterized by its omnipresence, free access and the so-called 'democratization' of information (Kapferer and Bastien, 2012). The experience is carried out almost anonymously by the user/customer via a mobile screen: according to WeAreSocial and Hootsuite, 92.4 per cent of worldwide internet users from 16 to 62 years old are connecting via mobile. Such a pervasive use of mobile redefines the behaviours of the new customers, and can be defined by the acronym introduced by Xavier Dalloz (Duvaut et al, 2020): 'ATAWAD', which stands for 'Anytime, Anywhere, Any Device'.

Anytime, anywhere: the mobile strategy evolves into the app focus for a more personalized omnichannel experience

The possibility of being connected everywhere has made 'mobile first adoption' the main objective pursued by early adopter brands since 2016: this was the year in which for the first time 'the combined traffic from mobile and tablet devices tipped the balance at 51.2 per cent, vs 48.7 per cent for desktop access' (Etherington, 2016).

The strategy to be potentially present on all devices always, which is still valuable after a few years, has evolved in focusing on the creation of integrated apps, available for iOS and Android, and can be seen in contrast to some of the main characteristics of the luxury industry, like exclusivity/rarity. The same can be stated for the ability to embrace the 'ATAWAD' strategy. An unfortunate part of the experience of western luxury customers is the long time spent waiting for a reply from a luxury brand contacted online via a contact form, emails, social media comments, SMS or WhatsApp messages. The geographical area from where the customer contacts the luxury brand has a deep influence on the quality of the service. Chinese customers, for example, expect to receive an immediate reply via WeChat when contacting a luxury brand via their WeChat account. The same can be said by US and Indian customers via WhatsApp. The Millennials first and then Generation Z expect the personal and simultaneous relationship they have in store to be replicated via app or other devices. In southern Europe, on the contrary, luxury brands lack real-time conversation, even when they rely on chat services onsite.

From the window to the homepage: the store becomes digital and vice versa

Screens replacing looks: store windows as cinemas or game rooms

Luxury customers might walk in the luxury districts or malls while keeping their eyes on their smartphone. Nevertheless, shop windows are more relevant than ever: the role of the visual merchandiser is going beyond the creation of looks or of a set design, by combining the ability to build connections with the online activity (Cant and Wiid, 2020). The collection as well as the set can be completely replaced by screens or art installations that have nothing (or little) in common with the store or the collection itself.

The concept store Luisaviaroma led the way in Italy to a completely different use of shop windows. Since the beginning of 2019, the big window of the physical store in Via Roma, Florence has been transformed into a big screen hosting video art installations or interactive videogames with required interaction from the public passing in front of the store. Collections are partially visible only at the entrance of the store, where a couple of mannequins welcome the customers. The use of the windows, linking art to fashion via a big screen, is justified by the desire to create engagement and emotional connections with younger luxury customers who are looking for something different than a setting for dreaming of an outfit. Even more, the introduction of a gaming pad in front of the window outside the store was a strategy to tap into gamification (Mohamed and Tini, 2020) and engage with Generations Z and Alpha, familiar with the gaming platforms.

QR codes: gates for new experiences

Before the pandemic, stickers with QR codes were already visible on the entry doors or windows of many luxury stores. By scanning those contemporary 'gates' with their mobile phones, customers were redirected to the homepage of the brand's e-commerce, deceiving their expectations. If the intention was to connect the homepage to the physical store, why use a QR code rather than the URL directly? After the Covid-19 pandemic, the adoption of QR codes became more frequent worldwide; nevertheless, most luxury brands were still underestimating the power of those tools.

QR codes are more than a possibility to drive visits from the physical store to the online website. As previously stated, this association generates frustration for customers who feel they lose time in scanning what I would like to consider examples of digital arts. QR codes can be personalized indeed and can be used strategically to involve customers in gaming activities or let them discover 'secret sections', exclusive pages that can be reached only from that specific sticker, in a specific store.

Using QR codes strategically can turn the experience into a 'treasure hunt', leveraging the power of entertainment and education (the edutainment approach) (Zuhal, 2012), depending on the scope of the experience. An example of strategic use of QR codes is made by the Parisian fashion brand Ami Paris. For Easter 2022, the brand launched its first-ever phygital 'Ami de Coeur Egg Hunt game' which took place in selected global cities, giving participants (customers, new customers, prospective customers) the chance to win prizes such as a limited-edition chocolate egg designed by the French pastry chef Yann Couvreur. Participants were asked to use their smartphones in different locations throughout these cities, finding and gathering as many hidden virtual eggs as they could, with a mechanism similar to existing games such as Pokémon GO (Tagwalk, 2022). To start the hunt, customers had access to the Ami website, where the section 'Egg Hunt' was visible on the top menu, landing then on a page with a QR code to scan. Once scanned, the experience started via mobile. Among the locations, the store was at the core of each quest, transforming the shopping experience into a new discovery.

Innovation at Printemps: from NFT ambitions to a physical pop-up for digital clothes in the Metaverse

Printemps, the Parisian luxury department store, passed through a renewal of their stores in Boulevard Haussmann as well as the website. A new e-commerce was released on 10 March 2022. As per the press release published by the company, this was 'conceived as a blended physical and digital universe (...) which invites customers to discover its very first immersive shop'. To promote purchases from the new platform, Printemps.com offered customers who made a purchase from the immersive boutique (not the e-commerce then, but the virtual boutique) the chance to enter a draw to win an NFT made in collaboration with contemporary French artist Romain Froquet.

By combining the immersive shopping experience and the contest to win NFTs, the company shows its interest in seducing new customers, in particular the younger generations attracted by the latest digital tools. Nevertheless, it must be noticed that the immersive shopping experience available is far from being as 'immersive' as it could be. The elements that prevent complete success are still due to technical limitations. Without the adoption of Oculus or any device to be worn to provide a 360-degree experience, the look and feel will be 2D. Even with the effort of recreating the store's dome, the view from the dome and the addition of sound, the experience is not as immersive as it could be or as gamers are used to having thanks to multiple devices.

To stand out from the competition, Printemps was the first department store to host a physical space for virtual try-on. By collaborating with the Los Angeles-based 'metafashion retailer' DRESSX, customers could use the physical space on the ground floor at Printemps to try virtual dresses or accessories. How? By using a digital kiosk available for six weeks from April 2022, visitors and customers were able to try and purchase a 100 per cent virtual wardrobe within an immersive universe combining fashion, artificial intelligence and augmented reality (Hirschmiller, 2022).

This represents the starting point for showing that the experience in-store is not contraposed to the virtual one. On the contrary, leveraging all the channels available – online and offline, the mobile, the APP ecosystem, as well as the Metaverse – is a great condition to welcome new luxury customers as well as the more experienced ones that might not be so familiar with the latest digital concepts and digital clothing opportunities.

Luxury and the Metaverse

The Metaverse is the way many tech corporations are envisioning the future. The science-fiction novel *Snow Crash* (Stephenson, 1992), where the term first appears, meant by this term a virtual reality, populated by users' avatars. The novel underlines as well the basic principle of the Metaverse: real and virtual worlds always remain strictly separate.

This separate universe is not without echoes of 'Second life', the online social platform developed by Linden Lab nearly two decades ago, where people created digital representations of themselves to socialize with others, pretty much fashionable from 2003 to 2007, when its virtual banks became involved in the subprime crisis (Chen, 2022). In the same article, Chen describes Metaverse as 'the convergence of two ideas that have been around for many years: virtual reality and a digital second life'.

From a technical point of view, today's Metaverse is neither a game nor a virtual theme park; at the moment, there is not a single protocol or platform for it. On the contrary, there are multiple platforms allowing different experiences. It is clear then that the 'Metaverse' has no agreed-upon definition. Nevertheless, according to Cathy Hackl, one of the most influential web3 and Metaverse strategists, Metaverse can be described as a successor state to the mobile internet, a group of shared experiences, between both physical and digital worlds, enabled by many different technologies, 'like virtual reality and augmented reality' (Hackl et al, 2022). Technologies like blockchain are already playing and will play a relevant role in the Metaverse's development, for data acquisition, data storage, data sharing, data interoperability and data privacy preservation (Gadekallu et al, 2022).

Surprisingly – if we think about the old luxury world, linked to heritage, tradition and highbrow style – luxury jumped immediately into this new world of opportunities opened by the Metaverse and NFTs, becoming very quickly a dominant actor, with brands like Gucci, Balenciaga and Louis Vuitton creating dedicated business units and hiring Heads of Metaverse.

Nevertheless, while the founder and President of LVMH, the major luxury group in the world, expresses some concern about the real utility of the Metaverse – 'it's not our objective to sell virtual sneakers for 10 euros' (Williams, 2022) – the CEO of Gucci, Marco Bizzarri, defines it as a long-term strategy and a 'very real' thing for the brand (McDowell, 2022). Mid-October 2022, around one year after having changed the name of 'Facebook' to 'Meta', Mark Zuckerberg was reported to define their own Metaverse platform as a 'sad and empty world', having fewer users than the famous previous similar experiment of 'Second Life' (Horwitz et al, 2022). We live in a world where future becomes history very soon and where only a few things become History with a capital H.

CASE STUDY Store observation activity

Luxury retail and the digital world are in constant and fast evolution and cannot be fixed on paper, unless we are talking about history. Renovations and changes in layout and visual merchandising are necessary and very frequent; it therefore is very difficult to have a fixed 'state of the art'. This is even more true in the digital world, where the pace of technological evolution is even faster. That is why our case discussion will be starting with an on-site observation of three examples of retail: Louis Vuitton, Apple and a third of your choice that represents, on the basis of what you have learnt so far, the epitome of luxury retail.

For the observation, take pictures (always ask for permission) and jot down handwritten notes (handwriting is different than typing and very important for creativity).

Then, answer the following questions and if you are more than one person – which would be the best way to perform this exercise – compare your answers within a group, in a 60-minute discussion:

- Jot down descriptions of the different places, as if you have to describe them for a novel; put some images in the middle to complete the description, indulge in interesting layout and merchandise details.

- Make a list of what makes the stores 'luxury': is everything in common? Make different columns and highlight similarities and differences.

- Try to buy – without necessarily completing the purchase – a product or service and carefully compare the two selling processes or ceremonies: which one do you believe is more appropriate for a brand defining itself as 'luxury'?

- How would you describe the experience overall: note at least five adjectives per store and compare them, including your personal feelings (e.g. did you feel welcomed, rejected, personnel were friendly, distant etc); give marks on the basis of the criteria you have defined for a luxury store.

- Compare the in-store experience you had with the online: are there differences? Is the online experience able to compare to one you live in-store? How could you improve the online/in-store experience if one is better?

- What are the services, experiences, details that make the difference in the best store? Describe them and see if you can export them into the other stores/businesses you have observed.

- What are the services and practices you have observed in other stores and places (not the three observed) that could be definitely useful to improve the experiences in the stores you have observed?

Chapter summary

In this chapter we have followed the evolution of retail and of the relationship between digital and luxury through the evolution of luxury retail. The relationship between luxury and digital was cold for a long time due to the antipodal marketing conceptions: one based on (artificial) rarity and exclusivity and on high prices, coupled with high demand, another based on the trade-off between demand and prices, traditional marketing and full accessibility. We have highlighted how wholesale retailers were at the origin of the evolution of both luxury retail and online luxury retail. In particular, we have highlighted how independent multi-brand stores and, among them, concept stores, a specific case of 'curated' stores, have opened the way to many innovations in luxury retail, making it more compatible with the digital world and with the idea of luxury for new generations. The case of Apple stores, initially reported in several circumstances by Bernard Arnault as inspired by the Louis Vuitton retail that was developed a few years before (Derrien, 2018; Vera, 2021), is taken by the authors as the epitome of luxury retail and integrated experience between online and offline, setting the trend of 'click and mortar'. Click and mortar, with a mix of different ways to ensure the bond with the customers, did not only allow the survival of traditional luxury brands during the 2020/2021 pandemic, but is set to open the way for a further evolution of online commerce and experience.

References

24 Sèvres (2017) Announcing a global address for fashion, www.lvmh.com/news-documents/press-releases/24-sevres-announcing-a-global-address-for-fashion/ (archived at https://perma.cc/MY9J-L9NQ)

Abboud, L (2022) Dior's Pietro Beccari: Dreams do not have a price tag, *Financial Times*, www.ft.com/content/eb7349fa-b8c3-4fc8-9830-a84587db15d5 (archived at https://perma.cc/EDT9-VKAA)

Adobe (2021) Thinking beyond the third-party cookie, https://business.adobe.com/content/dam/www/us/en/pdfs/Adobe_Thinking_Beyond_the_Third_Party_Cookie.pdf (archived at https://perma.cc/3TZY-A6N9)

Ahuja, K et al (2022) As the cookie crumbles, three strategies for advertisers to thrive, www.mckinsey.com/business-functions/growth-marketing-and-sales/our-insights/as-the-cookie-crumbles-three-strategies-for-advertisers-to-thrive (archived at https://perma.cc/CD6Q-CX89)

Aldrich, H (2010) Entrepreneurship. In N J Smelser and R Swedberg (eds) *The Handbook of Economic Sociology*, 2nd edition, Princeton University Press

Barber, B and Lobel, L S (1952) 'Fashion' in women's clothes and the American social system, *Social Forces*, **31** (2), pp 124–31, https://doi.org/10.2307/2573395 (archived at https://perma.cc/7H8M-DMT7)

Berry, C J (1994) *The Idea of Luxury: A conceptual and historical investigation*, Cambridge University Press

Bourdieu P and Delsaut, Y (1975) Le couturier et sa griffe: contribution à une théorie de la magie, *Actes de la recherche en sciences sociales*, **1** (1) Hiérarchie sociale des objets, pp 7–36

Brand Finance (2022) The annual report on the most valuable and strongest luxury & premium brands ranking, https://brandirectory.com/rankings/luxury-and-premium/table (archived at https://perma.cc/5ABN-R5QH)

Cant, M C and Wiid, J A (2020) Visual merchandising elements: Drivers of retail strategies? *The Journal of Applied Business Research,* **36** (5), pp 197–204

Chaffey, D and Smith, P R (2017) *Digital Marketing Excellence: Planning, optimizing and integrating online marketing*, 5th Edition, Routledge

Chen, B (2022) What's all the hype about the Metaverse? *New York Times*, www.nytimes.com/2022/01/18/technology/personaltech/metaverse-gaming-definition.html (archived at https://perma.cc/A7KV-KU32)

Crane, D (1997) Globalization, organizational size, and innovation in the French luxury fashion industry: Production of culture theory revisited, *Poetics* (Amsterdam) **24** (6), pp 393–414

Crane, D (2000) *Fashion and its Social Agendas: Class, gender, and identity in clothing*, University of Chicago Press

Crane, D (2019) Fashion and artification in the French luxury fashion industry, *Cultural Sociology*, **13** (3), pp 293–304, https://doi.org/10.1177/1749975519853667 (archived at https://perma.cc/M8JE-E8RR)

D'Arpizio, C and Levato, F (2021) Snap Chart: After another big year, online luxury sales approach a milestone, Bain and Company, www.bain.com/insights/online-luxury-sales-approach-a-milestone-snap-chart/ (archived at https://perma.cc/8D5B-9NQJ)

Derrien, J (2018) Steve Jobs a fait appel au patron de Louis Vuitton pour ouvrir ses Apple store, https://hypebeast.com/fr/2018/5/steve-jobs-louis-vuitton-bernard-arnault-apple-store (archived at https://perma.cc/6F7W-3VYN)

Duvaut, P et al (2020) *Internet of Augmented Me, I.AM: Empowering innovation for a new sustainable future*, Wiley

Etherington, D (2016) Mobile internet use passes desktop for the first time, study finds, *TechCrunch*, https://techcrunch.com/2016/11/01/mobile-internet-use-passes-desktop-for-the-first-time-study-finds/ (archived at https://perma.cc/CH4P-U432)

European Commission (n.d.) Cookies Policies, https://ec.europa.eu/info/cookies_en (archived at https://perma.cc/6EYG-TRDQ)

Fashion Network (2010) ASOS launches digital fashion marketplace, https://ww.fashionnetwork.com/news/asos-launches-digital-fashion-marketplace,139202.html (archived at https://perma.cc/J838-CYJJ)

Fuso, L (2020) The 'Olivetti style': modernity, beauty and functionality, *Design Wanted*, https://designwanted.com/brand-story-olivetti/ (archived at https://perma.cc/JLD7-T2HK)

Gadekallu, T R et al (2022) Blockchain for the Metaverse: A Review, https://arxiv.org/pdf/2203.09738.pdf (archived at https://perma.cc/TT25-8VQN)

Giusti, N (2009) *Introduzione allo studio della moda*, Il Mulino, Bologna

Giusti, N (2022) Field notes for the case study

Giusti, N and Colucci, M (2013) Field notes for a research on legitimation of creative fashion designers, University of Bologna, Management department (unpublished)

Glancey, J (2015) A History of the Department Store, *BBC Culture*, www.bbc.com/culture/bespoke/story/20150326-a-history-of-the-department-store/index.html (archived at https://perma.cc/89AD-KBB9)

Hackl, C, Lueth, D and Di Bartolo, T (2022) *Navigating the Metaverse: A guide to limitless possibilities in a Web 3.0 world*, Wiley

Hirsch, P M (1972) Processing fads and fashions: An organization-set analysis of cultural industry systems, *The American Journal of Sociology*, 77 (4), pp 639–59

Hirschmiller, S (2022) Why Printemps built its own metaverse online and teamed with DRESSX digital fashion in-store, *Forbes*, www.forbes.com/sites/stephaniehirschmiller/2022/04/11/printemps-builds-own-metaverse-and-partners-with-dressx/?sh=433fcc215743 (archived at https://perma.cc/T3MB-KX3V)

Horwitz, J, Rodrigues, S and Bobrowsky, M (2022) Company documents show Meta's flagship Metaverse falling short, *Wall Street Journal*, www.wsj.com/articles/meta-metaverse-horizon-worlds-zuckerberg-facebook-internal-documents-11665778961 (archived at https://perma.cc/87RJ-UTCE)

Kapferer, J N and Bastien, V (2009) The specificity of luxury management: Turning marketing upside down, *Journal of Brand Management*, **16** (5–6), pp 311–22 https://doi.org/10.1057/bm.2008.51 (archived at https://perma.cc/6CB6-RHPH)

Kapferer, J N and Bastien, V (2012) *The Luxury Strategy: Break the rules of marketing to build luxury brands*, 2nd edition, Kogan Page

Kawamura, Y (2004) The Japanese Revolution in Paris Fashion, *Fashion Theory*, **8** (2) pp 195–223, DOI: 10.2752/136270404778051771

Kemp, S (2022) More than 5 billion people now use the internet, *Wearesocial*, https://wearesocial.com/uk/blog/2022/04/more-than-5-billion-people-now-use-the-internet/ (archived at https://perma.cc/8FTU-DYWA)

Lindecrantz, E et al (2020) Personalizing the customer experience: Driving differentiation in retail, www.mckinsey.com/industries/retail/our-insights/personalizing-the-customer-experience-driving-differentiation-in-retail (archived at https://perma.cc/X5QL-JD45)

LuisaViaRoma (n.d.) In 1999, Panconesi took the LuisaViaRoma ethos and aesthetic worldwide by pioneering into e-commerce, www.luisaviaroma.com/it-it/crrunway/how-andrea-panconesi-turned-a-family-business-into-a-global-fashion-powerhouse (archived at https://perma.cc/SLT6-UVN9)

LVMH (2022a) LVMH Group milestones to the present. Explore the original creations, innovations and landmark events that have made the LVMH group what it is, www.lvmh.com/group/milestones-lvmh/1593-to-the-present/ (archived at https://perma.cc/HZ9X-U5FB)

LVMH (2022b) Press release: 2021 Full Year Results, https://r.lvmh-static.com/uploads/2022/01/press-release-2021-lvmh-full-year-results.pdf (archived at https://perma.cc/LM7D-DTAF)

LVMH (2022c) Translation of the French interim financial report sixmonth period ended June 30, 2022, https://r.lvmh-static.com/uploads/2022/07/lvmh_interim-financial-report-2022.pdf (archived at https://perma.cc/KN8B-KMUH)

MacRumors staff (2022) Apple Stores, www.macrumors.com/guide/apple-store/ (archived at https://perma.cc/QZ84-6LDA)

McCrindle, M and Fell, A (2021) *Generation Alpha*, Headline Publishing Group, London

McDowell, M (2022) Gucci CEO Bizzarri talks metaverse strategy and why it's 'already a very real place for us', *Vogue Business*, www.voguebusiness.com/technology/gucci-ceo-bizzarri-talks-metaverse-strategy-and-why-its-already-a-very-real-place-for-us (archived at https://perma.cc/PV9Z-VDWZ)

McKinsey (2022) What is the metaverse – and what does it mean for business? Podcast www.mckinsey.com/business-functions/mckinsey-digital/our-insights/what-is-the-metaverse-and-what-does-it-mean-for-business (archived at https://perma.cc/A5JR-ZKSF)

Mohamed, H and Tini, T (2020) Fashion and gaming: How luxury fashion brands use gamification, *Future Learn*, www.futurelearn.com/courses/fashion-and-gaming-how-luxury-fashion-brands-use-gamification (archived at https://perma.cc/N33J-KL8C)

Muret, D (2015) La naissance de Yoox Net-A-Porter Group ouvre une nouvelle ère, https://fr.fashionnetwork.com/news/La-naissance-de-yoox-net-a-porter-group-ouvre-une-nouvelle-ere-,476309.html (archived at https://perma.cc/N5PJ-PPAV)

Olivares, J (2016) *Richard Sapper*, Phaidon, London, NY

Olivetti, F A (n.d.) Camillo Olivetti: story of an Italian pioneer, https://artsandculture.google.com/story/-wUh8lOLDPHLIg?hl=en (archived at https://perma.cc/6P4H-F9WG)

Pine, B J and Gilmore, J H (1998) Welcome to the experience economy, *Harvard Business Review*, 97–105

Printemps (2022a) Printemps upgrades to Web 3.0, www.groupe-printemps.com/en/article/printemps-upgrades-web-30 (archived at https://perma.cc/H3MC-TMQY)

Printemps (2022b) Metafashion at Printemps Haussmann, www.groupe-printemps.com/en/article/metafashion-printemps-haussmann (archived at https://perma.cc/76AB-5628)

Przybylski, A K et al (2013) Motivational, emotional, and behavioral correlates of fear of missing out, *Computers in Human Behavior*, 29, pp 1841–48

Riot, E, Chamaret, C and Rigaud, E (2013) Murakami on the bag: Louis Vuitton's decommoditization strategy, *International Journal of Retail & Distribution Management*, 41 (11–12) pp 919–39

Ryan, T (2010) Disney opens first Apple-inspired store, *Forbes*, www. forbes.com/2010/07/12/disney-pixar-steve-jobs-markets-retailwire-apple-store.html?sh=274076897043 (archived at https://perma.cc/ HPD9-29HV)

Samir, C (2019) Forget about GDPR for a second: Ad-blockers are still a threat, *Reuters*, www.reutersagency.com/en/reuters-community/forget-about-gdpr-for-a-second-ad-blockers-are-still-a-threat/ (archived at https://perma.cc/5XA7-STBR)

Sapper (official website) (n.d.) https://richardsapperdesign.com/ (archived at https://perma.cc/BH27-X9AJ)

Schlender, B and Tetzeli, R (2015) *Becoming Steve Jobs: The evolution of a reckless upstart into a visionary leader*, Crown Business, New York

Sherman, L (2020) Case Study: The next wave of luxury e-commerce, *Business of Fashion*, www.businessoffashion.com/case-studies/luxury/ case-study-luxury-ecommerce-online-retail/ (archived at https://perma. cc/37AH-FF9X)

Snoek, J (2020) Zalando launches second-hand platform, *Retail Detail*, www.retaildetail.eu/news/fashion/zalando-launches-second-hand-platform/ (archived at https://perma.cc/LTX4-NMMC)

Stanfill, S (2021) G.B. Giorgini: Fashion, Florence and diplomacy, *ZoneModa Journal*, **11** (15), https://zmj.unibo.it/article/ view/13580/13270 (archived at https://perma.cc/H3NV-U8GP)

Stein, S (2021) It's been two decades since Apple opened its first store, *Forbes*, www.forbes.com/sites/sanfordstein/2021/05/19/apple-store-turns-twenty/?sh=757db24f31ac (archived at https://perma.cc/WG86-KVZM)

Stephenson, N (1992) *Snow Crash*, Bantam Books, New York

Tagwalk (2022) Ami hosts an easter egg hunt around the world, www. tag-walk.com/en/news/ami-hosts-an-easter-egg-hunt-around-the-world (archived at https://perma.cc/STA3-W9SV)

Theodosi, N (2017) Tinie Tempah plays host to celebrate the launch of LVMH's Clos19, *WWD*, https://wwd.com/fashion-news/fashion-scoops/ tinie-tempah-host-celebrate-launch-lvmh-clos-10885575/ (archived at https://perma.cc/67YX-ZQGV)

Tini, T (2022) Gaming, Metaverse and fashion: When being geek is chic. In *Brand Magic, The Brand Magic Book 2022*, Mauritius, https:// brandmagic.mu/ (archived at https://perma.cc/4QLV-47VN)

Vera, A (2021) Apple Store: Steve Jobs s'est-il inspiré de Louis Vuitton ? *PresseCitron*, www.presse-citron.net/un-francais-a-conseille-steve-jobs-au-lancement-des-apple-store/ (archived at https://perma.cc/J6R3-THTQ)

V&A (n.d.) Biba, www.vam.ac.uk/articles/biba (archived at https://perma.cc/3RXL-UMST)

Vogels, E A, Rainie, L and Anderson, J (2020) It's all just history repeating itself, www.pewresearch.org/internet/2020/06/30/its-all-just-history-repeating-itself/ (archived at https://perma.cc/8YNP-TDWP)

Vogue (2013) Luisa via Roma, la storia, www.vogue.it/moda/tendenze/2013/10/03/luisa-via-roma-storia (archived at https://perma.cc/SLF6-YRYX)

Wearesocial (2022) More than 5 billion people now use the internet, https://wearesocial.com/uk/blog/2022/04/more-than-5-billion-people-now-use-the-internet/ (archived at https://perma.cc/F7SS-P4SQ)

Wetlaufer, S (2001) The perfect paradox of star brands: An interview with Bernard Arnault of LVMH, *Harvard Business Review*, https://hbr.org/2001/10/the-perfect-paradox-of-star-brands-an-interview-with-bernard-arnault-of-lvmh (archived at https://perma.cc/88FF-V24Y)

Williams, R (2022) Bernard Arnault's take on the Metaverse, *Business of Fashion*, www.businessoffashion.com/news/luxury/bernard-arnaults-take-on-the-metaverse/ (archived at https://perma.cc/BZJ6-XX7X)

Yoox Net-à-Porter Group, official website, www.ynap.com/pages/about-us/who-we-are/history/ (archived at https://perma.cc/G6VJ-GCMX)

Zalando (2022) Zalando acquires majority stake in Highsnobiety, bringing together content and commerce, https://corporate.zalando.com/en/newsroom/news-stories/zalando-acquires-majority-stake-highsnobiety-bringing-together-content-and (archived at https://perma.cc/R8DQ-ZYEZ)

Zuhal, O (2012) Edutainment and learning. In N M Seel (ed) *Encyclopedia of the Sciences of Learning*, Springer, Boston

Developing profitable customer relationships through AI

07

ANNALISA TARQUINI-POLI
PHIL KLAUS

LEARNING OBJECTIVES

- To understand how AI is changing the way consumers make decisions and buy luxury goods and services.
- To understand how this shift in consumer behaviour is impacting luxury brands and customer experience management.
- To understand how luxury managers can improve the luxury customer experience and brand awareness implementing AI solutions.

Introduction

The technological revolution has changed the way clients purchase and interact with luxury products and services. The luxury retail industry is being profoundly transformed by digital and technological advancements. In particular, the direct-to-consumer (DTC) e-commerce model is altering the luxury retail landscape by making it simpler for new entrants to obtain market share (Eppe Beauloye, 2022). A sound and tailored digital strategy is essential for luxury firms to survive and thrive in today's market. With the rise of the internet, mobile devices and new technologies (e.g. non-fungible tokens (NFTs), blockchain and the Metaverse), luxury companies need to rethink their strategies to seize new business opportunities. Subsequently, companies need to rethink the way they build customer relationships.

Technology allows companies to collect and process large amounts of data. Luxury brands use new tools to perform their business more efficiently and effectively, and artificial intelligence (AI) is at the heart of this strategy.

AI is a field involving the ability of a mechanical device programmed to perform functions akin to learning and decision making. AI is used in many areas of business; for example, image, text and voice recognition, decision making, or to operate autonomous robots and vehicles.

AI is a branch of computer systems that refers to a technology that displays intelligent behaviour able to perform tasks that typically require human intelligence (Samoili et al, 2020).

Businesses and entire economies are being transformed by mobile and smart gadgets, robots, cloud technology and other technologies. McKinsey anticipates that by 2025 the economic impact will be between $14 trillion and $33 trillion per year (McKinsey & Company, 2021a).

There are multiple benefits for a company in using AI to make better use of existing customer data, one of which is to improve business process efficiency. Data processing at a pace and scale that humans alone would not be able to handle is the key to developing effective and efficient marketing and business strategies (Pratt, 2021).

AI can anticipate customers' preferences to offer products or services that both better match customers' expectations, and anticipate market trends. AI can shorten product and service go-to-market time span. AI offers opportunities to deliver better customer experiences (CX) and to improve brand loyalty (Bassano et al, 2020). AI has the potential to impact customer experience practices and to revolution-ize marketing decision-making processes. By integrating data with systems that process individual preferences, personal behaviour, feelings and emotional information, companies can gain useful information and design meaningful and customized customer experiences.

AI has changed the way consumers make purchasing decisions (Klaus and Zaichkowsky, 2020). Today's consumers require and look for both convenience and time savings, and they make their choices accordingly. Chat and voice-bots allow customers to save time and operate commands easily. Several companies have set up AI-based tools to facilitate customers' busy lives, allowing them to communicate with simple voice or text commands. AI can enhance the level of the CX personalization. Consumers expect offers mirroring their needs, but this process requires time and resources.

The question is, which businesses are most impacted by this change in consumer patterns? Klaus and Zaichkowsky (2020) highlight three:

- Branded businesses. These are companies that have substantially invested in branding and whose clients may now request a product by an attribute such as 'best price'. Algorithms have no brand loyalty. They assess a product's quality without regard for brand awareness. Voice-bots are also unaffected by visual triggers and do not consider packaging or product design sensorial stimulations.

- Brands that have traditionally differentiated themselves via outstanding human service and customer experience. The focus of customer experience management is moving away from interactions with brand representatives and offerings towards interactions with AI. When customers delegate their decision making to an algorithm, service's perceived influence is minimized, if not eliminated entirely.

- Any small company, including new start-ups. These small businesses can add a high-quality product with competitive pricing in the bot mix and it could become the most popular bot-pick right away, with no need for advertising. For example, in 2017, because customers searched by product category (e.g. yoga pants) rather than brand name (e.g. Lululemon), Amazon became the largest retailer of private-label clothes. This is an excellent example of how consumers benefit from AI since personal bots will be able to select the best features from all available options.

AI undoubtedly has the potential to improve marketing and CX strategies. The question is, how, when, and where can luxury companies benefit from AI?

Traditionally, luxury managers believe that they operate differently from other industries. Why do managers believe luxury consumers are different from other consumers? This notion of the luxury paradigm is based upon the way we conceptualize luxury and luxury purchasing behaviour. Researchers classify luxury brands according to their customers' spending power and different type of luxury such as absolute, aspirational and affordable (Brun and Castelli, 2013). Functional critical success factors (CSF) in the luxury context (Brun and Castelli, 2013), such as quality and craftsmanship, are not as important as more emotional key factors, such as CX. CX is the key marketing strategy (Atwal and Williams, 2017) 'because experience is replacing quality as the competitive battleground for marketing' (Klaus and Maklan, 2013, p 227). CX is the sum of all perceptions and feelings stemming from a customer's interaction with a brand over the duration of a true and authentic relationship, before, during, and after the sales (Klaus, 2015).

How is it conceivable that luxury customers, traditionally driven by direct interactions with the brand and its ambassadors, accept, embrace, and prefer brand interactions through technology (Klaus and Manthiou, 2020)? AI shifts the focus from a tool to a consumer benefit. Today's customer relationships are based on the experience delivered, not the channels used to deliver the experience. Customers are interested in time savings and convenience independent from with whom or what they interact.

Globally, luxury consumption is increasing; the digital era allows consumers a raised level of access to products and services. Think luxury e-commerce, once regarded as an inappropriate channel for luxury goods. This perception has changed completely. E-commerce is now a critical component for a luxury brand's survival. Luxury customers expect the buying process to fit their preferences for how, where and when they can find their favourite products or services. The online convenience and time-saving benefits apply for all consumer segments. For example, ultra-high net worth individuals state time savings, which can be achieved by AI, as a key driver of their purchasing decisions (Klaus et al, 2021). Luxury consumers are using online channels more and more often, a trend accelerated by the pandemic. Luxury customers are buying products that pre-pandemic were exclusively purchased after physical interactions with luxury products and brand representatives. An excellent example to highlight these changes is luxury yachts sales taking place on Zoom (Jackson, 2022). Today, the online luxury experience has reached a different level. It is indeed the end of luxury as we know it.

The purpose of this chapter is twofold. First, we highlight how AI has transformed the way people make decisions. We discuss how this shift in consumer behaviour is impacting luxury brands and CX management. Second, we aim to help luxury managers to improve CX and brand awareness by utilizing AI.

AI and the evolution of consumer decision making

In the last 80 years, the way customers make decisions has changed drastically, from strictly economic considerations (Telser, 1962) to today's AI utilization through smart devices (Wilson and Daugherty, 2018). The consumer experience has been shaped by brand concepts along the way. The pinnacle of the branding focus in the 1990s, as reported by Keller (1993) in the United States and Kapferer (1994) in Europe, stimulated hundreds of academic studies and several PhD theses about branding and brand management.

Improving the customer experience has become a difficult challenge for any luxury company because of the increase in customer expectations all the time. Companies that want to provide superior customer service must consider more factors than simply delivering a high-quality product on time through the correct channel. In addition to providing efficient service, they must seek new approaches to eliminate customer pain points throughout the entire purchase transaction (Daqar and Smoudy, 2019). The fast advancement of technology has opened tremendous opportunities for several sectors (Delponte and Tamburrini, 2018), especially in marketing, and AI is being employed more frequently in services, providing a significant source of innovation and causing disruptive changes in the value chain.

The evolution of AI

By the 1950s several scientists, mathematicians and philosophers were already familiar with the concept of AI. The human desire to 'forge the gods' has ancient roots, from the first-known automata, ancient Egyptian and Greek religious statues, to the automaton 'digesting duck' built in the mid-18th century (Newquist, 1994). But it was not until Alan Turing's work that the computational possibilities of AI could be understood (Turing, 2009). Turing's proposition is that if humans are able to use information and reason to solve problems and take decisions, then machines can do the same. Turing devised a test that became known as the 'Turing Test' or 'Imagination Game'. His goal was to find out whether a machine could engage in intelligent behaviour that could be interpreted as 'human'. The game consisted of placing a human being and a computer, both connected to a terminal, in front of a judge. The computer passed the test and was designated as 'intelligent' if the judge couldn't identify the difference between a human and a machine.

Access to computers became possible in the middle of the 1950s (Buchanan, 2005). The proof of AI concept was introduced in 1955 with the publication of *Logic Theorist* by Allen Newell (future Nobel laureate in economics), Herbert Simon and Cliff Shaw. The Logic Theorist was a program developed by the Research and Development (RAND) Corporation to simulate human problem-solving capacities.

In 1956 John McCarthy organized the first AI conference, establishing 'artificial intelligence' as a real scientific discipline. During the conference Herbert Simon and Allen Newell presented the first artificial intelligence program, Logic Theorist. AI thrived from 1957 to 1974, but the major deterrent to its progress was the lack of computer capacity (Anyoha, 2017).

AI enthusiasm began to diminish in the 1970s and 1980s, as scientists' claimed aspirations and ambitions proved to be too optimistic and ambitious.

Two factors rekindled AI in the 1980s: an extension of the algorithmic toolset and an increase in funding. 'Deep learning' techniques, popularized by John Hopfield and David Rumelhart, allowed computers to learn through experience. Edward Feigenbaum pioneered expert systems that emulated the decision-making process of a human expert.

The corporate community's interest in AI expanded in the 1980s, and many computer hardware companies focused their efforts on artificial intelligence. Following the typical trajectory of an economic bubble, interest declined. As a result, artificial intelligence research suffered another delay, this time lasting until the mid-1990s. Following this setback, artificial intelligence research shifted focus from intuition-based research to theoretical underpinnings, established mathematical conclusions and substantial experimentation. This partial rebirth, combined with the availability of ever-faster processors and new financing rounds, resulted in a change of fortune for AI (Anyoha, 2017).

Despite the absence of government investment, artificial intelligence has thrived. During the 1990s and 2000s, numerous artificial intelligence's key goals were accomplished. In 1997 IBM's Deep Blue beat Russian grandmaster Garry Kasparov, becoming the first machine to defeat a world chess champion. After the match, Kasparov said that the computer 'played like a god' (Thompson, 2022). Dragon Systems' speech recognition software was first installed on Windows in 1997. This was yet another significant stride forward, but this time in the direction of spoken language interpretation.

Machine learning was successfully applied to numerous problems in academia and industry in the first decades of the 21st century, thanks to innovative approaches, powerful hardware and the accumulation of massive data sets.

The fundamental limitation of computer storage that held back the development of AI 30 years ago was no longer an issue. Technological progress has accelerated at an astonishing speed in the last two decades, allowing the accomplishment of previously inconceivable ambitions.

We now live in the 'big data' era, in which we have the ability to collect massive volumes of data (Anyoha, 2017).

The fast-evolving technology development, with the increased calculation capacity and more sophisticated algorithms, has influenced the evolution of AI, but another aspect has given a new momentum to this evolution. AI now dominates every moment of our lives: our phones unlock with facial recognition, take us from one point to another, offer suggestions on possible travel destinations, and remember our preferences and tastes. It is precisely this dominance of technology in our lives that has enabled AI's impressive development. Consumers have unintentionally launched a process of AI improvement by continuing to utilize technology and providing access to millions of personal and non-personal data. The huge availability of data is what has set us apart from previous generations.

Data is the fuel for the development of the 'future economy' and AI is the tool for utilizing this massive data set. As a result, there is a basic relationship between population, economics and AI. Culturally, economically and technologically, we are in the midst of a momentous shift.

From the search for information to a decision-making tool: a new customer's journey

The emergence of the internet, and more recently social media, has completely transformed the way people shop. Traditionally, companies had a competitive advantage in the marketplace when they cut the cost of information search (Wu et al, 2004). Furthermore, brands used to be regarded as trustworthy because they offered reliable information about the quality of the purchase (Zeithaml, 1988). However, this information function of branding has now been replaced by the comparison ability of AI (Klaus and Zaichkowsky, 2020) and luxury digital consumption habits have now evolved throughout the consumer life cycle. Consumers' evaluation of the information provided by brands is often influenced by online interactions with various external individuals. These interactions occur because often peers, friends and family members show a lack of trust in the information provided by the luxury brand (Klaus, 2020).

In the digital era the new digital consumer is someone who uses mobile devices and the internet to seek and buy, making use of online content. They are conscious of their demands, and want to make purchasing decisions easier (Tkaczyk, 2016). Luxury digital consumers are much more than customers. They are not only informed persons who form their own opinions, but they also share their impressions, comments and experiences with others in real time. This confers a new power on the consumers, who challenge companies to offer more inviting interactions. This situation represents an opportunity for luxury companies. Brand strategists can establish a bond with the potential consumer before the purchase takes place. This shift from a monologue to a dialogue with the luxury consumer is in line with what luxury consumers desire – a more transparent and trustful conversation with the brand.

The digital consumer has become more conscious and demanding over time (Weinswig, 2016), especially when it comes to the luxury shopping experience, which must be perceived as personal and intentionally offered to the customer, whether or not the purchase takes place. This explains why a company's digital strategies are so important today. According to D'Arpizio et al (2020, pp 4–5) 'the luxury customer is present and increasingly active, dramatically rewriting the rule book of the industry. Brands will need to pivot to a new model to respond to customer's need when it comes to buying, consuming, and communicating.' A company's online presence is an important part of how customers learn about a brand, search for it, interact and hopefully become attached to it.

Digital disruption in choice: e-commerce evolution

Online retail started to take shape at the turn of the 2000s. Most of the luxury brands have been slow to embrace the digital revolution because of a diffused scepticism. According to them, consumers would have not migrated to online platforms for their purchases without being able to physically touch and scrutinize the products. At that time the most used e-commerce websites were selling books and toys. Amazon emerged as the 'best' service brand (Smith and Brynjolfsson, 2001), having been one of the first in online retail to start with books. On Amazon, customers were willing to spend more for the same goods. This was assumed to be correct because Amazon was regarded as a trustworthy service provider. Over the last two decades, Amazon has steadily grown its geographic reach and product offerings, while making online purchasing increasingly convenient for customers (Farah and Ramadan, 2017). In order to give the finest possible customer service experience, it has embraced a customer-centric retail approach (Prahalad and Ramaswamy, 2000).

At first, getting people to trust online buying in general was crucial; Amazon, on the other hand, built consumer confidence in online buying precisely by earning their trust. Amazon is now the market leader in online sales, with in-home voice assistants that connect to massive warehouses and distribution networks for millions of different consumer products (Dayton, 2020). Today, Amazon is the most popular online platform (Klaus and Zaichkowsky, 2022) and it represents a trend setter in the e-commerce business for many companies, including luxury. Its convenience, customer experience, geographical coverage, and return policies are challenging many brands. One of Amazon's latest extensions was its luxury store offering on its mobile app (Phelps, 2020). So, today we can find any kind of products and services offered online.

In 2017 Bain & Company predicted that the online channel will account for 25 per cent of the market value by 2025, and that online engagement will highly influence luxury purchases. According to a study by Klaus (2020) the convenience and flexibility that buying online offers are the main drivers for buying luxury goods online. This refers to both the restrictions imposed by shopping in stores, including in-store accessibility and lack of information about product availability, and the benefits, such as the larger selection available and the greater freedom offered by internet shopping. Thanks to accelerated adoption during Covid-19 with newly acquired consumers, online continues to develop at a rapid pace, increasing by 27 per cent from 2020 to 2021 to reach an expected €62 billion in market value in 2022. Brand-controlled websites now account for 40 per cent of all online traffic, up from 30 per cent in 2019 (D'Arpizio et al, 2021). Another point to consider is how voice bots are challenging visual online shopping. According to the Capgemini Digital Transformation Institute study (Capgemini, 2020) more than 50 per cent of consumers prefer the service offered by voice assistants, instead of traditional visual online shopping.

When it succeeds in generating efficiency over earlier models, technological innovation and its application in new industries is a disruptive force. Buying luxury goods online is a clear example. The digital era has disrupted traditional patterns of purchasing luxury products and services, opening up new frontiers previously unimaginable. Does this mean that the typical in-store luxury experience is no longer relevant? Research says no, but it highlights the difficulty of managing the 360-degree luxury customer experience (Klaus, 2020).

The phygital environment: where artificial intelligence and augmented reality meet

The (traditional) offline and the (modern) online realms are no longer distinct in the consumer journey, but rather part of a new dimension – the phygital environment (Petro, 2021). The new hybrid form of trade is a common global retail strategy that offers a new hybrid form of CX. Phygitality (Klaus, 2021) is the most complete omnichannel strategy, giving brands the ability to establish a consistent customer relationship with the consumers across all their touchpoints. This is in accordance with the CX research, which claims that CX must be understood and managed as a continuum between experiences and the channels through which they are delivered.

During the Covid-19 pandemic many consumers switched online to remain in touch with their beloved brands and to shop for their favourite products (Willersdorf et al, 2020). Companies who had previously invested in technologies were found ready and, despite the considerable loss, managed to survive (McKinsey & Company, 2021b). Due to the high competition online, a greater understanding of clients was required to provide more personalized offers. It is in these particular times that AI and additional sensory stimuli created by technologies like augmented reality (AR) and virtual reality (VR) produce phygital environments that are distinct from the real world.

Consumers and brands now have a more sustainable and fruitful relationship. AR applications offer a virtual alternative for consumers who are unable to touch and try on products such as watches, jewellery, clothing and beauty products, resulting in a better decision-making process and purchasing experience. Furthermore, AI enables brands to design targeted campaigns, obtain smart recommendations, and provide extensive customer support, all of which contribute to a trusted, preferred brand image (Inveon, 2021). Thanks to AI and its automated learning capabilities, personalized shopping experiences may now be offered not only to a specific target group, but also to a hyper-personalized audience (El Badia et al, 2021). Although these two technologies are completely different, they do share certain similarities: both are intended to offer a convenient and more sensory digital customer experience (Kime, 2011).

Many luxury brands, especially the most exclusive like Chanel and Hermès, were hesitant to move into the digital world, fearing that they would lose the personal connection with the end consumer in their retail stores. On the contrary, other luxury businesses are reinventing themselves by improving the consumer experience and experimenting with digital technology to meet their physical and emotional needs (DeAcetis, 2020). For example, Gucci, a 100-year-old brand, is reinterpreting its marketing strategies by collaborating with partners to deliver digital products such as virtual versions of its collections and products. The brand is actively adopting emerging technologies and digital marketing tools such as AR, VR and AI chatbots to create digital content to attract and interact with a younger audience (Hobbs, 2021). For instance, in 2021 the brand launched its first digital shoes, which can only be worn using AR (Gorman, 2021), and other virtual replicas of its collections for fashion-themed video games and VR apps where customers can dress up their avatars with Gucci products.

Another interesting case is the Louis Vuitton (LV) digital assistant chatbot on Facebook Messenger, which exploits AI to provide its customers with a more refined, customized, visual and interactive online experience (Eppe Beauloye, 2022). Particular emphasis has been placed on the search functions. Users can interact with the chatbot to discover the products available on the LV online catalogue, but also to receive advice on specific products and store locations. More importantly, the chatbot enables customers to share LV products on Facebook and receive votes on which ones to purchase.

A clear example of how luxury business looks at innovation is the partnership between LVMH and Viva Technology, Europe's biggest start-up and tech event (https://vivatechnology.com/). During the 2022 edition, LVMH announced the winners of the different categories, and one is dedicated to Data & Artificial Intelligence. The US start-up MarqVision received a special mention. Thanks to AI image recognition and semantic analysis, MarqVision spots counterfeit products that are sold online, helping brands to remove the fake products. Some luxury jewellery brands of the caliber of Tiffany and Bulgari are already trusting this technology. Bernard Arnault, CEO and Chairman of LVMH stated:

> At LVMH, Innovation is our lifeblood. It's what allows us to continually increase the desirability of our Maisons's products and services. The finalists of the 2022 Innovation Award will bring us their capacity to nourish the encounter between luxury and technology even more, as their entrepreneurial spirit joins and inspires our own (LVMH, 2022).

When a customer interacts with a luxury brand online, the brand learns new things about them, such as their tastes and preferences. In return, AI enables brands to provide more tailored experiences, resulting in increased sales through smart searches and suggestions. AR and digital technologies empower clients to make better decisions by allowing them to sample a greater range of products and combinations in minutes, independent of their location.

Trends in the luxury business change but one constant remains – the pursuit of client happiness. As long as this quest remains at the heart of luxury brands' strategies, the sector will continue to grow, thanks in part to the digital support provided by modern technology.

How AI is transforming digital marketing strategies

Historically, luxury customers have emphasized the importance of the relationship with a sales associate and the resulting customer experience while purchasing the desired product or service. Consumers' decision-making processes have been influenced by socio-emotional factors such as interactions with the company's human touchpoints and the subsequent brand perceptions (De Keyser et al, 2020). Favourable CX is triggered by positive interactions with a company's human touchpoints, which represent customers' perceptions of so-called soft skills (Klaus, 2020). Soft skills can increase trust and customer engagement (Heckman and Kautz, 2012), create a stronger brand perception and, finally, create brand loyalty (Dean, 2017).

On the other hand, according to a recent study, for some customers the lack of interaction is a reason for not shopping frequently online. The result is a double-edged truth. Thus, it appears that the direct relationship with sales representatives pushes the consumer away from the store and moves their purchases online. Most respondents stated that negative interactions with sales staff led them to avoid visiting retail stores so as not to feel 'judged' by the people working there (Klaus, 2020).

Chatbots are a tool used by marketers as a first virtual interaction with consumers, the main benefit being their efficiency. Thanks to their client profiling capacity, chatbots manage to translate customer expectations (Bassano et al, 2020). They can be found on landing pages to collect initial basic information and to send inquiries, available 24/7 without the need for the physical presence of a sales representative. The result is a better and more efficient CX.

In 2016 McKinsey forecast that by 2020, 85 per cent of US consumers would have interacted with brands using AI rather than humans (Campbell et al, 2020). Therefore, the key role of AI for brands and marketing is clear. But why has AI won such a high level of recognition in such a short time?

Foehr and Germelmann (2020), in a recent journal issue on trust, examined voice interaction technologies, and how they arouse emotions in consumers by interacting with them. The results show that the interaction between the customer and the voice bot is like interacting with a friend. Users perceive and establish trust in smart technologies in different ways. The main path is to link trust to the perceived personality of the voice technology interface. The other paths involve the software, the manufacturer and the device. The experience of communicating with a technology that can send messages of feeling and understanding in a human-like manner is critical to maintaining trust in the device.

This experience considerably outweighs the consumer's interactions with screens and tactical controls, to which we are less willing to delegate our decisions. Screens are two-dimensional surfaces on which several options can be displayed at the same time. The eye can analyse multiple options and compare them to one another, switching back and forth as needed. Consumers may use their devices to look for information or even seek guidance, but there is no emotional connection when they communicate with a screen.

Consumers are now more comfortable with decision making as a result of the humanization of technology through voice. The three main reasons why consumers delegate their decisions to bots are: 1) convenience; 2) feelings of control and trust; and 3) positive emotion. In the next sections these three factors will be discussed in more detail and then implications for service marketing professionals will be considered.

The new consumer: the convenience addict

The rise of technology has resulted in a convenience-addicted consumer. A vast stream of literature examines the various drives for consumers to shop. Convenience as a key factor in decision making is not a new concept (Kelley, 1958). In a study conducted to compare in-store with online shopping behaviour, results showed that convenience is the predominant reason for online shopping, preferred by 42.1 per cent of the respondents. The ease of buying any time and anywhere, and the time-saving process, are what consumers value. The possibility to compare products and price online follows with 22.9 per cent (Liu et al, 2013).

In 2018, Tim Wu, in an opinion piece published in the *New York Times*, talked about the tyranny of convenience: convenience is probably the most significant force driving lives and economies. Similarly, Evan Williams, a co-founder of Twitter, said 'Convenience decides everything'. Convenience appears to take precedence over what we would want to believe are our real preferences (Wu, 2018). Consumers took time to acquire a preference for convenience over other factors, but the modern consumer accepts it without question.

The rise of convenience as a key driver of customer experience and consumer behaviour is reflected by consumers' increasing use of emerging AI bot technologies. Despite the fact that consumers using voice assistants have less information about the products than when shopping in stores, other benefits emerge, like the physical and the cognitive time spent in the process. Consumers today value convenience and the time they save by shopping easily, and therefore appreciate companies able to provide convenience. This leads to brand loyalty (Lin, 2016). Consumers are drawn to AI bots for a variety of reasons, not the least of which is convenience. Voice adds several desired characteristics, making bots more likely to be the preferred service platform.

Control and trust

Aside from convenience and time savings, there should be another crucial ingredient at the heart of any transaction: trust (Klaus and Zaichkowsky, 2022). Trust is linked to the sensations and emotions that arise as a result of interacting with the device. When the interaction with the AI is human, trust develops. Research reveals that anthropomorphism mediates the relationship between focus and pleasure, as well as the type of connection one has with the AI (Foehr and Germelmann, 2020). AI is a social actor, and its characteristics influence an individual's response to it. As a result, anthropomorphism plays a critical role in the AI-human relationship, and it is a strategy that can reduce anxiety about uncertainty while also meeting social needs, by allowing a human-like connection with a non-human agent (Kim et al, 2019).

Consumers place trust in AI in both low-involvement and high-involvement decisions. In the first case, consumers feel free to share and store personal information with links to credit card and banking data to facilitate future deliveries. In the second case, humans' inability to analyse and compare complex forms of enormous data available in the marketplace may explain the trust placed in high-involvement decisions. If the consumer is pleased with the service and products received for low-involvement decisions, the shift to a more complex decision becomes easier. The favourable emotions received through vocal contact contribute to this trust.

Trust and emotions

Next to convenience, time efficiency represents another benefit in decision-making processes (Klaus and Zaichkowsky, 2022). Due to a rising sense of time scarcity (Whillans et al, 2017), time is considered a most precious possession, especially for wealthy customers (Klaus et al, 2021). Therefore, spending money on time-saving services increases customer happiness (Whillans et al, 2017). Additionally, consumers appreciate services that allow them to avoid negative experiences (Klaus and Edvardsson, 2017). This is in line with CX research that highlights the importance of designing brand strategies aimed at preventing bad CX rather than delighting customers (Ponsignon et al, 2015). Therefore, emotions are more valuable advantages in the decision-making process than expected and marketers need to focus on them rather than just on mere functional benefits.

The customer engages in long talks with the bot, which can give them positive feelings (Lopatovska et al, 2019). The voice-based interface turns the purchasing process into a conversational and spontaneous dialogue. Google, Apple and Amazon, among the world's most valuable businesses, are already utilizing this technology with Google Home, Apple HomePod and Amazon Echo, respectively. Brands recognize the value of voice and are increasingly focusing on choosing distinct, appealing voices in line with their brand image.

This is similar to trademarks such as unique logos, colours or tag lines, which have long been utilized by luxury brands as a distinctive element of the brand experience. The aim is for a unique voice to be recognized as a brand element and to represent a distinct personality, just like a voice does for a real human.

Consumers' enjoyment in interacting with AI in the decision-making process is also linked to their trust in the system. As previously mentioned, the trust placed in AI to offer the best option to the consumer for both high- and low-involvement decisions is crucial, and one of the elements that influence that trust is the voice interaction versus merely viewing through a screen (Foehr and Germelmann, 2020). Consumers are increasingly trusting their personal voice assistants to make decisions on their behalf as they utilize AI speech bots more regularly. And, if the purchase becomes more complex, AI may become increasingly trusted for high-involvement decisions. Consumers will be so dependent on AI that they will be hesitant to make their own decisions out of fear of making the wrong choice (Makridakis, 2017).

Implications and opportunities for service marketing professionals

Global trends indicate that online shopping will increase, and companies need to invest to meet the increasing demands of customers. Luxury consumers are aware that the online experience cannot replicate the in-store experience in terms of interactions, regardless of the segment, and managers must keep this in mind. They do, however, expect additional interactions and experiences outside of the usual in-store experience. A luxury customer does not compare the online shopping experience with other luxury brands, but with the way he or she can reach the goal to purchase a favourite product online. As a result, luxury clients compare the convenience and effectiveness of purchasing and using Alibaba, Amazon, Netflix or TripAdvisor to the online luxury experience.

AI is a game changer for any luxury brand and allows them to deliver personalization of the offer and an increased online CX. The integration of AI technology into the omnichannel strategy can be endless. An emphasis needs to be placed on consumers' increasing need for convenience, and this has multiple implications for service marketing practices.

Some suggestions for service marketing professionals:

- Don't use AI for the sake of using technology. The application of technology in retail should always be treated as a means and not as a goal. Customers can leave you if the solution doesn't work properly, but at the same time they can leave you if the brand doesn't provide AI solutions at all.

- The wrong AI solution can destroy CX and customer relations, therefore impacting customer loyalty. What is very important is that the use of AI needs to mirror the expected CX. It can happen that AI applications, especially apps, can destroy the CX and the customer relationship.

- Luxury is no exception. What kind of motivations, benefits and experiences are customers looking for while purchasing luxury goods online? It is about adding variety, not either/or. Decisions are made upon if it improves what your customers perceive as a good experience. Think about a new hierarchy of needs, where for the luxury customer convenience, reliability and time savings will always be more important than aspiration, social and hedonic value (for a full review please read Klaus et al, 2021).

Conclusion

To conclude, in our chapter, we highlighted how AI has transformed the way people make decisions nowadays. This important shift in consumer behaviour changes both how consumers buy luxury goods and services, and how luxury brands and CXs need to be managed.

References

Anyoha, R (2017) The history of artificial intelligence, https://sitn.hms. harvard.edu/flash/2017/history-artificial-intelligence/ (archived at https://perma.cc/78SU-XY49)

Atwal, G and Williams, A (2017) Luxury brand marketing–the experience is everything! In *Advances in Luxury Brand Management*, Palgrave Macmillan, Cham, pp 43–57

Bain & Company (2017) Luxury Goods Worldwide Market Study, Fall–Winter 2017, www.bain.com/insights/luxury-goods-worldwide-market-study-fall-winter-2017/ (archived at https://perma.cc/6ZXJ-XBCG)

Bassano, C, Barile, S, Saviano, M, Pietronudo, M C and Cosimato, S (2020) AI technologies & value co-creation in luxury context, *Proceedings of the 53rd Hawaii International Conference on System Sciences*

Brun, A and Castelli, C (2013) The nature of luxury: a consumer perspective, *International Journal of Retail & Distribution Management*, **41** (11/12), pp 823–47

Buchanan, B G (2005) A (very) brief history of artificial intelligence, *Ai Magazine*, **26** (4), p 53

Campbell, C, Sands, S, Ferraro, C, Tsao, H Y J and Mavrommatis, A (2020) From data to action: How marketers can leverage AI, *Business Horizons*, **63** (2), pp 227–43

Capgemini (2020) Empathetic Intelligence: How smart voice assistants are driving consumer convenience, www.capgemini.com/in-en/insights/expert-perspectives/empathetic-intelligence-how-smart-voice-assistants-are-driving-consumer-convenience/ (archived at https://perma.cc/2EX8-N5TF)

Daqar, M A A and Smoudy, A K (2019) The role of artificial intelligence on enhancing customer experience, *International Review of Management and Marketing*, **9** (4), p 22

D'Arpizio, C, Levato, F, Gault, C, de Montgolfier, J and Jaroudi, L (2021) From surging recovery to elegant advance: The evolving future of luxury, www.bain.com/insights/from-surging-recovery-to-elegant-advance-the-evolving-future-of-luxury/ (archived at https://perma.cc/Y2B7-38LQ)

D'Arpizio, C, Levato, F, Prete, F and de Montgolfier, J (2020) Eight themes that are rewriting the future of luxury goods, www.bain.com/insights/eight-themes-that-are-rewriting-the-future-of-luxury-goods/ (archived at https://perma.cc/J33Z-23AH)

Dayton, E (2020) Amazon statistics you should know: Opportunities to make the most of America's top online marketplace, *Big Commerce*, www.bigcommerce.com/blog/amazon-statistics/ (archived at https://perma.cc/V2UX-X7S5)

DeAcetis, J (2020) Relationship Goals: Luxury retail and technology make a perfect combo for customer, Forbes, www.forbes.com/sites/josephdeacetis/2020/08/15/relationship-goals-luxury-retail-and-technology-make-a-perfect-combo-for-customer/?sh=6bf7554c1275 (archived at https://perma.cc/2Y6E-9W5Y)

Dean, S A (2017) Soft skills needed for the 21st century workforce (Doctoral dissertation, Walden University)

De Keyser, A, Verleye, K, Lemon, K N, Keiningham, T L and Klaus, P (2020) Moving the customer experience field forward: introducing the touchpoints, context, qualities (TCQ) nomenclature, *Journal of Service Research*, **23** (4), pp 433–55

Delponte, L and Tamburrini, G (2018) European Artificial Intelligence (AI) leadership: The path for an integrated vision, European Parliament

El Badia, K, Doulkaid, A and Wahabi, R (2021) The impact of the co-production on the lived experience in a 'phygital' store: a value-based approach proposal of a model, *Revue Internationale des Sciences de Gestion*, **4** (4)

Eppe Beauloye, F (2022) How personalisation and artificial intelligence are transforming luxury retail online, *Luxe*, https://luxe.digital/business/digital-luxury-trends/how-personalisation-and-artificial-intelligence-are-transforming-luxury-retail-online/ (archived at https://perma.cc/3BBA-7HPJ)

Farah, M F and Ramadan, Z B (2017) Disruptions versus more disruptions: how the amazon dash button is altering consumer buying patterns, *Journal of Retailing and Consumer Services*, **39**, pp 54–61

Foehr, J and Germelmann, C C (2020) Alexa, can I trust you? Exploring consumer paths to trust in smart voice-interaction technologies, *Journal of the Association for Consumer Research*, **5** (2), pp 181–205

Gorman, A (2021) A virtual steal: the digital Gucci sneakers for sale at $17.99, *Guardian*, www.theguardian.com/fashion/2021/mar/19/a-virtual-steal-the-gucci-sneakers-for-sale-at-1799 (archived at https://perma.cc/X5JY-N8CG)

Heckman, J J and Kautz, T (2012) Hard evidence on soft skills, *Labour Economics*, **19** (4), pp 451–64

Hobbs, J (2021) How Gucci became the most popular luxury brand for gen Z on TikTok, www.vogue.com/article/vogue-club/why-gucci-is-the-most-popular-luxury-brand-on-tiktok (archived at https://perma.cc/M5YY-QCMH)

Jackson, R (2022) Boat Shows: Too many? Too few? Or just right? *Superyacht News*, www.superyachtnews.com/business/the-future-of-boat-shows-2022 (archived at https://perma.cc/4846-GWSY)

Kapferer, J N (1994) *Strategic Brand Management: New approaches to creating and evaluating brand equity*, Simon and Schuster

Keller, K L (1993) Conceptualizing, measuring, and managing customer-based brand equity, *Journal of Marketing*, 57 (1), pp 1–22

Kelley, E J (1958) The importance of convenience in consumer purchasing, *Journal of Marketing*, 23 (1), pp 132–38

Kim, A, Cho, M, Ahn, J and Sung, Y (2019) Effects of gender and relationship type on the response to artificial intelligence, *Cyberpsychology, Behavior, and Social Networking*, 22 (4), pp 249–53

Kime, S (2011) Engaging the Millennial, a case for augmented reality, *Luxury Society*, www.luxurysociety.com/en/articles/2011/02/engaging-the-millennial-a-case-for-augmented-reality (archived at https://perma.cc/6VEJ-DXZK)

Klaus, P (2015) *Measuring Customer Experience*, Palgrave Macmillan Books

Klaus, P P (2020) The end of the world as we know it? The influence of online channels on the luxury customer experience, *Journal of Retailing and Consumer Services*, 57

Klaus, P P (2021) Phygital–the emperor's new clothes? *Journal of Strategic Marketing*

Klaus, P and Edvardsson, B (2017) Relieving customers in service eco-systems – an empirical study of firms' value creation practices, QUIS 15 Symposium, Porto, Portugal

Klaus, P P and Maklan, S (2013) Towards a better measure of customer experience, *International Journal of Market Research*, 55 (2), pp 227–46

Klaus, P P and Manthiou, A (2020) Applying the EEE customer mindset in luxury: reevaluating customer experience research and practice during and after corona, *Journal of Service Management*, 31 (6), pp 1175–83

Klaus, P, Tarquini-Poli, A and Park, J (2021) Priceless time–the UHNWI's most precious possession: implications for international marketing theory and practice, *International Marketing Review*, 1 (2), pp 335–51

Klaus, P and Zaichkowsky, J (2020) AI voice bots: a services marketing research agenda, *Journal of Services Marketing*, **34** (3), pp 389–98

Klaus, P and Zaichkowsky, J L (2022) The convenience of shopping via voice AI: Introducing AIDM, *Journal of Retailing and Consumer Services*, **65**, p 102490

Inveon Insights (2021) Improving customer experience: AI and AR Applications, www.inveon.com/improving-customer-experience-ai-and-ar-applications (archived at https://perma.cc/C5AG-HV25)

Lin, C Y (2016) Perceived convenience retailer innovativeness: how does it affect consumers? *Management Decision*, **54** (4), pp 946–64

Liu, X, Burns, A C and Hou, Y (2013) Comparing online and in-store shopping behavior towards luxury goods, *International Journal of Retail & Distribution Management*, **41** (11/12)

Lopatovska, I, Velazquez, M, Richardson, R and Lai, G (2019) User sentiments towards intelligent personal assistants, *iConference 2019 Proceedings*

LVMH (2022) www.lvmh.com/news-documents/news/lvmh-announces-2022-innovation-award-prize-list-and-its-grand-winner-toshi-during-viva-technology/ (archived at https://perma.cc/8AQX-7GRJ)

Makridakis, S (2017) The forthcoming Artificial Intelligence (AI) revolution: Its impact on society and firms, *Futures*, **90**, pp 46–60

McKinsey & Company (2021a) The Internet of Things: Catching up to an accelerating opportunity, www.mckinsey.com/~/media/mckinsey/business%20functions/mckinsey%20digital/our%20insights/iot%20value%20set%20to%20accelerate%20through%202030%20where%20and%20how%20to%20capture%20it/the-internet-of-things-catching-up-to-an-accelerating-opportunity-final.pdf (archived at https://perma.cc/6Y5Z-CR6N)

McKinsey & Company (2021b) Solving the paradox of growth and profitability in e-commerce, www.mckinsey.com/industries/retail/our-insights/solving-the-paradox-of-growth-and-profitability-in-e-commerce (archived at https://perma.cc/WT6C-63SM)

Newquist, H P (1994) *The Brain Makers: Genius, ego, and greed in the quest for machines that think*, Macmillan, New York

Petro, G (2021) The 'Phygital' world: Reinventing the in-store experience digitally, *Forbes*, www.forbes.com/sites/gregpetro/2021/08/06/the-phygital-world-reinventing-the-in-store-experience-digitally/?sh=7719306f3863 (archived at https://perma.cc/ADT9-YY9M)

Phelps, N (2020) Amazon launches luxury stores on its mobile app with Oscar de la Renta as first brand partner, *Vogue*, www.vogue.com/article/amazon-launches-luxury-stores-oscar-de-la-renta (archived at https://perma.cc/KX4J-LXSV)

Ponsignon, F, Klaus, P and Maull, R S (2015) Experience co-creation in financial services: an empirical exploration, *Journal of Service Management*, **26** (2), pp 295–320

Prahalad, C K and Ramaswamy, V (2000) Co-opting customer competence, *Harvard Business Review*, **78** (1), pp 79–88

Pratt, M K (2021) 7 key benefits of AI for business, www.techtarget.com/searchenterpriseai/feature/6-key-benefits-of-AI-for-business (archived at https://perma.cc/QR7G-WNAY)

Samoili, S, Cobo, M L, Gomez, E, De Prato, G, Martinez-Plumed, F and Delipetrev, B (2020) AI Watch: Defining Artificial Intelligence. Towards an operational definition and taxonomy of artificial intelligence, JRC Research Reports

Smith, M D and Brynjolfsson, E (2001) Consumer decision-making at an internet ShopBot: brand still matters, *The Journal of Industrial Economics*, **49** (4), pp 541–58

Telser, L G (1962) The demand for branded goods as estimated from consumer panel data, *The Review of Economics and Statistics*, pp 300–24

Thompson, C (2022) What the history of AI tells us about its future, *Technology Review*, www.technologyreview.com/2022/02/18/1044709/ibm-deep-blue-ai-history/ (archived at https://perma.cc/S5RG-GR53)

Tkaczyk, J (2016) Digital consumer: trends and challenges. In: *The Impact of the Digital World on Management and Marketing*, Poltext

Turing, A M (2009) Computing machinery and intelligence. In *Parsing the Turing Test*, Springer, Dordrecht, pp 23–65

Weinswig, D (2016) Gen Z: Get ready for the most self-conscious, demanding consumer segment, *Fung Global Retail & Technology*, pp 1–19

Whillans, A V, Dunn, E W, Smeets, P, Bekkers, R and Norton, M I (2017) Buying time promotes happiness, *Proceedings of the National Academy of Sciences*, **114** (32), pp 8523–27

Willersdorf, S, Hazan, J, Ricci, G, Prénaud, A, Bianchi, F, Seara, J and Yang, V (2020) A New Era and a New Look for Luxury, www.bcg.com/publications/2020/new-era-and-new-look-for-luxury (archived at https://perma.cc/86T6-BHYJ)

Wilson, H J and Daugherty, P R (2018) Collaborative intelligence: Humans and AI are joining forces, *Harvard Business Review*, **96** (4), pp 114–23

Wu, T (2018) The Tyranny of Convenience, *The New York Times*, www. nytimes.com/2018/02/16/opinion/sunday/tyranny-convenience.html (archived at https://perma.cc/EWH4-R7FV)

Wu, D, Ray, G, Geng, X and Whinston, A (2004) Implications of reduced search cost and free riding in ecommerce, *Marketing Science*, **23** (2), pp 255–62

Zeithaml, V A (1988) Consumer perceptions of price, quality, and value: a means-end model and synthesis of evidence, *Journal of Marketing*, **52** (3), pp 2–22

PART THREE
New directions in luxury branding

Luxury in the Metaverse 08

The five forces of value creation for luxury brands in the Metaverse

ALESSANDRO BRUN
ALESSANDRO DONETTI

A technical introduction: blockchain, NFT and other digital devilish things

LEARNING OBJECTIVES

- To acquire the essential terminology as it relates to a new set of digital tools, from blockchain to web 3.
- To understand the functioning of NFTs and how they will allow us to generate and capture value.
- To identify the new five forces through which luxury brands can obtain a competitive advantage.
- To be able to exploit the paradigm of the creator economy, by looking at the Metaverse as an intersection of technological, economic and cultural perspectives.

Blockchain – not just for bitcoins

Blockchain technology is based on the principle of decentralized architecture. The internet works through a set of servers that belong to companies, as is commonly known. When the user interacts on X website of Y company, they are actually interacting with the company's servers. This centralized architecture has its benefits, such as greater ease of management, but it also has its weaknesses because since it is a centralized structure, the web services stop working if the servers fail. In addition, an essential point of these is the power, since the capacity of management, decision and control is accumulated in a single point of the network. This fact, linked to the new importance of data and its functionalities, has resulted in criticism and a change in social opinion about network privacy.

As an alternative, decentralized networks were born, where the nodes themselves support the network as servers, where each one manages the data and its processing, and there is collective coordination for decision making. This structure allows some of its nodes to fail since the other assets support the network. The problem comes with the complexity of managing and building the network, and taking responsibility for its actions. An example would be decision making, so that it really works correctly and there is no fraud, and as there is no node 'superior' to the others, it is necessary to ensure that users and data are accurate. The exact process in a centralized network is much simpler since the node, the company in question, makes the decision.

The ideal case is the self-managed network, where the network can manage itself and where all nodes are on the same level – a peer-to-peer network without the need for a central figure to maintain control. This concept already existed with technologies such as BitTorrent, an internet protocol designed to exchange large files located in several network nodes, thus lightening the work of the network, as opposed to being centralized in a single node. In the end, all users form the grid by storing parts of the files and then giving and receiving access with other users for its operation.

This technology took a giant leap forward when the bitcoin concept, self-defined as a peer-to-peer cash network, appeared anonymously on the internet under a pseudonym.

Bitcoin proposes grouping transactions into blocks and verifying them before adding them to the network to solve the synchronization problem. However, this method introduces a new problem as several users can co-exist, verifying blocks with different ones simultaneously, so the issue of simultaneous updating is maintained. The solution proposed by bitcoin is the computational 'payment' by solving a cryptographic problem in order to add the new block linked to the previous one, creating that chain. In this way, an effort is required, a 'proof of work' for participation; the sharing of the block to the network is authorized by solving the problem, known as mining. The technology adds the following condition to avoid two different verified blocks being added simultaneously and creating two different blockchains: the chain that adds a new block, and therefore is longer, is the one that will prevail. This operation can be performed by any user of the network who is motivated to do so since, in case of successfully mining the block, the user is economically rewarded as they have added the last line in the block, where it is 'paid' for the job performed.

A crucial point of the structure is its internal chain security. Each block has a unique identification code called a hash, created based on its content. The connection between blocks is made by referencing the previous block's hash as a transaction. This avoids the modification of the chain since, when the content of a block is changed, its code is modified and consequently that of all subsequent blocks. As the structure is governed by the longest chain, in the event of wanting to alter part of the chain, not only must the modified block be mined, but all subsequent blocks in order to exceed the length of the main chain and therefore become the valid one. Performing this action, known as a 51 per cent attack, is practically impossible since the user competes against the proofs of work of all the other users in each attempt to add a new block and would be able to succeed only in the case of having more than 50 per cent of the computational power. Therefore, this set of properties provides the chain with a high level of security, making it impossible to modify its data.

Typical blockchain applications are:

- **Cryptocurrency.** Firstly, from the idea of bitcoin, other cryptocurrencies were born as alternatives, copying the model and providing new features. The most important ones today are Ether (ETH), Litecoin (LTC), Cardano (ADA), Polkadot (DOT), Dogecoin (DOGE) and Tether (USDT).

- **Wallets.** A blockchain wallet is a digital wallet that allows you to store and manage all types of crypto-assets. It allows the user to have a wallet protected with a security protocol (e.g. passwords and seeds) and facilitates the transaction of these assets and even the conversion into local currencies. There are different types depending on the security against hacking, from webs and apps to physical hard drives or paper.

- **Smart contracts.** Smart contracts were born with Ethereum technology and are the basis for developing its applications. They are basically traditional contracts translated into computer programs stored on the blockchain. Their code digitizes the clauses of the contracts that will be executed automatically depending on the inputs, conditions and interaction with the chain. Smart contracts solve the problem of interpretability so that the results are predictable; they are public so that the clauses and their correct execution can be verified; but despite this, they can maintain privacy through the pseudonyms of the users.

- **Decentralized finance and tokens.** Decentralized finance is a term that refers to financial services based on blockchain technology. The main characteristic is the elimination of control by third parties such as banks or other institutions, streamlining the process, eliminating possible fees and making it accessible to anyone. This concept was also born from the hand of Ethereum with the implementation of smart contracts and the possibilities they offer. In this way, not only transfers between users have a place in the blockchain, but also other activities such as purchases, loans, insurance, crowdfunding or betting.

- **Decentralized autonomous organizations.** Following the idea of decentralization of power and distrust in institutions or superior figures, the concept of DAO was born. This is an organization designed to self-manage in a decentralized way – a digital business or project with a set of owners who decide its direction and strategy. Participation and membership are usually through tokens or a crypto capital contribution to the project. The community of anonymous users behind the pseudonyms is unknown and, theoretically, they participate because of the business potential, given that the project's smart contract and its goals are transparent. Decision making is an automated process carried out by voting, there are no vertical or horizontal influences from within the organization, and thanks to smart contracts, transparent and immediate answers, results can be obtained.

- **Non-fungible tokens**. Given their relevance, a specific section will be dedicated to this important application in the blockchain.
- **Web 3.0**. Web 3.0 is one of the most recent blockchain-based technologies, and although there are already some webs in operation, it is still in its development phase. Web 3.0 is a global registry, and the decentralization of the Web 2.0 we know today. The idea is to transfer and systematize the management and development in a decentralized way to prevent the current owners from profiting from user data through cookies and big data. According to its proponents, 'Web 3.0 will only reach its true potential when the majority of current and future web applications and websites have adopted a decentralized web infrastructure.'

Non-fungible tokens – a noteworthy financial tool, a necessary fashionista therapy, or a nimbly fading trend?

Let us open with a question to all our readers: when did you first hear people talking about NFTs?

The concept of non-fungible tokens (NFTs) has been around for quite some time (since 2014, to be precise), as the concept of the Metaverse and the idea of selling 'immaterial' things in a digital world. Most readers have probably heard talk of NFTs only recently.

Yet today it is important, for most of us, to get acquainted with the concept of the NFT. Let us try to explain why.

The brief story of NFTs

An NFT is a digital token that represents the ownership of a unique item. NFTs are 'minted' (i.e. coined, created) in the blockchain, through smart contracts that assign their ownership and manage their transferability. NFTs are 'non-fungible'. Fungible means *replaceable by another identical item; mutually interchangeable*. While coins and banknotes are fungible, NFTs are not, meaning that each individual NFT – being *unique* – has a value distinct from other similar tokens.

Besides being unique and non-fungible, NFTs have other characteristics: they are rare, they are proprietary (i.e. they have a specific ownership) and exclusive (i.e. they are indivisible, exactly like a concert ticket for a specific seat cannot be split into two valuable parts), and are transparent, as any activity (such as reselling an NFT that you recently purchased) can be publicly verified.

The value of an NFT

For people who are not used to the concept of NFTs, let alone owning digital assets (e.g. owning the 'original' of a digital picture, when you can just download a copy of it to your computer), the hype about some NFT drops (the minting and selling of a new NFT collection) may seem unjustified.

In case you didn't know...

- Twitter co-founder, Jack Dorsey sold his first tweet for $2.9 million. The tweet simply read 'just setting up my twttr' and the proceeds were donated to charity by Dorsey.

- Mike Winkelmann, the famous digital artist known as Beeple, sold an artwork obtained as the collage of 5,000 digital images, called 'Everydays, the first 5,000 days' for $69.3 million, making this the most expensive NFT to date, but also one of the most expensive creations of a living artist.

- The Bored Ape Yacht Club is a collection of 10,000 unique NFTs. Rarity is one of the reasons why these NFTs are valuable, but also the fact that the NFT owners have exclusive membership to an online hangout club called the swamp club. All 10,000 NFTs sold out in one day, for a reasonably cheap price (below $200), and now they are trading for north of $80,000 (this being 'the floor', or the lowest-priced NFT in the collection).

- A serigraphy from the street artist Banksy, bought for $95,000, was burnt, digitized and transformed into a piece of crypto-art, whose NFT sold for $380,000.

In luxury, several brands, such as Gucci and Louis Vuitton, are creating and launching their own NFT collections. So not only digital art can be sold through NFT: in the digital world, there is also room for sneakers, bags and more. The basic idea is to capture the interest of people desiring their avatars to 'look cool' with their Gucci sneakers and LV accessories.

But what is the value of an NFT?

In a very informative 2021 article in the *Harvard Business Review*, Steve Kaczynski and Scott Duke Kominers explain 'How NFTs create Value':

- They are an unprecedented way to design the market for digital assets defining clear property rights: before NFTs it was impossible to separate the 'owner' of a digital asset from just anyone who saved a copy of the same asset on their computer.

- NFTs – as blockchains – are programmable; as a consequence, NFTs can 'do things', so the creator can empower an NFT with added functionality, expanding its value and purpose over time, and providing utility to the owners, such as access to an exclusive club.

- Since the blockchain is public, it is possible to send (additional) products directly to anyone who owns a specific token.

- NFT's programmability supports new business models, notably the new royalty contract in which the original creator keeps getting a share of the revenues every time a certain crypto-artwork is resold.

Thus, according to Kaczynski and Kominers, 'owning an NFT effectively makes you an investor, a member of a club, a brand shareholder, and a participant in a loyalty program all at once'.

The Metaverse

First appearing in Neal Stephenson's sci-fi novel *Snow Crash*, published in 1992, this neologism is a blend (a portmanteau) of 'meta' (from Greek, a prefix meaning beyond – thus suggesting something transcending, or overarching) and 'universe'.

The first notable attempt to develop a parallel, virtual universe was Second Life, a virtual world platform launched in 2003. Today, for the digital native generations, the concept of spending the majority of their time in a virtual world is not perceived as a frightening dystopia. Gen X-ers, such as the authors of this chapter, may well go back to their teenage memories, and watch one of the sci-fi movies popular at the time (we'd like to think about Bladerunner, to mention one, or the US television series Knight Rider with the artificially intelligent speaking car named KITT).

Web 3 and value creation for luxury brands in the Metaverse

In January 1996, Bill Gates published a short essay entitled 'Content is King' on the Microsoft website. The Microsoft founder began writing his piece in this way:

> Content is where I expect much of the real money will be made on the internet, just as it was in broadcasting. The television revolution that began half a century ago spawned a number of industries, including the manufacturing of TV sets, but the long-term winners were those who used the medium to deliver information and entertainment.

Then he added:

> One of the exciting things about the internet is that anyone with a PC and a modem can publish whatever content they can create. In a sense, the internet is the multimedia equivalent of the photocopier. It allows material to be duplicated at low cost, no matter the size of the audience.

In his words, Gates showed that he understood that the internet would lay the foundations for the creator economy. However, it was an analysis well ahead of its time, and in fact Gates himself probably realized it, since he added, 'the long-term prospects are good, but I expect a lot of disappointment in the short term'. He then finished his short essay by writing, 'those who succeed will propel the internet forward as a marketplace of ideas, experiences and products, that is, a marketplace of content.'

As the internet has developed to date, Gates' prediction has not yet come true. In fact, in the last 20 years we passed through the second era of the internet, which has been characterized by the so-called 'attention economy', what is now called Web2. The second era of the internet started in the early 2000s, when the amount of information distributed through the web exploded and the attention of consumers became a scarce and therefore precious and valuable commodity. Many digital products and services have been offered so far for free in exchange for consumers' attention and related personal information. This all happened because the internet was not built to facilitate payment and, in general, the flow of money. Payments were not – and to a large extent still are not – integrated into the underlying infrastructure of the network, as they were considered too risky. And the lack of a payment infrastructure is precisely why so much of the internet has been and still is monetized through advertising. Rather than requiring users to pull out a credit card and type their information into a website, they have been monetized frictionlessly and indirectly through a different commodity: their attention. Social platforms have thus won the battle for consumers' attention and obtained the economic results that we all know. Just recall, for example, that Google and Facebook's advertising revenue combined represent more than half of the revenue of the global digital advertising market.

All that precipitated a shift in power from the old gatekeepers of media who controlled content creation and distribution – publishers, record labels and movie studios – to those who amassed consumer attention at scale.

This is the story of how Web2 broke the business model of media companies. Without native monetization methods built into Web2, the predominant business models were opaque, advertising-based and dependent on closed-garden networks, which gave an outsized advantage to social platforms. On the horizon, the advent of the third era of the internet, the so-called Web3, will unlock the opportunity for totally new business models and value chains that could lead to a truly creative golden age for the luxury industry.

From the attention economy to the creator economy

If the attention economy – centred on social platforms and fuelled by advertising – has characterized the Web2 era, a new generation of technologies will favour the transition to the creator economy. The number of content creators that characterized the second era of the internet was indeed very small, but the growth rate that can be expected for the next few years is extremely high. In fact, several studies have estimated a number of creators that is quickly growing from a few dozen million at the beginning of this decade, up to 200 million to date, of which more than 4 million have made it a profession with a stable source of income (Linktree, 2022). On the other hand, in several surveys I conducted, the percentage of young people belonging to generations Alpha and Z who declare they would like to become an 'online creator' is higher than 30 per cent, and for Millennials is higher than 20 per cent. Venture capitalists have become aware of this gigantic growth potential and have begun to fund dozens of start-ups which aim to encourage the development of creators. According to a recent study from CB Insights (2021), total funding for the creator economy reached $1.3 billion in the first half of 2021, a figure that represents an increase of 188 per cent compared to the whole of 2020. A large part of these funds has been allocated to start-ups active in the development of decentralized applications; that is, the applications that are expected to fuel Web3. It will be this transition – from Web2 to Web3 – that will create the technological infrastructure of the so-called Metaverse and fuel the development of the creation economy. In other words, decentralized applications will be the technological backbone of the Metaverse and the creation economy will be its economic backbone.

This means that the entire ecosystem of 'people's life in the Metaverse' will be fostered and fuelled by creativity, with a profound impact on both economic and cultural growth, and effects that will also span physical life. It would be a big mistake to consider the Metaverse only from a technological perspective, i.e. considering only the so-called immersive digital experiences provided through virtual reality technologies, like those that will be experienced in decentralized virtual worlds such as The Sandbox and Decentraland, or in centralized virtual worlds like Horizon from Meta. The Metaverse is much more diverse than immersive digital experiences only, since it is going to be an intersection of three different perspectives: technological, economic and cultural. In such an intersection creativity will be the driving force of consumer engagement, and it will be the keystone luxury brands will have to follow to be successful in the Metaverse. In other words, the Metaverse economy will be an economy based on creation, in which brands that create value will not be those that produce useful or beautiful things for consumers, but will be those brands that help creators to create useful or beautiful things. This paradigm shift will have a profound effect on the competitive forces luxury brands will have to use to create economic and social value. Therefore, knowledge of the value sources underlying the Metaverse provides the groundwork for a strategic agenda of actions.

In order to help brands to identify the value sources underlying the Metaverse, Alessandro Donetti developed a strategic analysis framework that is composed of the following five competitive forces:

- Genetic engineering of physical products and NFTs.
- Emotional connection through dynamic NFTs.
- Brand community mix and social tokens.
- Experiential ecosystems and social NFTs.
- Brand personification.

These competitive forces highlight the critical strengths and weaknesses of a brand's strategy in the Metaverse; they clarify the areas where strategic changes may yield the greatest payoff and highlight the places where Metaverse trends promise to hold the greatest significance as either opportunities or threats. Understanding these competitive forces also proves to be of extreme help in defining how to measure a brand's performance and ultimately its success in the Metaverse-based competitive environment of the future.

The five competitive forces

Genetic engineering of physical products and NFTs

In the physical world, the value of an object is governed by a few key dynamics, including its authenticity and its scarcity. In the digital world of abundance, where copies of a digital object are created and distributed with extreme ease, authenticity and scarcity create value just like in the physical world. The technology of non-fungible tokens has come to the fore in 2021 as a way to guarantee authenticity, the creation of scarcity and the right of ownership. Through NFTs any digital resource – be it an artwork, a piece of clothing, a video clip or an experience – can be made authentic, its exclusive ownership can be proved and its dissemination limited in a verifiable manner. At the end of May 2021 Gucci debuted with the first NFT from a luxury brand. The NFT – which accompanied a four-minute high-definition video clip – was auctioned by Christie's, from 25 May to 3 June, at a price of $20,000, and was sold for $25,000, later donated to UNICEF in order to support vaccination programmes in poor countries. The video clip was inspired by a collection named Aria, designed to celebrate the centenary of the brand. The debut of Gucci was followed by Louis Vuitton, who launched a video game – called Louis The Game – at the beginning of August 2021 to celebrate their 200 years of life. In the game were inserted 30 NFTs which, unlike the Gucci one, are just collectibles; they have no selling price and cannot be sold. The branded game allowed players to customize their characters with different Louis Vuitton monogram prints and colourways. In addition, it showed the history of the fashion house through postcards and old memorabilia.

After the first NFTs were used to celebrate the Gucci and LV centenaries, luxury brands started to use NFTs by associating them with digital and physical branded collectible items, bundled with exclusive experiences. The first-ever brand to move in this direction was Dolce & Gabbana, who auctioned nine NFTs belonging to a collection called 'Genesis Collection' at the end of September 2021. The collection was hosted by the luxury marketplace UNXD and was sold at a total price of 1,886 Ether, equivalent to approximately $5.6 million at that time.

The collection included high fashion and jewellery digital and physical items, and also provided an experiential component represented by exclusive access to the brand's fashion shows for a whole year together with private tours inside the atelier's brand in Milan. The experiential component of the jewellery items also included the digital display of the item for two weeks in the Milan flagship store, highlighting the name of the collector who had purchased the token, as well as digital displays in other stores across the world, with the buyer's name always prominently displayed.

In October 2021 it was the turn of Jimmy Choo – a British high fashion house, specializing in luxury shoes, handbags and accessories as well as fragrances – to launch its first NFT collection. The brand launched the collection on Binance's marketplace on 10 October 2021, stepping into the digital art world with the introduction of two types of NFT – a mystery box and an auction item. The mystery boxes contained a randomly assigned NFT of one of four digital card creations by the brand, with different levels of scarcity, from super rare to neutral, with the NFT revealed only after purchase. In addition to the mystery boxes, Jimmy Choo also auctioned an NFT of an exclusively designed trainer, one of a kind and available only in digital form.

Since then, many other luxury brands have followed similar approaches, launching collections of digital products combined with their corresponding physical 'twins', also giving access to physical experiences and artworks, or using NFTs in order to guarantee ownership and product authenticity, the latter case applied for instance by some watch brands.

The unique exception has been represented by Prada, which entered the NFT space at the beginning of 2022 with a user-generated, creator-owned art project in partnership with Adidas. Prada and Adidas selected 3,000 fans by raffle to turn their own original images into NFTs, leaving the ownership of the intellectual property rights to the individual creators, who were then able to sell the NFTs on secondary markets. The selected images were also combined as tiles into one mass patchwork NFT, designed by the digital artist and creative coder Zach Lieberman, and then auctioned on the digital art marketplace SuperRare and displayed as a large-scale installation in Prada and Adidas flagship stores. The auction of the patchwork NFT was won for 30 Ether – equal to €75,000 at that time – with 15 per cent of that value distributed among all individual image tile creators.

What has been done by luxury brands using NFTs since the first launch seems therefore inextricably intertwined with digital collectibles, as many brands' first step into the NFT waters has been to launch their own collections. That is, bringing a product line already existing in the real world into the Metaverse or creating new 'digital only' product lines that replicate physical products. Some brands have also added tokens that grant special perks like the possibility to live physical or digital exclusive experiences. They are projects that certainly expand the way consumers can interact with a brand and purchase its products; however, they still represent a traditional brand extension strategy; that is, they are adding beautiful things to the brand experience. But in this way, brands do not turn to creators, they do not actually help them in creating beautiful things, and so they risk losing sight of the disruptive change that is leading to the creation economy.

Granted, a vast majority of consumers still struggle to make sense of the 2021 NFT world of Bored Ape Yacht Club[1] and CryptoPunks,[2] and the usability of the underlying blockchain technology is still a long way from being consumer friendly. However, the NFT technology could be used by brands to give creators the possibility to 'mix' products designed by brands themselves, developing something like a 'genetic engineering' of physical branded products. For example, this is what the CryptoKicks patent – registered by Nike in December 2019 – would allow. According to Nike's patent, when a consumer buys an authentic, tangible pair of shoes – colloquially known as 'kicks'– a digital representation of a shoe is generated, linked to the buyer through an identification code, and assigned a non-fungible token, which will record certain 'genotype' information related to each shoe, such as colours, designs and various style attributes. The digital shoe and the cryptographic token collectively represent a 'CryptoKick', with all linking data recorded on the Ethereum blockchain. The digital representation may include a computer-generated avatar of the shoe or a limited-edition artist rendition of the shoe.

Using Nike's patented NFT technology, a buyer of a tangible pair of shoes is enabled to securely trade or sell that pair of shoes or its digital representation, and store the digital shoe in a cryptocurrency wallet or in another digital blockchain locker. According to Nike's patent, a buyer is also enabled to intermingle or 'breed' a digital shoe with another digital shoe to create a 'shoe offspring' and, based on rules of acceptable shoe manufacturability, have the newly bred shoe offspring custom made as a new tangible pair of shoes.

If all this should be applied to running shoes, for example, we can imagine a consumer who has bought a few pairs of shoes – and their associated NFTs – and is able to create a completely new model of running shoe by composing different shoe parts in a personalized way. In other words, if a buyer of two pairs of shoes prefers the sole and the heel of the first pair, and the tongue and the upper part of the second pair, they would be able to create a new sneaker that combines those favourite parts, creating an exclusive model that could be exhibited and sold individually. It's as though two 'parent sneakers' combine their DNA to create a pair of 'daughter sneakers' with a completely new design. This process would not obviously be unconstrained, as restrictions on the structure of a given shoe will limit what can be created. However, using the NFT technology, the entire offspring of a sneaker will be traceable on the blockchain, regardless of the number of reproductions that have been designed, and moreover, the creator – as well as the brand – will be able to earn a share of the proceeds from the sale of every single element of the offspring.

If a technology such as that registered by Nike was used by luxury brands and further integrated by some emerging NFT-based identification technologies that have appeared recently in the market – such as those of Veracity Protocol – it would be possible for virtually every consumer and buyer of an original luxury physical product to create an NFT from that physical product, taking into account the structural properties of its physical components, and then design a new original item. Creators could combine, for instance, sneakers and socks, armchairs and lamps, bags and tables, or whatever they like. In this way NFTs could stimulate profound and radical innovations in the design of a very large number of physical products, developing then completely new markets. In the same way, NFTs could also deeply revolutionize secondary markets of physical used products thanks to the possibility to trace the whole offspring of the original product. As Nike did, luxury brands might implement an NFT royalty standard that encodes a fraction of the value associated with every resale as well as involving creative consumers in after-sales activities in an unlimited number of different ways. The creation economy could get an enormous push, with economic benefits spanning from brands to millions of creators.

Emotional connection through dynamic NFTs

So far the NFTs I have referred to are of the static type, in other words they are programs stored on a blockchain – called smart contracts – that process static data recorded on the blockchain itself. Static data makes the most sense for many applications in the world of arts and collections, where NFTs became known to the public consciousness. After all, one of the biggest draws to NFTs is the permanency of data on decentralized, immutable blockchains. This immutability stops someone from, for example, creating an NFT with a picture of a cat and then changing it into a picture of a dog after it sells. However, it should be noted that a static NFT can still feature animated images, movies and all sorts of complexities that make NFTs so interesting for collectors, digital artists and creators.

It is the gaming world that has created a request for a new kind of non-fungible token, the so-called dynamic NFTs. Since interactivity is essential in gaming environments, dynamic NFTs may benefit from the ability to change. By making it possible to modify the data that is processed by smart contracts, game developers can create completely novel game mechanics, like for instance automatically minting, in real time, a new NFT when a player reaches a certain milestone such as a certain number of completed hat tricks or a certain number of enemies hit. While dynamic NFTs could bring more energy into gaming environments, their utility extends far beyond the gaming industry. Use cases have been presented in which a digital object is transformed according to the number of user views, bringing into play so-called visual liminality, represented for example by an image that is initially a sketch and becomes more detailed – and more beautiful – as the number of users who view it increases, or the image of a flower that blooms or withers when it receives more attention – that is, views. If you think about all this realized in three dimensions, the resulting effect is certainly engaging.

In any case, the extraordinary potential of dynamic NFTs could be fully grasped if they are used to create a connection between the blockchain and the physical world, incorporating real-world events, rather than the mere passing of time. Thinking, for instance, about applications in the governmental landscape, digital passports could be issued in a fraud-proof way through a connection to data outside the blockchain, which would offer the ability to query and verify personal credentials, as well as append data to a person's decentral-ized digital identity based on a real-world event. Land deeds could also be represented on the blockchain as dynamic NFTs that are au-tomatically appraised in real time by fetching data from local sensors on the Internet of Things, weather indices and property records. This would enable more objective, data-driven land valuations that could be leveraged as collateral. The above use cases are only a few exam-ples of the wide range of real-world goods and processes that could be represented as dynamic NFTs to generate a new class of auto-up-dating assets that are more liquid, data-driven and accessible.

On the other side, the possibility to incorporate the mere passing of time would unlock a new rich set of features for digital collecti-bles, to become impressive for collectors. Think, for example, about collectibles that grow in value over time, and those that do not show any sign of ageing, which decrease in value over time. Going further for collectors, while a static NFT would represent a football player always wearing the same shirt, a dynamic one would capture the player's team changes from one season to the next. Another example is provided by the image of a person who slowly ages or the image of a tree that loses and regains its leaves as seasons pass. These kinds of applications could stimulate a new form of emotional engagement between brands and consumers, started by a brand or based on cli-ents' usage of a luxury branded product. A brand could, for instance, continuously communicate with a client who has bought a handbag if it were tied to a dynamic NFT, saying, 'You bought a limited edi-tion bag and you got an NFT that proves it is authentic. Have a look at these videos which show how your bag was made and these pictures of how your bag can be styled.' Further, based upon usage, and which data is sent back to the blockchain and processed by the dynamic NFT, a brand could send personalized messages to its client in order to make the usage of the bag more appropriate or to suggest following a different style. The flow of real-world events – and the sensory involvement that could be derived from them – would trigger very positive emotional experiences for consumers, fostering stronger brand attachment.

If the applications I mentioned earlier could create higher emotional engagement between brands and consumers, they do not yet exploit the underlying technology of dynamic NFTs to generate value for creators and brands. It is in the engineering of physical products that the application of dynamic NFTs would be truly revolutionary and instrumental to generating economic value, both for creators and brands. If we go back to the example above related to the creation of a pair of 'daughter sneakers', we could imagine that the data processed by the NFT for the creation of the offspring is updated according to the usage of the 'parent sneakers'. Thus, it would be possible to design a new pair of shoes with physical characteristics that take into account how the shoes fit rather than how they touch the ground. It's quite easy to imagine the tremendous impact on brands' product innovation processes. Stimuli and opportunities for creators would be stellar, and those brands offering the opportunity to exploit them could reap extraordinary benefits in terms of value growth.

Brand community mix and social tokens

A key feature of the creator economy is that creators' activities are almost always collaborative – that is, creation efforts are driven by groups of creators rather than single individuals. YouTube creators, for instance, re-work videos that were previously made by other creators. But it's certainly TikTok that clearly showed collaborative creation at work. Videos are very often made by 'many hands', as the soundtrack of a video is created by one creator, the choreography by another, and so on.

Blockchain technologies can enormously stimulate and support collaborative creation mechanisms; in particular they can stimulate creators to work towards a common goal through the so-called DAOs, or decentralized autonomous organizations. DAOs are online communities owned and governed by their members; they were first popularized in the decentralized finance sector and have since been formed around communities with very different missions and goals, enforced into the blockchain. An interesting example is that of a former employee of the Cisco legal department, who at the beginning of 2022 created a DAO with the aim of acquiring the Denver Broncos, one of the most well-known US football teams, on sale for $4 billion. Another case is Football Club, a DAO created in the same period with the goal to become the largest football fan club in the world. Football Club prominently shows on its website a manifesto which reads:

> We believe the thing that makes our club the first of our kind is that instead of an initial fundraise or a run for immediate purchase of a team, our main goal is building out the most passionate global football community, where we will launch tons of incredible products and experiences for the football world along the way.

Or again, two South Korean DAOs were bidders in an auction at the end of January 2022 to buy a pair of bronze sculptures dating back to the year 563, considered national treasures by the Korean government. The two sculptures were auctioned by South Korea's oldest private art museum in Seoul – the Kansong Art Museum – which was struggling financially and was selling artworks to pay its debts. When the precious artworks received no offers, representatives of the two DAOs jointly contacted the museum to privately negotiate a purchase. The declared goal of the two DAOs was to prevent the two sculptures from entering into a private collection, no longer visible to the public.

On the other hand, DAOs can also be created to achieve a goal to create economic value, exploiting and rewarding creators' professional skills. In general, DAOs can be thought of as the organizational building blocks to build Web3's economic, social and cultural landscape. New DAOs are forming at such a rapid pace that it's almost impossible to count them, but it seems safe to say that at the end of April 2022 there were over 1,000 DAOs. Many of them have clear goals to create economic value for their members, like for instance the above-mentioned Decentraland – one of the most well-known blockchain-based virtual worlds. According to venture capital firm Andreessen Horowitz, as of end of April 2022, the total value of DAOs' balance sheet assets – the so-called 'treasury' – has been estimated to be approximately $11 billion, 60 per cent owned by the top 15 DAOs (Horowitz, 2022).

While almost all DAOs with the highest treasury values so far have been made up by developers with expertise in blockchain technologies, this does not prevent a brand from promoting the creation and development of DAOs together with creators that, in principle, could have any kind of professional skill. A brand could in fact promote blockchain-based communities, segmenting appropriately its customer base and its target audience, helping them to create successful brands, thus realizing a brand community mix. A brand community mix can thus be considered an ecosystem through which a 'parent brand' provides its support to creators so that they can create a brand, exploiting their professional skills, individually or together with other creators, members of the same community. It would be a sort of 'child brand' that could have different business goals, such as the creation and sale of physical or digital products, but also the creation of a platform to sell services in the physical world. Think, for example, about a DAO that could be established with the support of a luxury automotive brand aimed at creating a service platform similar to Uber. Another example could be a DAO created with the support of a luxury brand active in the home furniture market that is providing support to creators in order to establish a marketplace similar to Etsy. Countless examples could be imagined, and they could be provided by brands active in all segments of the luxury industry.

In order to foster the development of these blockchain-based communities, Web3 provides a particular kind of fungible token, called social tokens. Social tokens are fungible tokens issued by individual creators or communities that enable community members to collaborate and share ownership of the value created together. Social tokens are usually used for governance purposes – such as voting on community decisions – but they can be minted and issued by a DAO to reward members' behaviours. Some DAOs, for instance, have introduced the concept of 'seasons', which are periods of time where the community focuses on a certain set of goals, and members who are active and contribute towards those goals are given tokens as rewards related to the season. DeepDAO, a blockchain data source provider which tracked detailed information about around 180 DAOs, showed that at the end of April 2022, there were 1.7 million holders of social tokens, and about 500,000 of these holders actively participate in DAO governance. Many of these DAOs have decided to list their social tokens on cryptocurrency exchanges, making them freely tradable. In such a way, their tokens reflect the value at which a community's brand is 'priced' by the market and token holders can easily monetize their value. Early community members can use these markets to 'cash in' – just like early investors in start-ups – while potential new members can enter and give their contribution to grow the community's brand.

Social tokens are therefore a financial instrument that tracks the value created by each community of a brand community mix, as well as a magnet to attract other creators. The market value of social tokens would thus be a clear indicator of the success of a brand community mix that would financially reward both the parent brand and the creators of the brand's communities.

Experiential ecosystems and social NFTs

Consumers have, so far, the possibility to 'touch' a brand according to times, places and methods designed and created by brands themselves, rather than by their distributors or physical and digital retailers. If a consumer wants to buy a dress from a brand she likes, she enters into a store or visits the brand's website rather than the e-commerce site of a digital multi-brand retailer. If she just wants to 'see' how she would look wearing an outfit of her preferred brand, then she can take also a look at the brand's Instagram pages.

If we consider what we have seen so far in some virtual worlds of the Metaverse – like The Sandbox or Decentraland – even the touch points that brands are creating there look like they replicate the same structure as the physical reality. What is also offered in these virtual worlds is the possibility to buy digital and physical clothing, virtual gear or collectibles through NFTs, but this is also already possible when visiting some luxury retail stores across the physical world. For instance, in February 2022 Gucci announced it was building a virtual world in The Sandbox, planning for new engagement and immersive experiences as part of its Gucci Vault experimental online space. As part of the initiative, in the following month the luxury fashion giant also unveiled the Gucci Grail NFT project with digital accessories hub 10KTF, which featured digital outfits from 11 selected NFT collections including Bored Ape, World of Women and Cool Cats. In March 2022, Decentraland hosted the first-ever Metaverse Fashion Week, with appearances by over 60 high-fashion brands including Dolce & Gabbana, Dundas, Tommy Hilfiger, Philipp Plein, Fred Segal and Karl Lagerfeld. Even if the event was filled with brand-sponsored virtual catwalks, a virtual shopping district, live panels, concerts and interactive events, it was basically a virtual replica of what consumers can see and experience in real cities. I do not even think that a prominent goal should be to give visitors of these virtual branded touchpoints the possibility to express themselves and their creativity in the digital world via avatars, giving the possibility to try virtual products before buying them. If brands are laying the groundwork for future high-fashion and luxury experiences in the Metaverse by creating virtual touchpoints that are basically similar to what can be experienced in our cities, this would be a quite limited vision, and also not useful to create brand value through the Metaverse.

Paradoxically, it will be the Metaverse that will allow brands to finally give substance to the so-called experience economy, transforming completely the brand experience paradigms we have seen so far. Brands could offer consumers the possibility to create value through an ecosystem that rewards behaviours and experiences the brand itself is aimed to stimulate because they are consistent with its values and identity. It would be an experience-to-earn (E2E) ecosystem that would collect information about members who use it, and provide behavioural nudges to encourage more frequent, consistent or better behaviours to finally reward them. Meanwhile, the experiential ecosystem would reward brands' audience members for their current actions, nudging the daily activities they love more, until they reach the most coveted or exclusive experiences. For instance, a brand could simply reward an E2E member for the purchase of a digital product made during a virtual experience – thus replicating traditional loyalty programmes – but it could also reward behaviours and experiences realized in the physical reality that bring value, whether that be exploring a national park or a new city, playing tennis with a mate or seeing a band, taking care of physical and mental health, or supporting a charity.

All this will certainly be possible, since today many people are already tracking their daily real-life activities using smartphones, smartwatches and dedicated applications. In the future, the programmability of NFTs associated with Internet of Things technologies will broaden enormously the real-life domains that can be tracked.

The reward mechanism should be based on social NFTs, a particular class of NFT that brands will have to mint. So far, social NFTs have been issued mainly by social media influencers to monetize their content and reputation, build deeper connections with their fans and reward them in unique ways. For instance, when an influencer's fan buys a social NFT issued by the influencer, they could have access to a monthly call, a private community or discounts on the influencer's merchandise.

A brand could use social NFTs to reward its E2E ecosystem members for doing their daily activities, bringing new forms of value creation, going beyond the value creation model driven by brand-based experiences only, giving also value to social, self-care and self-development activities. When a person practises the 'right behaviour' they receive a social NFT, much rarer and more exclusive the more relevant and coherent the behaviour being practised, from simple rewards to unique privileges, such as the possibility to access exclusive experiences, in both the real and the virtual worlds. In this way, instead of creating virtual experiences that 'cannibalize' the real ones, brands would make them complementary, fuelling people's existing passions and exposing them to new, unique and intimate experiences.

Brands could also reward creators who contribute to the development of their E2E ecosystem, both for the virtual and the physical components. For the virtual components, brands could invite their audience to create individual parts of the experiential ecosystem by operating in a similar way to what is already practised by thousands of video gamers in the so-called play-to-earn (P2E) decentralized gaming platforms. For the physical components, creators could be free to propose the experiences they wish to offer to the brand's audience, whether that be yoga sessions rather than climbing an artificial vertical wall, a photography course, or charity activities. While P2E blockchain games rely on some level of skills such as those necessary to battle, breed or collect, which attracts gamers with the downtime, temerity and sometimes some starting funds to invest, in contrast, branded E2E ecosystems should reward people for investing in themselves, others and in brand values they believe in.

As Social Tokens can be listed on cryptocurrency exchanges, social NFTs could be sold in dedicated marketplaces created with the support of brands, and could give the possibility to access experiences of the E2E ecosystem of the same brand as well as those of other brands' ecosystems. The market value of social NFTs would contribute to developing a virtuous circle in which the behaviours that fuel personal and social growth serve as tokens for living increasingly 'valuable' experiences both in the virtual world and in real life. Finally, the market value of social NFTs would be a clear metric of the brand's E2E ecosystem success that would financially reward the brand itself, its audience and the creator members. An extraordinary combination of holistic growth that would fuel a continuous generation of value for the brand.

Brand personification

A fascinating brand management concept is the so-called personification of a brand; in other words, trying to understand how a brand would behave if it was a person – what are the things that it would prove to love and what would it prove to hate? Brand strategists so far, in order to give human traits to their brands in alignment with brand purpose and core values, have used a couple of brand personality frameworks, like those developed by Carl Jung and David Aaker.

For instance, the framework developed by Jung contains 12 personality archetypes which were outlined back in 1919. They cover the full range of personas, from those that make us feel secure and loved to those that excite us, ranging from the 'Innocent' to the wise and experienced 'Sage', from the 'Hero' to the 'Outlaw'.

Similarly, Aaker's framework identifies five dimensions of brand personality using concepts developed in personality psychology research.

Even if these frameworks – if properly used – can certainly help brand strategists to design a relationship between a brand and each member of its audience like a person-to-person relationship, some recent technologies related to the Metaverse will allow them to go much further, since they make it possible to design a brand as if it were an 'almost human being', with a name, a face, a tone of voice, and above all a behavioural style that embodies its personality, the reasons that lead the brand to act. All this will be possible through computer-created avatars that may have decidedly human features, behaviours and language, thanks to the combination of the latest holographic technologies with artificial intelligence. It would be a 'brand digital persona' with the brand's actions, inactions, silences and words weaved into it. Something similar to the 'virtual brand influencers' that are having so much success in China among young people. In fact, according to a report by Chinese video platform iQiyi, in 2019 64 per cent of Chinese people aged between 15 and 24 were fans of 'virtual idols' – the so-called virtual Key Opinion Leaders. Many researchers also agree on the fact that the percentage of Chinese Gen Z-ers that are fans of virtual idols significantly increased over 2020 and 2021, due to their high familiarity with digital technology which alleviated their loneliness during the pandemic period. Furthermore, several studies conducted in the last two years have highlighted that, for Chinese young people, the interaction with deliberately unrealistic virtual influencers can help overcome a particular sensation, called 'uncanny valley' by robotics researchers, which is experienced by people when they interact with anthropomorphic robots. Robotics researchers have experimentally shown that people experience a pleasant sensation by interacting with anthropomorphic robots that increases as the robots' resemblance to human figures increases, until a point where extreme realism produces a sharp decline in the pleasantness, arousing unpleasant sensations such as repulsion and restlessness.

Therefore, the design and development of a digital persona by brand strategists will no longer be an abstract activity, since to design and develop such an 'almost human being', strategists will have to not only decide how to dress the avatar, but also how the brand digital persona must behave and what it says to other 'inhabitants of the Metaverse' when it is close to them. Most likely, we can also assume, that this will be effective not only to target Chinese consumers but also Western ones.

On the other hand, brand strategists will be able to fully design and develop a brand digital persona consistent with brand purpose and values, only if brand leaders take a clear position on issues they often don't like to talk about. As I have personally experienced several times, many brands' CEOs find it difficult to answer questions such as 'What is the most important value for your brand?' or 'What does your brand hate?' or even 'What are people afraid of when they interact with your brand?'

To be clear, the design of a brand digital persona will only be possible under the condition of answering precisely and concretely those kinds of questions. In that way, a brand would no longer be represented only by its products rather than by its services, and not even by symbols or stories delivered to the brand's audience through different media, but rather it would be represented by digitally constructed 'almost human beings' that appear and 'live' alongside their audience, creating shared experiences and connecting in a semi-authentic way. Paradoxically, the 'invented reality' of the Metaverse will allow brands to leverage their digital persona to build deep connections with their audience, who will be able to interact with a brand as if it were a person. A Metaversian could be able to build a friendship with Google or participate in an event sitting next to Apple, build a friendship with Gucci, or participate in an event sitting next to her preferred luxury brand. A Metaversian could meet her favourite brand in a bar in the central square of a Metaverse virtual city, and start a conversation by asking 'What's your name?' or 'Do you prefer the sea or the mountains?' or even 'What do you do in your free time?' The answers the brand will give could lead to a new relationship and new encounters in other places in the Metaverse. Other brands could be represented by a chatty digital persona, who takes the initiative and starts talking about herself, her successes and her adventures, without asking any questions. Probably this kind of brand digital persona thinks that to make new friends it is necessary to 'make an impression'. It's exactly the same difference that exists in the real world between those brands that listen to their audience and those brands that talk continuously about their products rather than their services, saying how beautiful and useful they are, even if several studies have shown that over two-thirds of consumers prefer those brands that make them feel like people, demonstrating they know their deep desires and aspirations.

All these considerations highlight that in order to establish a profound relationship between a brand and an inhabitant of the Metaverse, in other words creating a friendship that lasts forever, the personality of a brand digital persona must be 'attractive' to the eyes (and ears) of the inhabitant, just like a real-world person who wants to be attractive to the people around her. Brand strategists will therefore have to learn to carefully design their brand personality, that is, their tone of voice, body language and above all their way of acting – what they are shown to love and hate through their behaviours. The last aspects are branding dimensions that are usually analysed in an abstract way, and now – paradoxically, with the Metaverse – will have to be instead designed methodically and with extreme attention to detail.

For example, according to the Jung framework, the Coca-Cola brand is believed to run on the Innocent archetype. Coca-Cola brand communication – one of the most appreciated in the world – is focused on depicting moments of simplicity, showing consumers who find fulfilment in daily moments that matter, like spending time with family and friends, but without talking to a friend called Coca-Cola. Applying the concepts we have described above, Coca-Cola brand strategists could add the brand digital persona to these daily moments, a persona who is talking with consumers, sharing their moments of simplicity in a direct and pleasant conversation. It's quite easy to understand that the relationship between the brand and its audience in the latter case could be much deeper.

The Metaversian competitive space is completely new and rapidly evolving. The considerations I have reported above are certainly not conclusive. However, it is clear that the Metaverse represents an intersection of technology, economy and culture where successful brands will not be those that sell products or experiences, but those that help creators to create successful products and experiences. In other words, in the Metaverse a brand will have to 'sell its values', and to do that, it will have to start thinking no longer as a company but as a nation's governing body, a nation where several communities live and share common values. Therefore, a brand will not only have to think about its own success, but will have to think about the economic, social and physical well-being of its nation's inhabitants, individually and as members of communities. A brand will have to provide the inhabitants of its nation not only with opportunities for playing and entertainment, but also opportunities to develop creatively new products and services, to make a contribution to the community they are part of. If a brand does not provide such opportunities, the inhabitants of its nation will move to another one. To achieve all this, it will be necessary to rethink in a profound way how brands are managed, their product development processes, marketing, sales and communication, as well as metrics used to measure brand performance. It will be necessary to measure not only cash flow and profit available for shareholders, but above all the economic and social value that creators and brand audience members have been able to generate thanks to the contribution of the brand itself. The most powerful growth generator of a brand's market cap will be in fact the market cap growth of the communities that have been created with the support of the brand itself. It will be an immense paradigm shift, both economic and managerial, that will require rethinking almost everything, even what is studied in business schools.

Notes

1 Bored Ape Yacht Club is a collection of 10,000 NFTs that was built on the Ethereum blockchain by a company called Yuga Labs. The collection features profile pictures of cartoon apes that are procedurally generated by an algorithm from over 170 possible traits, including expression, headwear, clothing, and more. The NFTs were originally sold in April 2021 for 0.08 Ether each – around $190 at that time – and were sold out in 12 hours. As of June 2022, the collection had totalized a total market volume of transactions of almost $3.5 billion, and was the first one in the total average value per single NFT ranking.

2 CryptoPunks is an NFT collection launched in June 2017 by a company called Larva Labs. In March 2022, the rights of the NFT collection were acquired by Yuga Labs. As of June 2022, the collection had totalized a total market volume of transactions of $2.35 billion, and was the second one in the total average value per single NFT ranking.

References

Aaker, J L (1997) Dimensions of brand personality, *Journal of Marketing Research*, **34** (3) pp 347–356

CB Insights (2021) The Creator Economy Market Map, www.cbinsights. com/research/creator-economy-market-map/ (archived at https://perma. cc/KV76-A22G)

Donetti, A (2022) Il Metaverso apre all'economia della creazione [blog], https://changes.unipol.it/technology/il-metaverso-apre-alleconomia-della-creazione (archived at https://perma.cc/RH4Z-Y3FA)

Horowitz, A (2022) State of Crypto 2022 – An Overview Report, https:// a16zcrypto.com/state-of-crypto-report-a16z-2022/ (archived at https:// perma.cc/BJ5E-M8A6)

Jung, C G (1954) Psychological Aspects of The Mother Archetype. In Read, H, Fordham, M and Adler, G (eds), *The Collected Works of C G Jung Volume 9*, Routledge: London

Kaczynski, S and Kominers, S D (2021) How NFTs create value, *Harvard Business Review*, https://hbr.org/2021/11/how-nfts-create-value (archived at https://perma.cc/P9C8-22YE)

Linktree (2022) Creator Report 2022, https://linktr.ee/creator-report/ (archived at https://perma.cc/W2Y2-GFMA)

The 'brand origin' dilemma

09

GLYN ATWAL
KLAUS HEINE

LEARNING OBJECTIVES

- To understand the different concepts related to brand origin.
- To assess the role and function of brand origin for luxury brands.
- To identify components of a brand origin strategy.
- To explore how luxury brands can overcome negative country of origin associations.

This chapter will discuss the importance of the country of origin of brands (CoB) in the luxury segment and how luxury brands can develop CoB strategies. We will also examine the challenges of CoB facing luxury brands originating from emerging markets as they expand outside of their home markets, with a focus on China and India. An overview of tactics will guide luxury brands to address potentially negative country associations. An outlook will discuss the future of CoB in an increasingly globalized marketing environment.

Conceptual definitions

The concept of Country of Origin (CoO) can be defined as an extrinsic product or service attribute indicating the country where a product or service was made, assembled, or both (Krupka et al, 2021). Within this context the CoO of products can be understood according to the following dimensions: Country of Manufacture (CoM), Country of Design (CoD), Country of Assembly (CoA) and Country of Parts or raw materials (CoP) (Aichner, 2013). For example, the fashion label Shaping New Tomorrow leverages a combination of these cues in its brand communications: 'Danish Design. Handmade in Portugal' (Shaping New Tomorrow, 2022).

However, there is a growing consensus that CoO needs to consider a wider range of attributes that has a greater focus on brand origin. Heine and Atwal (2022) discuss how CoO can be segmented into brand nationality (the brand's people-related roots), place of origin (the brand's location-related roots), brand stories (the brand's temporal roots), and brand traditions (the brand's cultural roots). For example, H Stern is a luxury jeweller founded by a German immigrant in Brazil. The company is headquartered in Rio de Janeiro and is present in 14 countries. Collections are based on many global influences but Brazil remains a frequent source of inspiration.

Indeed, Phau and Prendergast (2000) distinguished between the CoO of products and the country of origin of brands (CoB). According to Heine et al (2019, p 18), 'CoB can be defined as the country or countries where target consumers believe a brand originates from (CoB image)'. This definition is consistent with the concept of brand origin (BO) defined as the place, region or country to which the brand is perceived to belong by its target consumers (Tse and Gorn, 1993). This supports the argument that consumers place greater emphasis on the CoO image of brands and perceive the CoB as independent from manufacturing locations. For example, Apple's iPhone leverages its 'Designed in California' positioning to reduce possible negative effects related to the CoA (China) and CoP (Japan and South Korea).

Brand origin is of significant relevance for luxury brands as they deliver higher levels of symbolic, experiential and functional value (Berthon et al, 2009). According to Verlegh and Steenkamp (1999), CoO is not merely a cognitive cue for product quality, but it also relates to emotions, identity, pride and autobiographical memories. For example, Ralph Lauren is an iconic US fashion brand that incorporates the American lifestyle: 'From the designs of its apparels and accessories, to the dining experience offered in its restaurants, the Ralph Lauren brand stands as a symbol of America' (Roll, 2018). As argued by Heine et al (2019, p 17), the traditional approach of studying the effects of CoO information as extrinsic cues on product quality evaluation may no longer be adequate to fully understand CoO effects, because 'although it is widely accepted that the product quality of BMW is superior, some consumers may still decide to purchase an Alfa Romeo because of their enthusiasm for Italian *dolce vita*'.

This interpretation reinforces the argument that brand origin is a key component of the brand lifestyle, which is exemplified by many brand management strategies, such as the Bodega Argento vinery. According to its brand identity and style guide, 'When you buy Argento you buy Argentina, and when we sell Argento we sell Argentina. The characteristics of the wine are very Argentine and drinking it is like drinking in Argentina.' The brand adopts its country-of-origin image: 'It is sophisticated, real, proud, sociable, expressive, vibrant, and stirring' (Argento, 2013, p 2). Although we accept there is an important distinction between the two concepts of CoO and CoB, these concepts will be used synonymously in this chapter.

The strategic case for CoB

Heritage and tradition are intertwined with the identity of the luxury brand. According to Godey et al (2013), consumers recognize geographic and cultural origin as crucial characteristics of luxury brands. Research suggests that a favourable country image (e.g. Germany's strength in engineering) has a stronger impact on the quality evaluations of high-end and high-involvement products, which increases the likelihood of purchase (Godey et al, 2013). As Lojacono and Ru Yun Pan (2021, p 111) observe, CoO is critical in 'conveying a message about the quality, heritage, and craftsmanship of a company's products'. Indeed, there is evidence to suggest that consumers use CoO as a critical reference to evaluate product and brand performance for prestige brands, as reflected in customer reviews posted on e-commerce platforms such as Amazon:

> *Nice fit overall but the material is too thin, I am not sure because of the Country of Manufacturing compared to other GANT products I*

would say these are inferior. Probably they should care a bit more of the quality rather than just outsourcing in India and Bangladesh. On the long run they are going to lose customers and I will be one of them.
Reviewed by Luca R. on Amazon UK on 22 April 2022.

At this price I assumed this was made in France or at least in Europe, unfortunately, the pot is made in China. I am willing to pay a premium for products that are made in Europe but not for products that are made in China and only the great company name is on it... I would have expected more from Le Creuset (translated from the original German).
Reviewed by marfis on Amazon Germany on 28 March 2019.

Brand origin is generally seen in the luxury segment as contributing to brand equity (Jung et al, 2014; Yasin et al, 2007), brand distinctiveness (Yasin et al, 2007) and as a competitive advantage that helps increase trust and demand premium prices (Oetzel and Doh, 2009; Shukla, 2010). Interestingly, there is evidence to suggest that consumers low on status consumption use perceived strength of brand origin as an important cue for brand love (Siew et al, 2018).

It is within this broad context that many luxury brands, particularly European brands, have sought to build positive country-specific associations within specific areas of expertise such as French origins (cosmetics, wine, champagne), Italian design (shoes, fashion, accessories, jewellery), and Swiss craftsmanship (watches). As Laforet (2010, p 369) observes, 'Nations have individual fingerprints that are unique'.

CoB strategies

We outline the following CoO strategies based on Aichner (2014) to illustrate how luxury brands can leverage positive country image associations.

'Made in'

According to Aichner (2014, p 84), 'The use of the phrase "Made in ..." is the most frequent and easiest strategy used to communicate the CoO of a product.' Many Italian brands such as Brunello Cucinelli are keen to communicate their distinctive 'Made in Italy' label positioning. Italy enjoys positive country image associations such as passion, creativity and tradition that can have a positive effect on purchasing decisions. According to an Ipsos (2021a) study, meaning given by respondents to 'made in Italy' is first 'manufactured and assembled in Italy' (44 per cent), then 'raw materials are extracted from Italy' (37 per cent).

Quality and origin labels

The significance of terroir has received increasing attention, 'meant to represent an amalgam of history, tradition, specific soil composition and ethos emanating from a certain place' (Spielmann, 2014, p 182). Terroir can be regarded as an effective branding strategy to differentiate products within the wine sector (Bruwer and Johnson, 2010) and is considered as a synonym for authenticity (Charters and Spielmann, 2014). According to Beverland (2005, p 1005), authenticity or sincerity for luxury wine is achieved through 'relationship to place'. The Appellation d'Origine Protégée (AOP) model has become a legal reference to position prestige wines such as Burgundy wines and Champagne 'according to the reputation of their prestigious geographic indications' (Georgopoulos, 2014, p 41).

CoO embedded in the company name

Many European luxury brands have names that are explicitly related to their origin. For example, the name Bottega Veneta means 'Venetian shop' in Italian. Bulgari uses the Latin letter 'v' instead of 'u' to instil its historical connection to the city of Rome. Other brands such as Donna Karen New York explicitly carry the location of their origin in their names. Coach adopts a similar approach that includes 'New York' on its label. Likewise, Burberry's logo incorporates 'London' and 'England' to reinforce Britishness. Indeed, this phenomenon is not restricted to European brands. Qeelin expresses its strong Chinese identity with its brand name that refers to a Chinese national fruit. However, the CoO is not always as transparent because a brand's origin consists of different dimensions (Heine et al, 2019). For example,

Montblanc's actual CoB is German but its CoB image is French (or European) because of its brand name.

Use of the CoO language

Many French brands such as Hermès have a strong national CoB identity and consumers can spontaneously recognize the brand's origins, which can be attributed to the French pronunciation of the brand name. The use of language is widely used to leverage the CoO effect for marketing campaigns. For example, Longchamp's tagline 'très Paris' evokes the spirit of French *art de vivre*. The German car manufacturer Audi continues to use the 50-year-old tagline 'Vorsprung durch Technik' in its global communications.

Use of famous or stereotypical people from the CoO

Burberry has long partnered with a diverse selection of British personalities such as models (e.g. Kate Moss), musicians (e.g. Elton John) or brand ambassadors (e.g. Marcus Rashford) to underline its British origin. This national brand identity has been a consistent theme presented in Burberry fashion shows as underlined by chief creative officer Riccardo Tisci, 'The collection embodies an intangible essence that is Britishness, a unique fusion of honouring the beauty of the past, whilst also remaining focused on the future with thankfulness, hope and love' (Reuters, 2022).

Use of CoO flags and symbols

Many US brands make deliberate use of national symbols that are deeply embedded in their brand identity. For example, Ralph Lauren has been making Team USA's opening and closing ceremony uniforms since 2008. Harley Davidson concentrates on the brand lifestyle of motorcycling and more specifically on the subculture of American outlaw bikers.

Moreover, cultural heritage is symbolic of CoO that enables luxury brands to create an aura of status and sophistication that is rarely imitable. For example, Burberry is one of 816 royal warrant holders (credited as 'Weatherproofers' to the Queen and 'Outfitters' to the Prince of Wales). Royal patronage appears to have a positive effect on purchase intention. According to a research study, 57 per cent of Chinese consumers said the Royal association is important or very important in increasing desirability of British lifestyle brands (Wang, 2018).

Use of typical landscape or famous buildings from the CoO

The use of national landmarks is a CoO tactic for luxury brands to reconfirm a national identity in brand communication campaigns. For example, Longchamp's 'très Paris' video campaign is set against a series of iconic Parisian landmarks, including the Arc de Triomphe, Place Dauphine, Place de la Concorde, Tour Eiffel, Avenue Trudaine, Les Escalier Mont Cenis, Café Le Mansart and Les Bains.

Luxury made in... an emerging market

The bias against products from emerging countries was found to be of significant relevance within the luxury segment (Cordell, 1991; Manrai et al, 1998). As observed by Som and Das (2012, p 192), 'The country of origin remains, however, an unwanted burden for most high-end Asian brands because of the perception of low quality'. The 2021 Anholt-Ipsos Nation Brands Index (NBI) ranked Germany as the leading 'nation brand' followed by Canada, Japan and Italy, with China ranked 31 and India 40 out of 60 countries (Ipsos, 2021b).

However, anecdotal evidence suggests that consumer perceptions are changing, as noted by the growing market acceptance of design and creativity originating from emerging markets. The exhibition 'Africa Fashion' hosted at the V&A in London is a platform to acknowledge the vitality of design creativity stemming from the African continent. Fashion weeks have also become prominent showcases for emerging contemporary talent. For example, seven Chinese designers presented their work at the 2021 Paris Fashion Week. The increasing international success of brands originating from emerging markets can be partly attributed to the influence of soft power, defined as the country's ability to exert influence through attraction or persuasion rather than coercion (Nye, 2004). For example, South Korea's soft power is reflected through popular culture such as film and TV (e.g. *Parasite*, *Squid Game*), music (K-Pop) and fandoms – also the focus of the exhibition 'Hallyu! The Korean Wave' at London's V&A. According to the Global Soft Power Index 2022, the United States headed the ranking but China was ranked fourth, its highest position ever and overtaking Japan in Asia (Brand Finance, 2022).

In Asia and especially in China, consumers are increasingly interested in home-grown high-end brands, which goes along with a wave of newly emerging luxury brand start-ups in China. The brand purpose of Shang Xia is representative for many of the young Chinese high-end brands (Heine and Atwal, 2022). This trend is driven by the young and fashion-conscious avant-garde, mainly from Shanghai, who are increasingly proud to be Chinese. At the same time, these changes in consumer preferences are yet to reach mainstream audiences (Liu et al, 2020). European brand origin is still seen as the gold standard in the luxury category. This creates a dilemma for high-end start-ups from emerging markets. On the one hand, they want to differentiate from established luxury brands with their (Chinese) brand origin, but on the other hand, they face challenges in managing still prevailing negative country image associations (e.g. low prestige value: Yang et al, 2019).

Below we outline how luxury brands originating from emerging markets can develop strategies to allay consumers' negative impressions of country image association without compromising brand authenticity. It is also a reminder that prestige brands from emerging markets can leverage their brand origin as a positive brand asset.

Demonstrate quality

Outstanding product quality that often reflects craftsmanship has been long considered as a defining characteristic of luxury brands. Kapferer and Michaut (2015) found that 'exceptional quality' was the first attribute listed when self-declared French luxury consumers were asked which attributes defined luxury. This implies that luxury brands originating from emerging markets need to ensure that product or service quality is at least on a par with or preferably exceeds international standards, 'Companies need to think about quality, as well as design, style and all other aspects of a customer experience that together make up the brand' (Som and Das, 2012, p 191).

Although many references of quality are subjective, luxury brands can demonstrate product excellence and thereby performance superiority. Hidesign, an Indian enterprise which continues to expand internationally, has managed to position itself as an authentic ethical luxury fashion brand. The brand places emphasis on traditional handcraftsmanship skills and techniques and has helped to shape a distinctive brand identity, as underlined by a long-standing slogan: 'Real Leather Crafted the Forgotten Way'. Its #*GoSlow with Hidesign* campaign stresses that its Atelier spends 42 days hand crafting a single bag, underscoring its commitment to craftsmanship that rivals many European brands.

Furthermore, internationally recognized awards can provide a compelling case for brands to deliver outstanding performance on a global scale. For example, Nashik (India)-based Sula Vineyards exports to over 30 countries and publicizes many of its awards such as Decanter World Wine Awards (Silver). Awards help Sula Vineyards to build an international reputation and to gain 'permission' to compete against brands that originate from established wine-growing countries and regions.

Instil innovation

It is acknowledged that most luxury brands attempt to embody the notion of innovation. This phenomenon is very much evident within the fashion sector where innovation is synonymous with creation. Every industry has its distinct approach towards innovation but in luxury industries, 'innovations take the form of design processes that manifest into new products, services, and experiences, but also new organizational processes, such as novel marketing strategies' (Carvajal Pérez et al, 2020, p 141).

It is within this holistic definition of innovation that brands can demonstrate innovation to overcome potential negative country associations. For example, Deshpandé and Raina (2011) observe how the organizational culture at the Taj Group has given the Indian company a distinctive and competitive advantage within the hospitality sector.

Sawhney et al (2006) identified dimensions of business innovation 'anchored by the offerings a company creates, the customers it serves, the processes it employs and the points of presence it uses to take its offerings to market'. SHEIN is reportedly the largest online-only fashion company in the world (the United States is the company's largest market). The Chinese-owned company has reinvented the fast fashion model and 'introduced the speed and effervescence of Chinese e-commerce to the outside world in three ways: via an integrated supply chain, data-driven design, and a grasp of the social media hype cycle' (*The Economist*, 2022). Although SHEIN is not a luxury brand, its approach to innovation that has established the concept of ultra-fast fashion 'supposes a rupture, whether in terms of consumer behaviour, or how things are done in a company' (Hoffmann and Lecamp 2015, p 38).

Celebrate cultural identity

Brands can leverage their cultural identity that is closely associated with their country of origin. It is within this context that there is a positive product/service-country match that is coherent with the cultural resources route: 'In certain product categories, originating from a particular emerging market *adds* value to the brand' (Kumar and Steenkamp, 2013, p 145).

Chinese brands such as Herborist create authenticity by leveraging 'Traditional Chinese Medicine' (TCM), a branch of traditional medicine based on more than 3,500 years of Chinese medical practice. In a similar vein, Forrest Essentials is an Indian luxury beauty brand that is identified by the brand's ancient rituals of Ayurveda. Indeed, the increasing international market success of the Brazilian beauty brand natura is based on its associations with Brazilian biodiversity.

For example, castanha-based products use the fruit that in traditional Amazonian communities is pressed by hand to produce a nourishing white milk.

Other brands attempt to take advantage of positive cultural cues that are clearly distinctive to the country of origin. Shang Xia opened a boutique in Paris in 2013 that is renowned for reviving old Chinese craftsmanship traditions (e.g. bamboo marquetry, bamboo weaving, eggshell porcelain-making, cashmere felt artwork and Kesi embroidery), reflected in many of its objects and furniture.

Emphasize storytelling

Storytelling is a widely used marketing technique that anchors the brand's image. This also incorporates myths that 'live high above "normal" stories; they are meta-narratives, existing beyond time and space, illuminating our realities from afar with their magical magnetism and radiant power' (Schaefer and Kuehlwein, 2015, p 123). Ralph Lauren creates a fantasy of the lifestyle of an American, aristocratic elite whereas Tiffany's is associated with the Hollywood movie *Breakfast at Tiffany's*.

Brands originating from emerging markets can use similar storytelling techniques that are related to the brand's narrative, point of difference and set of values. For example, Royal Enfield, quintessentially an Indian brand but rooted in British biking history, is gaining market share outside of the Indian market. Although not strictly luxury, the motorcycle brand plays tribute to its heritage such as the 'Flying Flea', a lightweight 125cc motorcycle designed during World War II to be dropped by parachute. This is underlined by Hughes et al (2016, p 359), who support the argument that the brand's story 'can reveal its unique history or a symbolic event that develops a connection between the community and the brand'.

Hybrid positioning

There is a case for luxury brands originating from emerging markets not to be typically tied to a single country of origin, but to associate with countries that are perceived to have a more prestigious country image. Godart and Zhao (2014) introduced the notion of brand hybridity. The authors argue that low-hybridity brands draw their inspiration mainly from one country and high-hybridity brands are characterized by a mix of elements of two or more cultures into a multicultural brand identity. Heine et al (2019) identified six types of hybrid brand identities in the Chinese luxury segment. For example, Qeelin emphasizes its Chinese-ness with country-specific symbols in its jewellery designs combined with an association with its foreign founders and owners.

Likewise, Hidesign, with a manufacturing base in Pondicherry in India, exhibits a multicultural aesthetic with design studios in Milan and London. Moreover, the label creates synergies with myriad country identities. For example, models and music used in communication campaigns represent a diverse range of ethnicities and styles respectively. Collections also celebrate global designs and inspirations such as Zen (inspired by the Japanese art of seeing into the nature of one's own being), Memphis (inspired by the Memphis era of design during the 1980s) and a Scandicci collection based on designs that have their origins in Tuscany.

CoO – an outdated concept?

Brand strategists may argue that CoO is an outdated concept. Manrai et al (1998) recommend a 'non-country branding' for luxury brands from developing countries to improve perceived product quality. This approach is evident within the fashion category. For example, there is virtually no reference to SHEIN's Chinese ownership. The corporate website states, 'SHEIN is a global fashion and lifestyle e-retailer committed to making the beauty of fashion accessible to all' (SHEIN, 2022). Likewise, the Chinese swimwear brand Cupshe, which is gaining market share in the United States (Wu, 2022) is, according to its corporate website, 'a beachwear brand inspired by and created for the most vibrant, fun, and fearless women all over the world' (Cupshe, 2022). Indeed, a 'neutral' or 'non-country' branding approach may be applicable to all brands, including luxury, regardless of CoO for the following reasons.

First, there is evidence to suggest that consumers are becoming more informed about luxury brands and no longer need CoO as a cue to evaluate performance. Deloitte (2021, p 20) reported that consumers are becoming more educated about luxury timepieces and 'the "Made in Switzerland" designation is no longer a draw'. Surprisingly, the study revealed only 15 per cent of Chinese consumers consider country of origin to be important when choosing a watch. Indeed, the growing popularity of digital garments and fashion non-fungible tokens (NFTs) such as the Gucci Virtual 25 could even mean that brand origin as a cue for quality will become even less relevant.

Second, consumers are increasingly willing to accept that brand identity is a result of a fusion of diverse cultural influences and rarely represents one national identity. Indeed, many traditional luxury brands continue to draw inspiration from a diverse range of cultural sources. For example, Dior's 2020 cruise collection was positioned as 'a dialogue between the Dior wardrobe and African fashion' that centred around Wax, a fabric emblematic of the African continent (LVMH, 2019). This phenomenon is highlighted in the success of the streetwear category among younger cohorts: 'The boundaries between fashion, art, luxury and street feel like they are no longer there' (Financial Times, 2020). This phenomenon appears to be consistent with many luxury brand collaborations, such as Burberry x Supreme and Gucci x North Face, that are based on a fusion of national cultural identities.

Moreover, consumers are demanding greater diversity and are increasingly challenging cultural stereotyping. Ralph Lauren, who have received criticism 'for marketing a fantasy package of the WASP life' (WASP is an acronym for (in the United States) White Anglo-Saxon Protestant) (Granta, 2021, p 90) recently launched a collaboration with Morehouse and Spelman colleges to honour the legacy of Black students. Interestingly, a global survey reported that 23 per cent of 18–25-year-old survey respondents took notice of representative advertising at the time of purchase for apparel and footwear, which increased to 28 per cent for beauty and personal care (Deloitte, 2021).

Third, country image associations can change. This can have implications to the extent that consumers are impacted by images of national brands. For example, Ipsos (2021b) reported UK relative reputation weaknesses on perceptions of the welcoming nature of its people and protecting the environment. As a result, luxury brands need to consider a neutral image to avoid a possible backlash against changing perceptions towards a country.

Indeed, consumers may avoid a brand because they feel animosity towards the country from which the brand originates or believe that purchasing foreign-made products is unpatriotic (Klein et al, 1998; Shimp and Sharma, 1987). For example, the 2012 anti-Japan boycott saw Japanese businesses in China incur an estimated $100 million in damages (Jing Daily, 2022). Japan's Shiseido launched China-only brands such as Aupres and Urara 'which are less likely to be targeted by nationalistic consumers during boycotts' (Jing Daily, 2022).

Conclusion

Brand origin is integral to the luxury brand identity. Luxury brands that enjoy a positive country image can leverage these associations through a range of tactics. Many European luxury brands integrate explicit and implicit cues in their marketing strategies. In a similar vein, US brands that are broadly positioned as accessible or 'masstige' use image impressions to create an emotional association. However, the dilemma facing many prestige brands stemming from emerging markets is how to overcome potentially negative country of origin associations. Examples show how brands originating from China and India have developed different strategies to create positive dimensions of the CoO image. This is key as prestige brands originating from emerging markets seek to expand their international market presence. However, luxury executives need to critically assess a 'non-country branding' strategy in response to a rapidly changing luxury market landscape.

Takeaways

- The CoO image of luxury brands can influence prestige/quality evaluations and purchase intention.
- Luxury brands can leverage positive country image associations – especially with the use of origin labels, CoO language, country ambassadors, as well as CoO flags and symbols.
- Luxury brands from emerging markets need to manage potentially negative country image associations – especially with a focus on quality, innovation and cultural identity.
- Luxury executives can consider a 'neutral' or 'non-country branding' approach as a valid future strategy.

CASE STUDY   Guochao: Redefining 'Made in China'

Guochao ('Guo' = country and 'Chao' = fashionable) refers to 'modern consumer goods that are infused with Chinese cultural elements as a key selling point' (Brooker, 2022). The trend towards guochao can be attributed to the rise of nationalism in China that according to Atwal (2021) is consistent with the rise of Chinese identity, design and style that has become 'an ingenious code for celebrating Chinese culture and self-expression'. According to McKinsey & Co (2021), the share of respondents who say they would buy a local Chinese brand over a foreign brand increased from 15 per cent in 2011 to 85 per cent in 2020.

The growing popularity of guochao is reflected in many categories. For instance, local brands reported 38 per cent share of the sportswear market in 2020 (McKinsey & Co, 2021). Domestic sportswear brands Li-Ning and Anta have reported significant increases in sales (Rozario, 2021). Anta used the patriotic theme 'China has got Anta for sports lovers' for the Tokyo Olympics in 2020. The continual market success of Chinese sportswear brands is putting competitive pressure on the likes of Nike and Adidas.

Guochao, which has mainly been associated with Chinese brands that according to Ma (2021) are 'spurred by the movement that turned "Made in China" into "Designed in China"' has also attracted the attention of non-Chinese brands. For instance, international luxury brands are exploring how to insert Chinese cultural codes into luxury products and services. For example, Dior's 2021 fall menswear collection was influenced by Chinese techniques, craftsmanship and culture (Yuan, 2021). Similarly, the collaboration between Canada Goose and Angel Chen used bold colour and visual symbols of Chinese identity (Bargeron, 2021).

However, not all efforts to integrate Chinese cultural elements resonate with Chinese consumers. For example, Norwegian Cruise Lines launched a new ship, the *Norwegian Joy*, specifically for the Chinese market, that featured typical Chinese features, including teahouses and karaoke rooms. However, this adaptation failed because Chinese passengers were, in fact, seeking a more Western-style experience (Sang and Ulrich, 2021).

The significant consumer interest in guochao that is 'driven by Chinese products becoming more competitive through attractive design, enhanced features, and improved performance' (McKinsey & Co, 2021) raises important questions for future prestige marketing strategies. Is guochao redefining what 'Made in China' really means? Can guochao expand beyond Chinese borders?

Discussion question

Is Guochao an opportunity or a threat for international luxury brands?

References

Aichner, T (2014) Country-of-origin marketing: A list of typical strategies with examples, *Journal of Brand Management*, **21**, pp 81–93

Argento (2013) *Argento Brand Identity and Style Guide*, http://www. logo-dizajn.com/wp-content/uploads/2014/12/Argento-Brend-Identitet. pdf (archived at https://perma.cc/C77L-8UF9)

Atwal, G (2021) Luxury brand success in China: Rewriting the code, *Jing Daily*, https://jingdaily.com/china-luxury-marketing-canada-goose-lv/ (archived at https://perma.cc/E87Z-HJWU)

Bargeron, S (2021) Why Canada Goose can't get enough Angel Chen, *Jing Daily*, https://jingdaily.com/angel-chen-canada-goose-collab/ (archived at https://perma.cc/W3X2-GTPL)

Berthon, P R, Pitt, L F, Parent, M and Berthon, J-P (2009) *Aesthetics and ephemerality: observing and preserving the luxury brand*, *California Management Review*, **52** (1), pp 45–66

Beverland, M (2005) Crafting brand authenticity: The case of luxury wines, *Journal of Management Studies*, 42 (5), pp 1003–29

Brand Finance (2022) Global Soft Power Index 2022: USA bounces back better to top of nation brand ranking, https://brandfinance.com/press-releases/global-soft-power-index-2022-usa-bounces-back-better-to-top-of-nation-brand-ranking (archived at https://perma.cc/FYU6-3957)

Brooker, A (2022) Guochao's rising prices open a door for global luxury brands in China, *Jing Daily*, https://jingdaily.com/guochaos-rising-prices-open-a-door-for-global-luxury-brands-in-china/ (archived at https://perma.cc/NNY2-U2QE)

Bruwer, J and Johnson, R (2010) Place-based marketing and regional branding strategy perspectives in the California wine industry, *Journal of Consumer Marketing*, 27 (1), pp 51–56

Carvajal Pérez, D, Le Masson, P, Weil, B, Araud, A and Chaperon, V (2020) Creative heritage: Overcoming tensions between innovation and tradition in the luxury industry, *Creativity & Innovation Management*, 29, pp 140–51

Charters, S and Spielmann, N (2014) The characteristics of strong territorial brands: The case of champagne, *Journal of Business Research*, 67 (7), pp 1461–67

Cordell, V V (1991) Competitive context and price as moderators of country-of-origin preferences, *Journal of Academy Marketing Science*, 19 (2), pp 123–28

Cupshe (2022) Our Story, https://uk.cupshe.com/pages/about-us (archived at https://perma.cc/H8KD-53PV)

Deloitte (2021) Authentically inclusive marketing, www2.deloitte.com/xe/en/insights/topics/marketing-and-sales-operations/global-marketing-trends/2022/diversity-and-inclusion-in-marketing.html (archived at https://perma.cc/S8HP-UUZG)

Deshpandé, R and Raina, A (2011) The ordinary heroes of the Taj, *Harvard Business Review*, December, pp 119–23

Financial Times (2020) Does streetwear have a future?, 4/5 January, www.ft.com/content/34cbe1c8-2350-11ea-b8a1-584213ee7b2b (archived at https://perma.cc/7R2M-E9U7)

Georgopoulos, T (2014) Wine law: Concepts; methods, issues and prospects. In S Charters and J Gallo (eds) *Wine Business Management*, Pearson, Montreuil

Godart, F and Zhao, Y (2014) Drivers of China's desire for luxury and consequences for luxury brands. In G Atwal and D Bryson (eds) *Luxury Brands in Emerging Markets*, Palgrave, Basingstoke

Godey, B, Pederzoli, D, Aiello, G, Donvito, R, Wiedmann, K and Hennigs, N (2013) A cross-cultural exploratory content analysis of the perception of luxury from six countries, *Journal of Product & Brand Management*, **22** (3), pp 229–37

Granta, F (2021) *Fashion Criticism: An anthology*, Bloomsbury Publishing

Heine, K and Atwal, G (2022) Growing luxury brands through culture-driven innovation, *Strategic Change*, to be published

Heine, K, Atwal, G and He, J (2019) Managing country-of-origin affiliations for luxury brand-building in China, *Australasian Marketing Journal*, **27** (1), pp 14–23

Hoffmann, J and Lecamp, L (2015) *Independent Luxury*, Palgrave Macmillan, Basingstoke

Hughes, M U, Bendoni, W K and Pehlivan, E (2016) Storygiving as a co-creation tool for luxury brands in the age of the internet: a love story by tiffany and thousands of lovers, *Journal of Product and Brand Management*, **25** (4), pp 357–64

Ipsos (2021a) Be-Italy! Exploring the dynamics of Italy's international reputation, www.ipsos.com/en/be-italy-exploring-dynamics-italys-international-reputation (archived at https://perma.cc/F959-HNRH)

Ipsos (2021b) Germany maintains top 'nation brand' ranking, Canada and Japan overtake the United Kingdom to round out the top three, www.ipsos.com/sites/default/files/ct/news/documents/2021-10/NBI-2021-ipsos.pdf (archived at https://perma.cc/3KR5-P2BB)

Jing Daily (2022) What luxury brands need to know about scandal in China, https://jingdaily.com/avoid-brand-boycott-shiseido-puig/ (archived at https://perma.cc/K5RF-JHL8)

Jung, H J, Lee, Y, Kim, H and Yang, H (2014) Impacts of country images on luxury fashion brand: facilitating with the brand resonance model, *Journal of Fashion Marking and Management*, **18** (2), pp 187–205

Kapferer, J N and Michaut, A (2015) Luxury and sustainability: a common future? The match depends on how consumers define luxury, *Luxury Research Journal*, **1** (1), pp 3–17

Klein, J G, Ettenson, R and Morris, M D (1998) The animosity of foreign product purchase: an empirical test in the People's Republic of China, *Journal of Marketing*, **62** (1), pp 89–100

Krupka, Z, Mirt, M and Ozreti-Došen, D (2021) The importance of country-of-origin construct dimensions in destination brand building, *Market-Tržište*, **33** (2), pp 221–38

Kumar, N and Steenkamp, J-B E M (2013) *Brand Breakout*, Palgrave Macmillan, Basingstoke

Laforet, S (2010) *Managing Brands: A contemporary perspective*, McGraw-Hill, London

Liu, Y, Karimi, S and Yuen, T W (2020) 'Support your country and buy Chinese Brands' – Would Chinese consumers buy it? *Journal of Marketing Communications*, **26** (2), pp 130–44

Lojacono, G and Ru Yun Pan, L (2021) *Resilience of Luxury Companies in Times of Change*, De Gruyter

LVMH (2019) Dior 2020 Cruise Collection celebrates Africa, www.lvmh.com/news-documents/news/dior-2020-cruise-collection-celebrates-africa/ (archived at https://perma.cc/4R6M-KE38)

Ma, A (2021) 3 ways foreign luxury brands can tap into China's Guochao trend, *Jing Daily*, https://jingdaily.com/china-guochao-western-brands-dior-lining/ (archived at https://perma.cc/RDP4-8WS9)

Manrai, L A, Lascu, D N and Manrai, A K (1998) Interactive effects on country of origin and product category on product evaluation, *International Business Review*, 7 (6), pp 591–615

McKinsey & Co (2021) Five consumer trends shaping the next decade of growth in China, www.mckinsey.com/cn/our-insights/our-insights/five-consumer-trends-shaping-the-next-decade-of-growth-in-china (archived at https://perma.cc/Z4H8-TGVS)

Nye, J S (2004) *Bound to Lead: The changing nature of American power*, Public Affairs, New York

Oetzel, J and Doh, J P (2009) MNEs and development: a review and reconceptualization, *Journal of World Business*, **44**, pp 108–20

Phau, I and Prendergast, G (2000) Conceptualizing the country of origin of brand, *Journal of Marketing Communications*, 6 (3), pp 159–70

Reuters (2022) Burberry celebrates British culture in London live show return, www.reuters.com/world/uk/burberry-celebrates-british-culture-london-live-show-return-2022-03-11/ (archived at https://perma.cc/K34Q-ELUQ)

Roll, M (2018) Ralph Lauren – A Brand Capturing the American Spirit, https://martinroll.com/resources/articles/strategy/ralph-lauren-a-brand-capturing-the-american-spirit/ (archived at https://perma.cc/PG3C-2SDN)

Rozario, K (2021) Nike feels the burn as Anta and Li-Ning continue their winning streak, *Jing Daily*, https://jingdaily.com/nike-anta-li-ning-sports-china-march/ (archived at https://perma.cc/Q829-3EPF)

Sang, L and Ulrich, K (2021) *Winning in China: 8 stories of success and failure in the world's largest economy*, Wharton School Press

Sawhney, M, Wolcott, R C and Arroniz, I (2006) The 12 different ways for companies to innovate, *MIT Sloan Management Review*, 47 (3), pp 75–81

Schaefer, W and Kuehlwein, J P (2015) *Rethinking Prestige Branding: Secrets of the ueber-brands*, Kogan Page, London

Shaping New Tomorrow (2022) Changing the way we think traditional menswear, https://shapingnewtomorrow.com/pages/about-us (archived at https://perma.cc/GGV2-KXN3)

SHEIN (2022) About us, www.shein.com/About-Us-a-117.html (archived at https://perma.cc/8JTB-T7QK)

Shimp, T and Sharma, S (1987) Consumer ethnocentrism: construction and validation of the CETSCALE, *Journal of Marketing Research*, 24 (3), pp 280–89

Shukla, P (2010) Status consumption in cross-national context: socio-psychological brand and situational antecedents, *International Marketing Review*, 27 (1), pp 108–29

Siew, S-W, Minor, M S and Felix, R (2018) The influence of perceived strength of brand origin on willingness to pay more for luxury goods, *Journal of Brand Management*, 25 (6), pp 591–605

Som, A and Das, S (2012) The rise of Indian luxury brands. In G Atwal and S Jain (eds) *The Luxury Market in India: Maharajas to masses*, Palgrave Macmillan, Basingstoke

Spielmann, N (2014) Promotion and events in the wine business. In S Charters and J Gallo (eds), *Wine Business Management*, Montreuil: Pearson

The Economist (2022) How much of a risk is opacity for China's Shein? www.economist.com/business/2022/04/16/how-much-of-a-risk-is-opacity-for-chinas-shein (archived at https://perma.cc/9H5R-SKHN)

Tse, D K and Gorn, G J (1993) An experiment on the salience of country-of-origin in the era of global brands, *Journal of International Marketing*, 1 (1), pp 57–76

Verlegh, P W J and Steenkamp, J B E M (1999) A review and meta-analysis of country-of-origin research, *Journal of Economic Psychology*, 20 (5), pp 521–46

Wang, Q (2018) *Four perspectives on the Royal Wedding*, https://warwick.ac.uk/newsandevents/knowledgecentre/society/sociology/royalwedding/ (archived at https://perma.cc/GJZ2-YKPD)

Wu, N (2022) Chinese swimwear brand Cupshe makes waves in the US, *Jing Daily*, https://jingdaily.com/cupshe-chinese-swimwear-dtc-amazon/ (archived at https://perma.cc/5Q9G-9RZ8)

Yang, S, Jiménez, F R, Hadjimarcou, J and Frankwick, G L (2019) Functional and social value of Chinese brands, *Journal of Global Marketing*, **32** (3), pp 200–15

Yasin, N M, Noor, M N and Mohamad, O (2007) Does image of country-of-origin matter to brand equity? *Journal of Product & Brand Management*, **16** (1), pp 38–48

Yuan, M (2021) Dior's Guochao menswear collection avoids cultural clichés, *Jing Daily*, https://jingdaily.com/diors-guochao-menswear-collection-avoids-cultural-cliches/ (archived at https://perma.cc/25W7-VSD5)

The niche world of ultra-luxury brands 10

A unique set of customers and how to act differently to serve them

MATTEO ATTI

LEARNING OBJECTIVES

- To understand the spectrum of luxury marketing.
- To understand the needs and desires of UHNWI.
- To understand the value of creating a luxury niche and how to execute it.
- To understand the power of communication and human connection across every stage of the marketing and sales cycle.

Introduction

This chapter explores the particular concerns of uber-luxury marketing and how niche brands can build and sustain a profitable business. It explains how such brands should not seek to emulate the mega-luxury conglomerates, but instead seek to leverage their own advantages by taking an ultra-targeted approach.

Successful luxury brands are required to be unique, innovative, insightful and hyper-segmented. They take a human-to-human approach over the traditional B2C or B2B models to reach a critical, demanding, cash-rich and time-poor audience looking for experiences and emotional responses over mere products or services.

The chapter also takes a look at what the next generation of ultra-wealthy individuals are spending their time and money on.

The world of luxury marketing is actually a universe

When people think of luxury, most tend to visualize fashion, jewellery or fragrance brands that are attainable and aspirational for many. The luxury world is dominated by mega brands and luxury groups such as LVMH, Chanel, or high-end car marques who have the marketing might and mass-market appeal to launch multiple products across many price points to the widest audience.

But there is a whole universe of brands that only service a handful of customers. Smaller companies that fill all the moments of the day of an ultra-high net worth individual (UHNWI), from waking up to sleeping and all the time in between. Think of antique furniture, fine art, fine dining at home, private travel, housing, social entertainment, and all sorts of collectibles and personal passions, from golf to racing horses. This is particularly true since the outbreak of Covid, as the rich have got wealthier even as the general population struggles with increasing costs of living (Picchi, 2021).

A recent report, The Art Market 2022, reveals strong recovery of the market, with a return to live sales and events, while online sales continued to grow. The sixth edition of the Art Basel and UBS Global Art Market Report, written by cultural economist Dr Clare McAndrew (2022), founder of Arts Economics, and published by Art Basel and UBS, presents the results of a comprehensive and macro-level analysis of the global art market in 2021, including a survey examining the behaviours of high-net-worth collectors across 10 markets. It found that on average, collectors purchased more art and antiques in 2021 than they did in 2019 and 2020, with the median expenditure on fine art, decorative art and antiques rising from $72,000 in 2019 to $126,000 in 2020, before more than doubling in 2021 to $274,000. Following its biggest fall in sales in 10 years in 2020, the global art market recovered strongly in 2021, it reports, with aggregate sales of art and antiques by dealers and auction houses reaching an estimated $65.1 billion, up 29 per cent from 2020, with values also surpassing the pre-pandemic levels of 2019.

It is not just art. Bain & Company reported in 2022 that the personal luxury goods market has experienced a V-shaped rebound, reaching €288 billion in value. In its luxury 2022 Spring Update – 'Rerouting the Future' (D'Arpizio and Levato, 2021), Bain & Company estimates market growth to reach €360–380 billion by 2025.

The Luxury Institute announced key findings from its 2022 qualitative survey of its Global Luxury Expert Network members, comprising prominent luxury goods and services CEOs, C-levels and consultants, as well as additional top-tier luxury executives and experts, with the biggest winners predicted to be travel and leisure (Luxury Institute, 2022).

Milton Pedraza, CEO of the Luxury Institute said: 'We must gauge real consumer sentiment by category, and by brand, and act accordingly to eliminate waste and mobilize to gain share right now. For brands with courage and resources, it is time to take advantage of the confusion and fear by investing for the future.' He recommends that brands invest in talent, game-changing innovation, ethically sourced, direct-from-the-customer predictive data and insights, analytics, and in recruiting and nurturing emotionally intelligent front-line expertise.

Meanwhile, US real estate brokerage Redfin saw sales of luxury homes in the United States rise by 41.6 per cent year over year in the first quarter of 2021, far outpacing sales growth in every other segment of the housing market. By comparison, sales of affordable homes increased only 7 per cent and sales of mid-priced homes climbed a mere 5.9 per cent (Katz, 2021; Vinogradov and Datwani, 2021).

Although UHNWI, each with private wealth in excess of $30 million, represent only 1.2 per cent of the world's HNWI population (which includes all people with wealth over $1 million), their combined net worth of $35.5 trillion accounts for a substantial 34 per cent share, underlining the huge stock of global wealth held by this select group of around 300,000 individuals, according to the Wealth X World Ultra Wealth 2021 report (Imberg et al, 2021).

While the demand trends are showing clear opportunities for growth at the higher end of the luxury market, gone are the days where reputation and know-how were the leading criteria to succeed in high luxury. Successful niche luxury brands are required to be unique, innovative, insightful and hyper-segmented.

Uber luxury is priceless but comes at a price

Think of bespoke hypercars, personalized wellness creams and treatments, flats on yachts circling the world, one-off creations to celebrate milestones, bespoke champagne made to your taste. UHNWI are seeking experiences, unique moments to remember or investing in bespoke couture, artwork, motors, jewellery, private jets – products and services that bring joy or save time.

There has been intense growth in the super-exclusive UHNWI world – both in terms of how many there are and their propensity to spend more, more often. So, how to address and engage this very special audience?

The growing space in uber luxury – and how niche brands can take advantage

There is a new space opening at the top of the luxury universe and the brands that get it right can build resilient businesses to cater to the wealthiest people in the world. Getting it wrong, though, is risky and luxury marketers must reimagine the way they connect, emote and relate.

Starting a new high-luxury brand, or growing an existing one, is not easy. Reasons include high price points, scarcity of clients, and low purchase frequency, where even fans would not convert often. Add to that the limitations of the distribution channels, considering that the traditional retail model would not work as it generates high daily recurring costs versus occasional purchases.

In a world where mega-luxury conglomerates can dominate in terms of share of voice, media budgets and recognition, niche brands will struggle to stand out if they are battling in the same media environments.

A company such as Chanel can spend upwards of 13 per cent of its gross revenues on marketing. In financials for 2020 it reported revenues of $10.1 billion, with $1.36 billion spent on brand support activities (Paton, 2021). A niche player will spend as little as – or less than – 1 per cent, with most of its investment going back to product and service optimization.

At the same time, niche brands hold a powerful advantage if they get their offerings right, and marketers for those brands must adapt their ways of communicating. Instead of aspiring to build massive brand awareness, niche brands can leverage their strength in unique products, particularly when playing in the very small, private worlds of UHNW individuals.

They can move from *aspirational* to *inspirational*, communicating only at times and in ways that create meaningful marketing.

It's time to change perspective

Niche brands are often told: You play in a small playground, your audience is small, you are small, your voice is small.

In reality, because they play in a small playground, their market share is potentially 100 per cent. A brand can certainly become the biggest and make its voice the loudest in a very specific realm, rather than trying to muscle in on the established luxury mega brand market.

A niche marketer simply won't be able to ask Google or Facebook to target people worth over $100 million at the touch of a button – because that doesn't exist as a segment. Nor should they accept the widely available, pre-set mass-marketing tools that could end up approaching consumers who cannot afford the product, risking both diluting investment and upsetting an audience that feels excluded.

Engaging with the elites requires marketers to take a unique approach – and the distinctive markers of high personalization and attention to detail that are woven into all aspects of ultra-luxury communications are probably some of the purest expressions of marketing techniques.

Niche marketing is hyper-focused and highly personalized. That means it can be hyper-effective since people statistically respond better to personalization (Morgan, 2020).

This is also why it is hard to find good, publicly quoted examples of marketing to the ultra-high-end market – few people receive these communiques and fewer still will publicize them.

Where and how should niche brands look to invest?

1 **Carefully vet the context.** You don't want your brand to seem out of place or be associated with the wrong environment or news cycle event. Better not to speak than to speak out of place.

2 **Every impression counts.** Prepare to spend a long time on creating the perfect message, testing and reassessing it against every age, culture and life path in the world.

3 **Engage with just the right people.** Place even more attention on targeting your message correctly, since your highly targeted message would fall on deaf ears in any other case.

4 **Be respectful.** Even in a digitally dominated channel mix, one-to-one marketing to UHNWI requires building a tangible perception of respect for the reader. How can you show them that you care?

5 **Paint your picture with multiple strokes.** While your audience should receive multiple impressions of your message across different intersecting channels, no message should be repeated in the same way. You would not even do that to a person you meet on your way to work every day, right?

6 **No message can be the wrong message.** You only have one chance before a UHNWI decides to move on and discard your brand as irrelevant.

7 Make a difference. No message can be perceived as a waste of their time, or there might not be another chance to be considered again.

How the modern UHNW marketer should look and behave

Never forget that luxury marketing is designed for the customer. So, here are a few tips on how to live and act by it:

1 Start your day by remembering that you are not the target market.

2 Never try to impress those whose lifestyles exceed your own.

3 Never see your product or brand in a subservient status – its desirability comes from your projected confidence in its superior quality.

Once the brand accepts its audience's and its own position in the marketing conversation, it can move from exclusive (leaving people out, protecting its world) to inclusive marketing (welcoming people in, sharing its world).

Generation next and new niches

The events of 2020 had a bearing on wealth performance by age, according to the Wealth X report (Imberg et al, 2021). With most UHNWI being self-made (72 per cent at the last count), it is important to watch out for this next generation and the trends that are driving them today and tomorrow.

Technology as a primary industry accounts for a greater proportion of individuals in this group. The wealth of many such individuals was boosted over the course of the year as digitalization expanded rapidly during the surge in home working, online shopping and personal leisure pursuits.

The fortunes of the under-50s, the youngest and by far the smallest UHNWI cohort in absolute number, grew by the largest margin, contributing nearly two-thirds of the overall 2 per cent annual rise in total UHNW wealth. Meanwhile, Millennials (Gen Y) and Gen Z customers will continue to assert their position as critical growth levers for the luxury sector in 2022, a generational shift that will continue to accelerate as their wealth and expectations rise.

Together, these younger generations of affluent consumers are set to account for 70 per cent of the luxury market by 2025 according to Bain & Company (D'Arpizio and Levato, 2021). Yet, they are still under-served by many luxury brands, and could become the target audience for nimbler high-end luxury companies.

This is why it is critical to focus not only on marketing just the core attributes of the brand itself, its history and unique knowledge, but to consider carefully how the brand can intercept the new ways in which its potential customers move and behave. As we write, some trends are taking the lead and should be considered as key opportunities for all niche brands to establish a conversation with their prospective audience:

- **Artificial intelligence.** Advances in AI will help marketers deliver exceptional, personalized customer experiences, not only in the digital sphere but through every touchpoint.

- **The Metaverse.** At the crossroads of digital, gaming, augmented reality and virtual reality, it represents another significant opportunity for niche luxury brands both online and offline, creating products and services catered to a very specific, and recognizable, niche.

- **Non-fungible tokens.** NFTs are assets that carry a unique digital identity and can be traded between users on a public blockchain. Experts are still debating whether this is a growing trend or a fad, but potential interest has been demonstrated by artist Beeple, who sold a piece for $69.3 million in 2021 (Brown, 2021). Analysts at Morgan Stanley expect the luxury NFT and Metaverse market to reach $56 billion by 2030, opening an entirely new world of traded assets (Lee, 2021).

- **Social life sources.** As behaviours shift, the social side of life is facing changes too. In a recent survey, nearly 7 in 10 of Northrop & Johnson's UHNW yachting clients used social media regularly, with

LinkedIn (36 per cent), YouTube (35 per cent) and Facebook (34 per cent) each cited by about one-third of respondents. Instagram, which is popular with travel marketers, had a 25 per cent response, followed by Twitter at 13 per cent and WeChat at 4 per cent (St.Denis, 2020).

- **Subtle influences.** Silent influencers, whether within a private or public setting, are also having an effect. Take luxe fashion brand The Row, which has spent minimal amounts on marketing since launching in 2006, with no traditional advertising at all. Instead, its 'stealth wealth' attraction or *quiet luxury* presence lay in timeless style, with no logos or branding (Sherman, 2019). The Row has never shared images of celebrities wearing the brand on social media, and its account is filled with look book images from collections and various artworks. Yet recently, several illustrious celebrities – Kendall Jenner, Chrissy Teigen and Zoe Kravitz, for instance – are tagging the brand on social media. Coincidence? And what does that mean for the brand's future marketing plans?

Conscious consumption – purpose in practice

A whole new set of topics are shifting expectations and requirements, particularly among Millennials and Gen Z, and in the past five years two emerged with prominence: sustainability and conscious consumption.

Says Claudia D'Arpizio (2021), partner at Bain & Company: 'Where once it was all about status, logos and exclusivity, luxury brands are now actors in social conversations, driven by a renewed sense of purpose and responsibility.' In the UK alone, some £3 trillion will change hands to the next generations in 2023. And critical for them are Environmental, Social and Governance (ESG) actions.

Responding to their new priorities, VistaJet, one of the largest business aviation providers in the world, recently committed to becoming carbon neutral by 2025, leading in a sector often not seen as engaged in environmental responsibility (VistaJet, 2022).

'This means changing the way we operate, to benefit not only our clients, but the whole global community. The industry as a whole must step up to combat climate change and its impact today – it's the right thing to do and we all have to act now,' said its founder and chairman, Thomas Flohr. Not only do they see it as the right thing to do – it is also what customers are increasingly demanding.

It is not just about announcements. Third-party audits are the only way to ensure companies are meeting their pledges and reporting transparently about them. Extensive greenhouse gas (GHG) emissions and Task Force on Climate-related Financial Disclosures (TCFD) audits enabled VistaJet to identify the carbon footprint of its operations and offices worldwide, in order to define further sustainability opportunities and priorities (VistaJet, 2022).

Transformative initiatives, such as investment in sustainable aviation fuel and emission reduction through development of routing AI, are critical components of its investment in the future, while communications to customers make the brand and its clients proceed hand in hand to change the way the product is used and its impact on the larger global community is reduced.

ESG is not only about carbon footprint, though. Brands that respond to social responsibility calls are becoming more and more relevant in a highly attentive customer world. During the Covid-19 pandemic, with commercial aviation at a standstill, VistaJet offered complimentary empty leg flights for government repatriations and medical materials transportation to help ensure that those with critical travel requirements were able to keep moving (VistaJet, 2020).

This is seen across all sectors. A study highlighted by Accenture suggests that the newer generations of consumers hold stronger ethical buying values (Curtis et al, 2021). Over 60 per cent of the new generation of consumers are attracted to brands based on the company's ethical values and purpose. The consultancy also believes that consumer demand for purpose-driven brands means that companies who amplify their positive social and environmental impacts will also maximize their revenues.

By 2030, it predicts, Millennials will hold five times as much wealth as they have today and are expected to inherit over $68 trillion from their predecessors in the Great Transfer of Wealth. 'The bottom line is that having a purpose is good business,' said Brian Wipple, CEO of Accenture Interactive. 'It is the business of the future!' (UN Global Compact Media, nd).

A move into ESG and purpose-led discourse, though, has to be true to the brand and substantially affect its core business model. Brands looking to prove their sustainability and community credentials must walk the talk and be transparent about ambitions and outcomes.

Making business marketing personal

We highlighted the need to stop thinking in terms of business-to-business or business-to-consumer, instead highlighting human-to-human interactions and communications that span the entire sales and marketing cycle. At the end of the day, as business leaders or decision makers, we are all people.

As critical as reaching UHNWI in their personal environments, emotional rationality is another tool to be carefully considered. Stakeholders and shareholders want results for the short, medium and long term and will demand transparency and value for money. But are they really evaluating messages with only a look at the bottom line? How are the leaders of the largest companies in the world really influenced?

Three key points make all the difference in today's transactional world, be they personal or organizational:

- we make decisions faster;
- we want to listen less;
- we look for few, strong facts to guide us.

But here's what's unique about niche marketing to corporations. Business purchase decisions are typically higher value and higher stakes than consumer purchases. They involve more influencers and stakeholders, greater complexity and more distinct stages.

The *Wall Street Journal* intelligence report, looking at B2B purchase decision journeys among large companies ($250M+ revenue) in 2021 in technology, finance, professional services and marketing services, revealed some interesting insights about the triggers to initiate a search for a new product, service or vendor, the time taken to complete the journey, as well as which stakeholders are involved (Vinogradov and Datwani, 2021). The decision stages identified were three:

Pre-decision:

- The time between when they last selected a supplier for the given category and when the 'trigger' occurred that prompted them to actively begin searching for and deciding on a new supplier.

Search, evaluation and shortlisting:

- Search: the period between the trigger for the new supplier and the initial search.
- Evaluation and shortlisting: the time when the organization arrived at a 'shortlist' of likely candidates.

Final decision:

- The final review of shortlisted candidates to the ultimate buying decision.

Interviews showed that:

- Search for new partners can be triggered at any point in time, by either internal or external circumstances.
- The decision journey can take from as little as six weeks up to seven months.
- There are typically three job functions or departments involved in the decision, with IT/technology as the department most frequently involved across all regions and purchase categories, followed by senior leadership (c-suites, boards, etc), risk management and finance roles.
- On average, organizations consider between two and four potential providers, from the initial stage of research and exploration.

Here's where *emotional rationality* comes in:

- At the outset of their journey, decision makers already have greater familiarity with the winning versus losing brands.

- Decision makers have stronger emotional connections – especially trust and confidence – with winning versus losing brands at each journey's stage.

The use of the decision makers' preferred type of content also informs the final decision, as the emotional impacts of brand exposure in various channels, and the selection of the media and context in which the messages are displayed, drive fundamental differences in the perception of the considered brands:

- Decision makers cite case studies, videos and thought leadership research as the most highly valued types of content to inform their decisions.

- The media channels preferred by B2B decision makers include brand websites, business news and trade media outlets, as well as social media platforms and discussions with brand sales representatives.

- Networking at a trade show is appealing to decision makers.

- Trust and confidence, in both winning and losing brands, are enhanced by ongoing media and marketing exposure. Feelings of trust, in particular, can be strengthened by brand exposure in business news and trade media.

Listen, observe, adapt and engage

Whether debating services for personal or corporate use, luxury brands are catering to highly educated, knowledgeable customers who are working hard to identify which brands to associate themselves with. As their decisions can influence very large revenues, establishing a trustful relationship in the most carefully vetted channels and with the right tools will have to start way before the purchase decision is activated.

Though the approaches to reaching the right individuals differ subtly between business and personal contexts, there are important considerations to keep in mind across the two.

Here are some key learnings:

- Collecting data is critical. Privacy-compliant, first-party data is vital, particularly that which taps into the behavioural.

- Be primed to constantly adapt as new preferences and groups come on the horizon. Select the key cores of your strategy to deliver to your chosen audience.

- Listening is key. This is a two-way conversation, so without listening how can you hope to understand those who you hope to connect and build a relationship with?

- Human-to-human is the solution, aided by powerful technology. That tech increasingly allows marketers to fine-tune audiences and deliver messages and services effectively and purposefully.

- Finally, stay true to your promise. Trust is the glue that binds a long-term and meaningful relationship between vendor and customer.

Glossary

Conscious consumption: a new way of buying for the better. As opposed to conspicuous consumption where consumers wanted to flaunt their wealth, the trend now is to spend dollars in a more community-led way.

Emotional rationality: all decisions, business and personal, are said to be underlined by rationality. But beneath that, the emotional aspect is key. Both should be considered in tandem.

Human-to-human marketing: this is about remembering or identifying that this is not just a simple sales cycle. We are not – yet – bot-to-bot.

Inclusive marketing: at the lower end of the luxury market there can be a tendency to 'show don't tell' – i.e. here's what you could have, if only you could afford it – focusing on the aspirational aspect of selling. Inclusive marketing invites everyone in, while not targeting people unnecessarily.

Business cases

CASE STUDY   Private jets: how megatrends can be applied to a niche industry

Founded in 2004, VistaJet revolutionized business aviation by pioneering a new way to fly: access to a global fleet without any of the responsibilities of owning an aircraft. It realized that ownership itself was no longer a status symbol for a growing niche of ultra-high-net-worth individuals (UHNWI) who were looking for experiences that made their life better, easier, quicker and happier while underlining their focus on trends such as shared economy, quality of life and value for money.

VistaJet says it stands for being simple, efficient, reliable and global with a focus on giving services that set the new standards of excellence.

It has grown to offer access to a global fleet of silver and red jets, offering an unparalleled cabin experience, flying into and out of the hardest-to-reach destinations. To date, VistaJet passengers have flown to over 1,900 airports in 96 per cent of the world's countries, making it the first and only global aviation company.

The signature Program membership, a bespoke flight hour subscription plan, offers guaranteed aircraft availability at a fixed hourly rate, with no depreciation and no capital risk, as well as on-demand flights for less frequent flyers.

The company continues to evolve. Whereas once the world of chartered aviation was seen as a business expense, now the company is seeing growth in personally motivated travel and has evolved its marketing to service this niche. Request for door-to-door integrated services has grown threefold since the start of the pandemic, with the company saying that the 'working from anywhere' trend has forced a blend of the two categories like never before.

From a fully enabled business suite to a restful family space, its cabins are equipped for all needs. Fine bed linen, cashmere blankets, Christofle silverware and porcelain, a curated library by Heywood Hill and an on-board entertainment system ensure a home away from home environment. All passengers can enjoy a private dining selection, created in partnership with some of the world's most renowned chefs and restaurants.

Recognizing that the flight is only one part of the travel experience, VistaJet has introduced a number of programmes that either make the most of passengers' time in the air or help them enjoy experiences beyond the airport. It is about creating unique moments to remember, whatever the occasion.

VistaJet identified the importance of catering to the wider family when flying, be that keeping children entertained or allowing pets to enjoy the cabin space without having to be put in the hold. To support that need, its cabin crew is Norland-trained, and it offers bespoke parties in the sky – anything from a Mad Hatter's Tea Party to shooting movies or completing a secret spy mission. It has created bespoke Explorer Backpacks, personalized to the individual child's age and their travel destination, to be used both on board and for days afterwards; as well as family activity hampers, full of activities to create together.

VistaPet was launched because one in four members flies with their pet. It was designed in collaboration with experienced veterinary practitioners, coaches, dieticians and groomers to respond to the unique needs and challenges faced when travelling with animals. Pre-flight fear of flying courses are offered in partnership with The Dog House to prepare for a comfortable in-flight experience. The training desensitizes dogs to what they could experience during a flight, such as the sound of jet engines, cabin air pressure, and the movements of air turbulence.

Small moments matter too. On discovering a frequent elderly flier always requested tiramisu, the vice president of private dining delivered his own personal tiramisu recipe to his chef. They made a single portion for her to enjoy on her next flight, a family-sized portion to take home, and a note explaining that it came from his grandmother's own recipe.

VistaJet knows it is not just a travel company but an experience one, shaped by more than just time spent on board.

A very private world

To complete its unique set of services, VistaJet has also curated a portfolio of the world's finest accommodations and partners – from favourite suites, residences, ski lodges and yachts to private islands and exceptional estates, with a focus on privacy and personalized service.

Partnering with a network of world-leading travel experts and properties, including Pelorus, Kisawa, EYOS, Guest, Wilderness Safaris and Based on a True Story, it started offering a host of personal services to create unforgettable moments – the ultimate notion of private travel.

The company also continued to build programmes that tie into its members' passions, such as art, sport and wine.

Some 80 per cent of VistaJet members are art collectors and many share their passion for the arts by lending artworks to the most prominent museums around the world, as well as supporting their growth through patronage and donations. To support clients in pursuing their passion, VistaJet members now enjoy VIP access to Frieze Art Fairs worldwide and can enjoy each exhibition with private tours by leading art curators, as well as priority preview in a virtual environment only accessible from the privacy of the jet cabin.

Its global wine programme provides bespoke access and personal introductions to the world's best winemakers and wine clubs. Members can request round-the-world wine itineraries and personal tours of the finest vineyards and wine regions, as well as access to wine auctions and events with fine wine traders and collectors.

VistaJet's golf programme aims to further inspire customers in their love of the sport, granting members access to some of the most private courses, tournaments, golf experiences and destinations, as well as meeting global champions on the courses, including Jon Rahm and Phil Mickelson.

Marketing is data driven, personalized, low key and designed only to hit members and prospective clients when it is relevant. In creating moments that matter, VistaJet also knows that its marketing is only effective in those other moments that matter to cut through the growing mountain of communications its audiences face.

Be bold, and do it your own way.

Discussion points

- How important is ownership over experience and vice-versa, and why is the latter a growing trend?
- How has marketing evolved from the traditional business-to-business and business-to-consumer mentality?
- What does this mean for marketers building niche programmes aimed at UHNWI?
- What does it mean for the products and services they offer?
- How can niche brands tap into the experiential trend?
- What does that mean for the conventional view of sector-based marketing?
- Can different niches be developed under the umbrella brand and why might this be worth considering?

SOURCE VistaJet website and corporate information.

CASE STUDY Putting the personal experience into luxury ownership

At once both a heritage and niche brand, Rolls-Royce is in the rarefied position of being known by everyone but marketing to a select few. And it is paying dividends. The car marque is steeped in the past but preparing for the future.

In this case study we will outline how the company is marketing to its customer base across the sales cycle and repositioning itself for the future.

Rolls-Royce revealed it had higher sales in 2021 than in any other year of its 117-year history (Rolls-Royce, 2022) because the pandemic, claims the marque, made the super-rich realize that life can be short (Churchman, 2022).

Rolls-Royce was created as a wholly owned subsidiary of BMW in 1998, after BMW licensed the rights to the Rolls-Royce brand name and logo from Rolls-Royce Holdings plc and acquired the rights to the Spirit of Ecstasy.

The company delivered 5,586 motor cars to clients around the world in 2021, up 49 per cent on 2020. This overall figure includes all-time record sales in most regions, including Greater China, the Americas and Asia-Pacific, and in multiple countries across the globe.

Chief Executive Torsten Muller-Otvos claimed in a virtual press conference that it is 'very much due to Covid that the entire luxury business is booming worldwide'.

People were encouraged to invest in 'what I would call the nice, lovely things in the world'. Winning brands are changing with – or ahead of – the times and emphasize the added purpose, happiness and enrichment that products and services can bring.

Power and luxury go together with freedom. With power and money, UHNWI can choose what they want to have and what they want to represent.

For Rolls-Royce that has meant an evolution of its strategy, with an acceleration towards an electric future and a commitment to serving its customer from the moment it has a touchpoint to far beyond the sale. Buying a Rolls-Royce is both a costly and a timely process and the British-founded marque makes a virtue of this.

A single car can take some six months to build, with nearly every task completed by hand, and customers offered the chance to customize nearly every aspect of it. They are kept up to date on progress with bespoke video communications. It is not just about offering premium products, such as a palette of 44,000 colours, but a long-lasting premium experience and ongoing relationship as well.

Black Badge and bespoke – a level beyond

Bespoke commissions are at record levels. Examples include the Phantom Oribe, co-created with Hermès, alongside the Phantom Tempus, and Black Badge Wraith and Black Badge Dawn Landspeed Collection cars.

Coachbuild becoming a permanent fixture in its future portfolio, in 2021 it announced its first all-electric car, Spectre, with plans to launch in late 2023, and the company is committed to an 'all-electric future'.

Of its growing Black Badge programme, introduced in 2016, Rolls-Royce says: 'Black Badge is for those who reject conformity and live on their own terms. It's for the innovators, trailblazers, rule-breakers – and above all – those who dare.'

Black Badge now accounts for more than 27 per cent of all Rolls-Royce sales. In layman's terms, Black Badge is a trim level that adds more luxury, more power, improved handling and a darkened aesthetic.

According to the company, there is no requirement for structured approaches to market research. The brand understands its customers because the execution of its product is achieved in close personal collaboration with them. Its senior executives integrate themselves into their clients' lifestyles, knowing many personally and often defining future projects not by internal codenames but by the name of the first client who requested it.

Marketing has included the creation of an animation, with NFT creator, artist and illustrator Mason London and supporting events such as London Craft Week, as well as a redesign of its showrooms worldwide, including the Mayfair flagship. It encourages owners to attend exclusive events and buy sought-after accessories.

An app called Whispers, launched at the onset of the global pandemic, acts as a gateway for clients to immerse themselves in a digital world of luxury, curated by the brand. It also offers a suite of online live video options to enable real-time communication with the marque's executives, product experts and craftspeople.

Clients may also view their motor car live on the production line, at the marque's manufactory – witnessing the 'marriage' when the powertrain meets the chassis, or the fitting of the Spirit of Ecstasy.

Members can even virtually exhibit their automotive collections for the network of fellow Rolls-Royce clients to peruse and admire. With the ability to search by name, location and even by car, members are able to connect with local, like-minded members, for both business and leisure purposes.

Rolls-Royce is daring to be different in a new era of luxury, investing and embracing the future of fuel and travel while acknowledging that luxury goes beyond ownership alone.

Discussion points

- How can a brand leverage its heritage while underlining future ambitions?
- What can new niche brands learn from heritage companies such as Rolls-Royce?
- How can they ensure they leverage their own advantages over more well-known competitors?
- Why is bespoke a growing trend and what does it mean for marketers?
- How should marketers approach the pre- and post-sale relationship?
- In an age when time matters and on-demand is growing, how can brands build anticipation?
- How important is it to appeal to a newer, more sustainable audience and how can marketers effectively do that without being accused of green-washing?
- How important are collaborations in the modern marketer's playbook?
- Few brands today can afford an effective showroom presence. What are the pros and cons?

SOURCE Rolls-Royce Motor Cars website and corporate information.

References

Brown, A (2021) Beeple NFT sells for $69.3 million, becoming most-expensive ever, *Forbes*, 11 March, www.forbes.com/sites/abrambrown/2021/03/11/beeple-art-sells-for-693-million-becoming-most-expensive-nft-ever (archived at https://perma.cc/C9XV-2SBT)

Churchman, L (2022) Covid death toll drove Rolls-Royce to record car sales as rich adopted 'life's too short' mentality, says CEO, *Independent*, www.independent.co.uk/news/uk/home-news/covid-deaths-rolls-royce-sales-torsten-muller-otvos-b1991080.html (archived at https://perma.cc/DKA9-SEZF)

Curtis, M et al (2021) *Life Reimagined: Mapping the motivations that matter for today's consumers*, Accenture

D'Arpizio, C and Levato, F (2021) Luxury market rebounds in 2021, set to return to historic growth trajectory, Bain & Company

Imberg, M, Shaban, M and Warburton, S (2021) The World Ultra Wealth Report 2021

Katz, L (2021) Luxury-home sales rise 42% in first quarter, far outpacing 7% growth in affordable-home sales, *Redfin*, 21 April, www.redfin.com/news/luxury-versus-affordable-housing-market-q1-2021/ (archived at https://perma.cc/3RP9-SNMS)

Lee, I (2021) Luxury NFTs could become a $56 billion market by 2030 and could see 'dramatically' increased demand thanks to the metaverse, Morgan Stanley says, *Markets Insider*, 16 November, https://markets.businessinsider.com/news/currencies/luxury-nfts-metaverse-56-billion-market-revenue-2030-morgan-stanley-2021-11 (archived at https://perma.cc/N2CK-UDAS)

Luxury Institute (2022) Luxury Institute: Experts predict what's next for the global luxury industry, *Cision*, www.prnewswire.com/news-releases/luxury-institute-experts-predict-whats-next-for-the-global-luxury-industry-301567012.html (archived at https://perma.cc/DH77-FW4M)

McAndrew, C (2022) The Art Basel and UBS Global Art Market Report, https://artbasel.com/about/initiatives/the-art-market (archived at https://perma.cc/J2TU-USP2)

Morgan, B (2020) 50 stats showing the power of personalization, *Forbes*, 18 February, www.forbes.com/sites/blakemorgan/2020/02/18/50-stats-showing-the-power-of-personalization (archived at https://perma.cc/4TQ9-432M)

Paton, E (2021) In a year of lows for luxury, Chanel's spending on itself reached new highs, *New York Times*, 15 June, www.nytimes.com/2021/06/15/business/in-a-year-of-lows-for-luxury-chanels-spending-on-itself-reached-new-highs.html (archived at https://perma.cc/6G6S-EZ7W)

Picchi, A (2021) Billionaires got 54% richer during pandemic, sparking calls for 'wealth tax', *CBS News*, 31 March, www.cbsnews.com/news/billionaire-wealth-covid-pandemic-12-trillion-jeff-bezos-wealth-tax/ (archived at https://perma.cc/P4SQ-2DME)

Rolls-Royce (2022) Press release: Rolls-Royce motor cars reports record annual results for 2021, www.press.rolls-roycemotorcars.com/rolls-royce-motor-cars-pressclub/article/detail/T0363813EN/rolls-royce-motor-cars-reports-record-annual-results-for-2021 (archived at https://perma.cc/XNQ3-PYHS)

Sherman, L (2019) BOF: The Row: What makes the quiet luxury label work, Robert Burke associates, http://www.robertburkeassociates.com/press1/2019/9/9/the-row-what-makes-the-quiet-luxury-label-work (archived at https://perma.cc/29AS-XFQN)

St.Denis, J (2020) Media use by ultra high net worth individuals 2020, Northrop & Johnson, www.northropandjohnson.com/navigator-news/advice/a-study-on-media-use-by-ultra-high-net-worth-individuals (archived at https://perma.cc/6TUM-QWHF)

UN Global Compact Media (no date) How brands are attracting socially conscious consumers and creating change in the world, UN Global Compact, www.unglobalcompact.org/take-action/purpose-driven-marketing (archived at https://perma.cc/BQS6-4C9J)

Vinogradov, P and Datwani, H (2021) How B2B firms can thrive in the future of sales, *The Wall Street Journal*, 18 October. https://deloitte.wsj.com/articles/how-b2b-firms-can-thrive-in-the-future-of-sales-01634577325 (archived at https://perma.cc/7NL3-BTRH)

VistaJet (2020) VistaJet offers global infrastructure to support governments and medical organizations, *VistaJet*, www.vistajet.com/en-gb/news/vistajet-offers-global-infrastructure/ (archived at https://perma.cc/DC3M-LDGT)

VistaJet (2022) Sustainability in Aviation, www.vistajet.com/en-gb/about-us/sustainability/ (archived at https://perma.cc/US9D-5WVY)

The old is the new 'new'   11

Emerging business models in the luxury field: renting and resale

ROBERTA CRESPI
ALICE GUZZETTI

LEARNING OBJECTIVES

- To introduce the concept of emerging consumption models based on collaborative consumption.
- To provide a thorough and practical understanding of how luxury collaborative consumption is developing.
- To understand renting and resale options for luxury brands.

Introduction

Over the past decade, technological innovations, increased digitalization of customer exchanges and the rise of experiential consumption have revolutionized many industries and resulted in some fundamental restructuring (Holmqvist et al, 2020; Christodoulides et al, 2021).

Consumers, especially younger ones, now expect immediacy, availability, and instant gratification, so many logics of fast fashion have also been embraced by the luxury industry. As a generation who grew up digital, they are less enthralled with owning goods, since they are experimenting with ways to access goods besides purchasing, ranging from clothes and music to homes or vehicles.

Young people want items that align with their values, desires and identity, and demand a more democratic luxury that is convenient, seamless and flexible. This has resulted in a boom of new means to access luxury; unconventional forms of consumption are emerging, shifting the focus from 'having-to-being and from owning-to-experiencing' (Cristini et al, 2017, p 101).

After all, we have long shared things with family and friends, and the internet and the sophistication of digital devices, further accelerated by lockdowns, have facilitated commercial sharing and trading among peers (Gibson et al, 2018; Widlok, 2017), contributing to the success of the so-called sharing economy.

The sharing economy is an umbrella concept that encompasses several theoretical constructs including **collaborative consumption,** defined as an economic model based on sharing, second-hand purchasing and renting or leasing products and services (Iran and Schrader, 2017; Hamari et al, 2015; Möhlmann, 2015; Botsman, 2013). Collaborative consumption involves temporary or permanent consumption and peer-to-peer or business-to-consumer exchanges platforms (Kumar et al, 2018). By integrating the concept of the sharing economy into the clothing sector, collaborative fashion consumption provides consumers with alternative options to the classic model of purchasing garments, and people participate in an organized system of acquisition and distribution of previously owned clothes or accessories for a fee. Moreover, facilitated by technological advances, the secondary market has substantially expanded opportunities for consumers to dispose of apparel while recouping some of their previous investment by reselling or renting still-valuable items (Sihvonen and Turunen, 2016). A good example of this trend is the three-day sale organized by the Kardashian–Jenner sisters with The RealReal, proposing a vast assortment of designer items from their rich closets.

New business models in the luxury field

In the luxury field, the most diffused collaborative consumption business models are **resale** and **renting**. Both these practices rely on the redistribution of existing garments, but while resale is characterized by the opportunity to acquire individual ownership of unwanted or underused products, through renting the consumer pays to access the use of products owned by others.

The factors influencing the collaborative luxury consumption business model can vary with: (a) type of product category, such as occasion wear and casual wear; (b) ownership of the goods (corporate ownership vs consumer ownership); (c) channel of distribution (offline vs online).

Both the models are expected to grow significantly in the next few years. The resale luxury market is estimated at €33 billion in 2021, up from 2017 proportionally more than the luxury market of new products (+65 per cent resale vs +12 per cent new) (D'Arpizio and Levato, 2022), and it is predicted to grow annually at a rate of 10–15 per cent over the next decade (Berg et al, 2021), while luxury fashion's rental market is ready for takeoff, as interest in the funding rounds of several platforms by luxury conglomerates or venture capital companies demonstrates. By Rotation, a peer-to-peer fashion rental platform, has raised $3 million in seed funding in 2022, while the previous year Kering participated in Cocoon's funding round, acquiring a 5 per cent stake.

Accordingly, ThredUp (2021), indicates that the closet of the future will host around 20 per cent resale and rental clothes over the next 10 years.

Implications for the luxury consumer

The assertion that luxury consumers might prefer temporal access, rather than ownership, conflicts with a long heritage of research that identifies the importance of ownership and possessions as a deeply rooted human preference (Beggan 1992; Belk, 1988; Morewedge and Giblin, 2015; Pierce et al, 2001; Richins, 2004). Nevertheless, although they are hardly a rival to the mainstream fashion industry, renting and resale represent a substantial change in how some consumers relate to apparel ownership (Sherman, 2018).

Historically, second-hand clothing and renting were stigmatized as the domain of low-income consumers, unable to afford the higher-priced first-hand apparel (Crane, 2000). But, coinciding with a change in consumer attitudes towards second-hand goods, and combined with a taste for retro apparel and demand for individuality against the mass customization of fast fashion, there has been a steady growth in the secondary clothes markets (Beard, 2008), even in markets where consumers typically regret wearing used clothes (Cervellon et al, 2012).

Collaborative consumption services are democratizing high-end fashion and luxury, challenging what is valued as luxury and how it is valued as well as the traditional long-term relationships consumers form with luxury objects. Some of the qualities that made certain objects luxuries, collectible and valuable have disappeared in the sharing economy, for example scarcity, rarity, uniqueness, inaccessibility and permanence. Luxury goods are now readily available and easily accessible for aspirational consumers, making it difficult to interpret luxury as being a sign of exclusivity. Indeed, the sharing economy can be a lifestyle facilitator (Bernthal et al, 2005), where consumers can participate in more affluent lifestyles that they cannot afford via traditional ownership-based paths. Less affluent consumers now have the possibility to buy an affordable version of the same item, without engaging in counterfeiting or acquiring pseudo-luxury items such as affordable lines of products or merchandise.

The increase in demand for access also calls into question the role that ownership and possession of the object play in luxury and its status signalling. Nowadays, status and luxury are not necessarily attached to solid forms of objects and traditional ownership. In a large-scale anonymous city where people may not even know their neighbours, high-status pre-owned items may be a way to leverage higher-income lifestyle goods that otherwise would be unaffordable.

Collaborative luxury consumption could be also considered a signal of status among specific sub-cultures of consumers, perceived as a smarter and more sustainable choice against consumerism. Materialistic consumers may engage in collaborative consumption too, as they might feel an identical or a higher perceived ownership attitude towards purchased versus rented luxury (Krekels et al, 2020), and psychological ownership might satisfy consumers' need for ownership (Fritze et al, 2020).

Motivations to adopt

Consumers are motivated to engage in collaborative luxury consumption by two broad categories of reasons (Guzzetti et al, 2021): **utilitarian** factors and **hedonic** motivations.

The attractiveness of the price is found to be a main driver to engage in collaborative consumption where it represents a goal-oriented behaviour (Lawson et al, 2016; Edbring et al, 2016; Möhlmann, 2015; Bardhi and Eckhardt, 2012; Durgee and O'Connor, 1995). For renting, it can also avoid the responsibilities associated with owning goods such as maintenance, storage, disposal or refund (Yuan and Shen, 2019; Wittkowski et al, 2013). Individuals may also feel a sense of freedom by being able to preview a good and to postpone the purchasing decision (Park and Joyner-Armstrong, 2017) or even to avoid purchasing (Park and Joyner-Armstrong, 2019). Pre-owned and shared products give the opportunity to rethink fashion more circularly, through the refinement of consumption choices (Machado et al, 2019) and to lengthen the life cycle of clothes. Indeed, encouraging consumers to think about consigning their clothes is an interesting concept and could affect consumers' purchasing decisions, for example selecting more durable, luxury brands versus purchasing more, or more frequently, affordable products. Concepts such as 'buy less, buy better' (Cline, 2016) or 'slow fashion' are rising (Pierre-Louis, 2019).

The hedonic motivations are driven by recreational and experience-related factors: the excitement of the bargain and treasure hunting for pre-loved goods (Ferraro et al, 2016; Bardhi and Arnould, 2005), the nostalgic pleasure of finding objects from the past, and self-expression through pieces and variety of items for consumers highly involved in fashion (Kessous and Valette-Florence, 2019). Consumers seek novelty, fun and change through variety-seeking behaviour (Kahn, 1995). The acquisition of used luxury products is also linked to social climbing and status (Kessous and Valette-Florence, 2019; Pantano and Stylos, 2020).

Barriers to adoption

Collaborative luxury consumption included obstacles to its adoption, mainly related to consumer concerns about the service provider. The absence of guarantees, trust issues, level of difficulty in usage and degree of familiarity with sharing platforms are significant predictors discouraging inexperienced consumers from participating in re-commerce websites (Becker-Leifhold, 2018). Other perceived barriers included resistance toward habit transformation (Armstrong et al, 2015), and hygiene concerns, especially in the case of clothes, because people are worried about the transmission of diseases from previous owners, odour, and dirtiness (Armstrong et al, 2015; Catulli et al, 2013).

In the case of second-hand and renting, platform users also claimed the lack of choice as a driver to not engage in collaborative luxury consumption. The problem of finding the right model, size, price or colour makes it inconvenient to choose used clothes, for example.

In China, specifically, consumers are heavily concerned about the financial risks of counterfeit products since the secondary market has long been unregulated, and about engaging in the social risks of being associated with products that are inferior goods for low-income consumers (Lang and Zhang, 2019).

Implications for luxury brands

Traditionally, consumer perceptions of the prestige of luxury brands stem, at least in part, from the exclusivity of the brands (Wiedmann et al, 2007). This recent shift in the mode of product acquisition for luxury brands may render them less exclusive and, ultimately, have an effect on these brands.

We see also implications for the relationships and brand loyalty that consumers develop with luxury brands. According to Bardhi et al (2020) wider access will make consumers more committed to the luxury product category, but not particularly committed to a brand or specific luxury objects, and in renting, they identify with displaying high-end brand names, but not a particular brand name.

For luxury brands, this implies there might be lower levels of brand loyalty, as variety and ease of access become more important to consumers than expressing one's identity via a particular brand. Moreover, once luxury brands are accessible via renting, as opposed to only being available for purchase, the equity of the brands is negatively affected (Yuan and Shen, 2019). Specifically, where a brand was higher priced, brand credibility and brand leadership were diluted once the available mode of acquisition for the brand changed to include renting.

Anyway, the nature of luxury is changing, so resilience and adaptability are required for brands to stay relevant. At the same time, the emergence of multi-million-dollar platforms (e.g. Luxury Closet, Uber Lux and Rent the Runway) that offer new forms of digitalized and experiential luxury to consumers has forced traditional luxury retailers and brands to rethink their strategies, with Ralph Lauren launching a rental scheme (Puhak, 2021) and Selfridges reselling second-hand luxury brands (Marriott, 2019).

These changes also offer new opportunities for brands. For example, when retailers introduce a rental business, it reduces the illegal behaviour of those 'customers' that acquire a fashion item before a special event, wear it and then return it after a few days asking for a refund (Yuan and Shen, 2019). The return rate of party dresses could be 35–75 per cent and the biggest return day of the year is January 2, as the party dresses are just used for a New Year party (Recode, 2017). The retailer, the renter, and the entire retail system could perform better when the renter and retailer are integrated into one group.

Key points in the fashion collaborative consumption value chain

Compared to a traditional retail business, either selling first-hand or second-hand products, there are touchpoints that characterize the renting and resale company's 'value chain'. Both the models share, more or less, the need to pay attention to the following activities: assortment procurement, inventory management, delivery and return logistics, and the pricing policy choice.

Assortment procurement

Acquiring goods is an ongoing activity that characterizes all companies whose client is the final customer. Companies have two choices for collecting the assortment.

Purchasing the right inventory

Creating an appealing assortment of items requires considerable investment. At Rent the Runway, about a third of its revenue is spent on fulfilment costs. This could be reduced if a company buys fewer clothes, but this can lead customers to complain about the poor selection. Companies spend capital to buy products, but specifically in renting, revenue comes at a slower pace as the garment is rented out; indeed each item typically requires multiple rentals to justify the cost. Moreover, companies should consider the depreciation of inventory; clothing naturally diminishes in value through wear and tear and as trends fall out of favour, which makes depreciation a significant factor in the company's business model.

Through consignment

Not having to carry the costs of inventory is less risky and represents one advantage for peer-to-peer companies like Vestiaire Collective, or for companies like My Wardrobe HQ whose revenues come from consignment partnerships with brands. The result is a light inventory and therefore a very scalable business model. However, for peer-to-peer platforms this may mean a lack of control over the quality of the items exchanged by users, which may impact the image of the service provider.

Inventory management

Typically, this consists of all the back-end activities linked to storing and tracking the inventory: storage of items, implementation of a tracking system, photographing every single item and development of the product's sheet, insurance policy, repair of the item and, in case of renting, cleaning after use. A business model where the inventory is not owned by the company means easier management, because not as many stages are involved. The choice of the product category to focus on impacts on the complexity of these processes too. Vivrelle, for example, offers rental of jewellery and other accessories which are easier to process and don't require dry-cleaning and frequent reparations. For many start-ups or in-house services of clothes, storage and cleaning can prove to be cost-prohibitive, and make them resistant to the economies of scale.

Delivery and return logistics

The logistics of sending clothes to customers and arranging for their return is a major issue for the secondary market. In the case of rental, shipping and returns are extremely expensive since for every single transaction a shipment implies a return, unlike retail. So, the pricing of the service should absorb and pay off these costs. The logistics also involve tracking of the items and strict supervision of the renting time by customers, with the development of a system of penalties in case of delays or product damage. Frictions in the timing, caused by other users or by the company itself, may cause delays in exchanges or the creation of waitlists. In particular, delays in the renting of occasion-wear or long waitlists may undermine customers' satisfaction and deter users from proceeding with the rental.

The pricing policy choice

Setting a competitive price is crucial for a resale platform, in order to be appealing to clients and to potential sellers. Typically, deciding the right price for a pre-loved piece involves considering its scarcity. If the item is considered a classic or is part of a brand's permanent collection, demand is usually consistent and high. Seasonal items may no longer be in such high demand, so their value is depreciated, whereas limited editions could be valued more than the original retail price. In peer-to-peer resale platforms, sellers set the price directly based on the condition of the product, which should be congruent with the reality. Many websites help sellers with a resale calculator, and others employ third-party software. The platform gets a percentage on the transaction. Under the current commission model, Vestiaire Collective takes 25 per cent of the sale price for anything between $170 and $2,300, with the percentage decreasing with pricier items and a flat 17 per cent for anything below $170.

Even in renting, getting the right pricing policy is crucial. If it's too cheap, brands won't make a margin. If it's too expensive, consumers won't rent. Brands have to balance the cost of the product with both its lifespan and consumer demand. The most successful business operating in the rental sector, Rent the Runway, made the subscription payment method its 'hero product' based on different levels of subscription, soon adopted by the majority of the players. However, it doesn't represent the only option available because sometimes rental services elaborate different pricing according to the category of item, and neither does it guarantee the success of a model. If the subscription-based model ensures a recurring revenue stream that allows a company to keep growing, in a recessionary environment, it turned out to be the main source of loss, because consumers are turned off by a recurring bill. Instead, they were eager to spend less for a few days' rental of a high-end dress. Moreover, the subscription fee should be justified by the product selection and its quality. In order to make sense, in a subscription rental service the monthly fee shouldn't exceed the value of the product and the selection should be sufficiently large to induce users to engage in a long-term commitment. For example, Dressmate, a fashion rental social network, became oversaturated with fast-fashion garments that were too cheap to justify the pricing of the subscription.

Renting

Introduction

Over the last decade, fashion renting services have sprung up. The concept was pioneered by Rent the Runway in 2009, which reached a unicorn status with a reported valuation of $750 million in 2020 (Roof, 2020), and its success has inspired brands and companies. When it was launched it offered shoppers an affordable alternative to buying handfuls of new dresses for occasions every year. It began pivoting its business model to subscription, where consumers can pay a monthly fee to access a number of items. Today, subscriptions are still the company's revenue driver and the model has been adopted by almost all the players operating in the business.

Small niche rental start-ups also saw new opportunities in the market, including menswear rental or accessories. However, the majority of projects are still hyper-local and city-based, attracting customers through word of mouth, a model logistically not feasible to scale beyond its current reach. Indeed, many providers still suffer from insufficient consumer demand (Needleman and Loten, 2014) and remain 'small, losing money, and surviving on venture capital' (Cusumano, 2018, p 27).

In Europe, My Wardrobe HQ's UK-based rental service was launched in 2019, and works on a consignment model and developing partnerships with brands, for example Burberry and Harrods; it focused on the higher end of the fashion spectrum, as occasion-wear rental is currently more popular in the European market than everyday clothing.

But the Covid-19 crisis hit rental hard. Many services saw an immediate impact when lockdowns began, since a massive number of customers paused or cancelled their subscriptions. Some rental companies were scared of losing nearly their entire customer base and some others were forced to shutter entirely (for example By Rotation or Armarium).

Some years later, despite early traumas and uncertainty, the future of luxury renting has yet to be announced and the pandemic may actually have boosted its relevance. On the rental side, after the government's announcement that lockdown restrictions would lift, rental companies saw their website traffic surge and are optimistic about a quick recovery. On the other hand, consumers, demanding more sustainable fashion options, have realized that owning a big closet may be a waste of space. The e-commerce platforms empowered by the pandemic acceleration in digitalization, and the normalization of wearing second-hand clothes, contributed to inducing consumers to engage in rental. Indeed, a recent trend adopted by many rental companies is the option to purchase products, or a buy-and-sell option, where customers can opt to buy something at a discounted rate without having to rent it first.

The luxury brand perspective on renting

The way in which luxury brands are dipping their toes in the rental market is actually cautious and indicates interest in the phenomenon guided by uncertainty over its success. The luxury sector, which thrives on strictly controlling the distribution, price and presentation of its products, was for many years leery of the rapid growth of resale and rental platforms, but players are increasingly experimenting in the space, seeing an opportunity to burnish their sustainability credentials with consumers and test the waters of new business models. For brands, rental offers some of the same benefits as resale, opening luxury houses to a much larger audience that cannot afford the retail price, and serving as an acquisition channel for first-time customers. Rental can also help brands learn from customers who use the service, offering insights into consumer behaviour and product design that they can feed back to their teams.

Rental business can also represent a revenue stream for luxury brands. According to the LuxCo 2030 Report by Bain & Company and Positive Luxury (D'Arpizio et al, 2021), when an item gets rented 20 times, for instance, it generates a profit margin of more than 40 per cent, shifting the focus on the product life-cycle value. Items that endure several rentals can generate higher revenue per item than selling them. Moreover, according to the report, rental could represent 10 per cent of revenue by 2030 for a brand that embraces it. In addition, renting is a way of taking advantage of excess inventory as a smarter, more innovative alternative to end-of-season promotions, and of gauging the relevance of archive collections.

Recently, the luxury giant Kering has invested in the new funding round of Cocoon, a London-based handbag subscription service, suggesting a sign of luxury's growing interest in this modality of consumption. Kering's investment is part of the luxury group's wider strategy to explore disruptive trends in the market by taking small stakes in emerging technologies and services. Ralph Lauren is the first major luxury brand to offer clothing rentals, launching 'The Lauren Look', a \$125 per month subscription service powered by CaaStle that allows consumers to rent items from its lower-priced Lauren Ralph Lauren line.

Burberry developed a partnership with My Wardrobe HQ, according to which the platform's users can rent one trenchcoat for £170 a week, or buy one second-hand for £750. Hancocks London, a long-established historic jeweller, has begun renting bejewelled tiaras to brides enamoured with TV series such as *Bridgerton* and *Downton Abbey*. However, despite the enthusiasm of a younger generation, the potential of rental and subscription models remains open to question. For the specific case of the renting of high jewellery, bridal and gifting purchases tend to be highly emotional – the piece holding long-term meaning and personal value. Given the hedonic nature of this category for a significant part of the market, it is hard to see it becoming a big piece of the pie.

The business models operating in the fashion renting market

There are several business models currently operating in the fashion rental market: multi-brand rental platforms, brand partnerships with multi-brand rental platforms, peer-to-peer rental platforms, brand partnership with business-to-business rental platforms, in-house renting and brand investment:

- **Multi-brand rental platforms.** They can be either big players or small, niche start-ups. Rent the Runway and Le Tote, the two market leaders in the United States, buy the items directly and sometimes work on consignment with brands. Often, larger multi-brand rental companies develop partnerships with brands to purchase their excess inventory, or work with designers to create pieces specifically for the platform. Many players are currently introducing the possibility to buy products after renting them.

- **Brand partnership with multi-brand rental platforms.** A partnership with an established rental platform offers brands a relatively risk-free option that requires minimal logistic effort. It also offers a marketing and customer acquisition opportunity alongside income, but leaves the brand with no infrastructure of its own to build on, because all the items are handled directly by the brand itself. Burberry and Harrods, for example, partnered with My Wardrobe HQ, and Ganni, Rixo, House of Sunny and Jacquemus partnered with Rotaro. The rental platform oversees the marketing activities, optimizes the buying process and collects millions of data points, which are regularly shared with brand partners. It also gives brands access to tens of thousands of new potential customers.

- **Peer-to-peer rental platforms.** These typically operate on a small scale, like Hurr Collective or By Rotation, both UK-based. At By Rotation, a marketplace for Londoners, the quality of the exchanged goods is guaranteed by avoiding the exchange of high street items with a value lower than £100. In China, an example of peer-to-peer rental platform was YCloset provided by Alibaba, which had over 1 million users but shut down in 2021. These platforms' key advantages over larger services like multi-brand rental platforms is that their selection grows and evolves along with their users' closets, and the decentralized approach, because they leave most of the logistics to their customers, reducing their own costs. Many peer-to-peer platforms delegate the cleaning and the shipment of the goods to customers. To keep this model thriving, the base of users must be populated by a small number of fashionistas and passionate consumers, who are committed to sustain the effort of good maintenance.

- **Brand partnership with business-to-business rental platforms.** Each brand partnering with white-label platforms rents only its own clothes, while the service provider handles the majority of the operations. The service platform usually takes care of the logistics and tech for partner brands, from shipping and dry-cleaning to onsite payment gateways and inventory tracking. The platform also shares anonymized data and learnings gathered from its client base with each brand. All the brands have to do is allocate products and align the internal processes, fine-tuning pricing and analysing which products perform well. For a luxury brand, working with a white-label platform is the middle ground between building a rental business in-house and working with a third-party rental site. Ralph Lauren partnered with CaaStle, and Ganni launched its rental platform, Ganni Repeat, in September 2019, partnering with Danish white-label platform Continued Fashion.

- **In-house renting.** Urban Outfitters Inc's Nuuly has been a pioneer in developing its own rental service from scratch building a dedicated 300,000-square-foot warehouse close to its head office, along with an in-house laundry facility. It took about a year to put the tech in place and hire a workforce of about 80 people needed to run the operation. Nuuly gathers clothes from its flagship brand, plus Free People and Anthropologie. My List Bloomingdale's is the first department store to launch its own rental service (temporarily suspended after Covid). Setting up a rental operation in-house is challenging regardless of brand size, not least because there are many costly and time-consuming operational must-haves to factor in. Clothes need to be cleaned, inventory needs storing and tracking, and styles need to be insured to protect lenders against accidental damage by borrowers. Everything is different to the retail business, down to the fact that the clothing is not a liability on the balance sheet anymore, but an asset that depreciates over time.

- **Brand investment.** This represents the less involving, as well as less risky, form of shares acquisition in the rental business. Typically, it takes the form of the acquisition, from a big brand or group, of a stake in multi-brand rental platforms, peer-to-peer rental platforms, or in B2B platforms.

Table 11.1 Business models operating in the fashion rental market (non-exhaustive list)

Multi-brand rental platforms	Brand partnership with multi-brand rental platforms	Peer-to-peer rental platform	Brand partnership with business-to-business rental platforms	In-house renting	Brand investment
2004 • Bag Borrow or Steal *2009* • Rent The Runway • Mine4Nine *2012* • Le Tote *2014* • Drexcode *2015* • Bag Romance *2018* • Onloan • Nova Octo Vivrelle *2019* • Cocoon • My Wardrobe HQ • Rotaro *2020* • Luxury Fashion Rentals	*2021* • Burberry with My Wardrobe HQ • Harrods with My Wardrobe HQ • Ganni with Rotaro & Hurr Collective • Jacquemus with Rotaro	*2015* • YCloset *2017* • Tulerie • Hurr Collective *2019* • By Rotation	*2018* • Gwynnie Bee with CaaStle *2019* • Ganni with Continued Fashion • Banana Republic with CaaStle *2021* • Ralph Lauren with CaaStle	*2018* • Vince with Vince Unfold *2019* • Twinset with pleasedontbuy • Selfridges • Urban Outfitters with Nuuly • Bloomingdale with My List (temporarily suspended) *2021* • Hancocks London	*2021* • Kering invests in Cocoon

SOURCE Authors' elaboration, 2022

CASE STUDY   Twinset – Pleasedontbuy

Twinset, an apparel company founded in 1987 in Italy and today 100 per cent owned by Carlyle Group, is positioned in the accessible luxury market segment. The collections, which initially focused on sophisticated knitwear, expanded over the years to offer both apparel and accessories.

In 2019, thanks to the original idea of the company's CEO Alessandro Varisco, Twinset launched the first Italian rental business, offering a rental collection of ceremony and special event dresses exclusively tailored and 100 per cent made in Italy. The service, after an interruption during lockdowns, is currently available in four European countries, with the 'Try On' option (the chance to try on the clothes at no charge in all the Twinset boutiques) only available in Italy. The rental service works on single-time renting (not by subscription): the cost ranges from €40 to €230, inclusive of insurance and shipment, for clothes with a retail selling price in the range of €2,000-€3,000, available for a period of four to eight days.

A wide product offering and a great range of sizes are the strength of the service, combined with the ease of collecting the clothes, which are delivered in-store or shipped directly to the customer's home.

The company itself, with its internal laundry and tailoring, meticulously checks and reconditions the clothes after they have been hired and returned. The garments are treated with hydrocarbon washing, which uses odourless new-generation solvents that are mild and kind to the fabrics as well as to the environment.

In partnership with influencers and celebrities, the aim is to reach social media-savvy consumers and to teach them to consume responsibly.

As said before, the intuition for this new business came to Alessandro Varisco in 2018 during the Christmas period while looking at a Netflix TV series where a young lawyer was complaining about the number of dresses, very similar to one another, she had to buy for being compliant with her role and her social life. Besides the initial money investment, the dresses needed to be maintained and stored and as a result she lived in a house transformed into a closet.

Alessandro Varisco decided to analyse the data coming from the company's CRM and came to the belief there was an interesting business opportunity. In a very short time, he presented the idea to the Carlyle Group and created a very young, dedicated team inside Twinset for the development of this project. The name 'pleasedontbuy' came to Varisco by chance when he was listening to the song 'Please Don't Go'. The target client is a little younger than the current one; however, thanks to the dedicated website and especially the try-on option, it has been possible to make young prospects aware of a product of high quality, 100 per cent Italian made with precious silk fabrics and rich embroideries.

Young people are very active on social media where they need to change their outfits very often. The rental business is a good way to engage them in the Twinset environment, also increasing the cross-selling. The original young target group has expanded over time and today the clients of the rental business also include baby boomer-generation women.

The company didn't suffer from cannibalization of customers, as the rental business is additional to the traditional sales business. According to the CEO, around 70 per cent of the rental clients are new clients. While this new business has proved to be interesting for the brand, it's still a work in progress. Now the company is thinking of limiting the number of rentals of each item to 10, even if normally a dress can be rented for 15 events, to maintain a product that is resellable in the second-hand market.

At the moment the rented dresses can't be purchased while they are in their rental period but when the company dismisses a batch of pleasedontbuy products, those are sold at 10 per cent of their original price. Over time the company enlarged the type of dresses to now include kids' apparel, special event outfits like for Miss Italia or the Venice Film Festival (where recently a pleasedontbuy dress won the best-dressed award of Hollywood) or for graduations and job interviews.

Everyday dresses are not considered in this business, as with pleasedontbuy, Twinset is acting as a style consultant for special events.

This business is capable of generating profits as a dress is normally rented eight times, but its cost is recouped with three or four rentals and then after this it is sold as a second-hand product, totally amortized.

As profitable as this business is, it is not exempt from negative aspects. The most negative aspect of this experience according to the CEO is that the company was obliged to charge an insurance fee as sometimes the condition of the returned dresses is so poor that it is impossible to rent them again. More recently the increases in transportation costs have affected the margins of this business, but for the moment this is not a great problem considering also that those who are now renting a dress could become loyal customers for all the Twinset products. Indeed, this is an interesting business opportunity for any luxury brand. Not only is it a profitable business, but it also acts as a means to bring youngsters closer and attach them through quality service, increasing their loyalty to the brand.

Questions for discussion

- Which are the challenges a luxury company may face in entering the rental business?
- Which business strategy was adopted by Twinset in order to not impact their sales?
- Can the strategies undertaken by Twinset be adopted by high-end luxury brands?
- In your opinion, does the rental business affect the luxury industry?

Resale

Introduction

The global second-hand fashion market was worth approximately $130 billion in 2021, with major markets like the United States continuing their double-digit growth at least until 2025 (Lee and Malik, 2021), and with a not yet fully expressed potential for further development, as proved by the numerous investments in start-ups and by the various acquisitions of shares of companies operating in this field. According to a recent analysis by BoF, these financial operations demonstrate interest towards a phenomenon that is perceived as the new frontier of this sector, and also as a new possible distribution channel, exactly as e-commerce was in the past (Malik and Lee, 2021).

There are multiple drivers for resale that continue to strengthen and reinforce:

- **Favourable demographics,** as younger generations are more likely to buy and sell second-hand – and not likely to 'age out' of this practice given their unique perspective on valuing experiences more than goods and access more than ownership.
- **Customer desire for variety** and self-expression with unique pieces.
- **Reduced stigma around second-hand,** as more people joining makes resale more mainstream.

- **Circularity**, as second-hand shopping can inherently be more sustainable than new, first-hand fashion consumption.

- **Limited editions and drop culture**, where the scarcity of drops drives resale activity (often at a premium to the retail price), especially for streetwear and sneakers.

- **Platforms sophistication**, which offer more inventory with better features and streamlined user journeys that reduce frictions in participation.

- **Technologies** that enable authentication and traceability (for example NFTs).

- **B2B start-ups** that facilitate brands to enter into this market without extensive effort.

- **The excess of inventories** (both from the company side and from private sellers).

The luxury brand perspective

Luxury was historically averse to resale, fearing it could be a boost for the diffusion of counterfeiting products. The opposition of some historical houses like Chanel is well established; the brand remains embroiled in a lengthy lawsuit with The RealReal, claiming that only its own stores are qualified to sell authentic Chanel and the resale site's authentication experts cannot be trusted. The suit is reflective of the sector's early resistance to the market. Hermès and Chanel still refuse to sell their most appreciated leather goods online, but they've seen their control slipping away as iconic bags like Birkin or Chanel 11.12 became top sellers on resale sites.

Neither Hermès nor Chanel seem to be suffering from that, but if the desirability of core category items falls, it could potentially create problems down the product pyramid, creating higher margin and higher sales volume, but impacting on appeal. Indeed, the secondary market remains problematic for a sector that is all about **perception**, **exclusivity** and **scarcity**. Limiting the supply ensures brands have strict control over the distribution channels. Second-hand products are available at every moment, so the supply increases and competes with new product distribution, legitimating brands' fear of cannibalization. When the interplay between supply and demand on resale sites reveals these products to be more ubiquitous and less valuable than expected, the perception of exclusivity starts to break down. However, according to industry experts, rather than cannibalizing full-price sales, second-hand products sold at lower prices **widen the market for luxury goods** and provide more **affordable entry points** to high-end brands, thereby serving as a gateway for first-time buyers, because the customer segments of the second-hand and primary luxury markets are totally different (Kansara, 2020). Engaging in resale is a way to acquire young aspirational customers who do not stigmatize first-hand consumption.

The second-hand market exists, whether the luxury brand wants it to or not, and it comes also with reward, so a number of brands are rolling out their own approaches to resale. For the luxury players it could be a chance to polish their **sustainability** credentials. In the near term, the buzz around the initiatives could help to clean up their reputations among environmentally conscious shoppers, as well as a new channel to **monetize** their own unsold inventories and returned products. There's also an opportunity to build **consumer loyalty**. Luxury brands partnering with resale sites have offered sellers store credit in return for their pre-loved items. Brands also see opportunity in the way resale highlights their products' **enduring value**: the shock of a Chanel flap bag, on average priced at over $6,000, is reduced when clients keep in mind the part of that investment they could recoup should they want to sell the item later, thus boosting the perceived affordability.

To sum up, there are many ways the secondary market can help luxury brands:

1 **Further reach.** It is quite normal for a luxury brand to sell lower-priced items like small accessories or beauty products as an entry-level access to the brand for aspirational and low-income consumers. The resale market can provide a similar result. Partnering too with a well-established reseller allows luxury brands to tap into a new, younger customer base.

2 **Fuel sales of first-hand products.** The majority of consumers engage in the second-hand market to then fulfil a new first-hand product and they are likely to trade up to a new product in the next purchase. Moreover, on the seller side, some brands offer private consignors vouchers or store credit to spend in boutiques (for instance Burberry or Stella McCartney). Resale allows them to recruit new customers, at the same time as deepening engagement with existing ones.

3 **Increase profits with vintage items.** Vintage pieces are a great opportunity to play on nostalgic feelings, to boost the second-hand market with archive pieces coming directly from the brands or from a selected customer base.

4 **Enrich storytelling.** If luxury is predicated on quality and heritage, the secondary market seems useful in proving it, because it's actually a superior quality product that retains its value over time.

5 **Track product life cycles.** In-house resale gives brands the ability to track a product's life in the secondary market and make more informed decisions when developing new collections and setting pricing policies.

6 **Tighten control.** Regulating, directly or in partnership with resellers, the sales of pre-loved items could be a great opportunity for a luxury brand to avoid counterfeit trading and to assure IP protection.

However, while the reasons to engage with resale are tempting, the second-hand market comes at the same time with risks, and not all luxury brands should embrace it.

Besides the aforementioned reasons for luxury brands to be reluctant in engaging resale from an ontological point of view, arranging it is an expensive activity. In fact, to operate in the resale market a company must be able to adequately present all the items, independently from their typology and resale value. All of them must be authentic, well presented and sellable, requiring financial resources and specific capabilities that makes it hard for even multi-brand companies like The RealReal to generate profits. Consequently, for most of the single brands, embracing resale is even more difficult than for multi-brand; they still have to cover such high fixed costs, without the possibility to exploit scale economies for these activities, due to the much smaller number of products offered. Therefore, some brands may decide to enter the resale market more to enhance customer loyalty than to gain additional revenues.

The business models operating in the fashion resale market

For a long time the second-hand market has been synonymous with independent small shops, often dusty, with very limited presence in e-commerce, probably limited only to the 'eBay option'. Instead, more recently, riding the wave of Gen Z and Millennial consumers' attraction for sustainability and digital tools, pushed even harder by the pandemic, we have seen the flourishing of new e-commerce platforms like Vestiaire Collective and The RealReal, able to present appealing pre-loved products offered with interesting side services. The luxury resale space has completely changed and several business models flourished: multi-brand resale platforms, brand partnership with multi-brand resale platforms, peer-to-peer resale platforms, brand partnership with business-to-business resale platforms, in-house resale and brand investment:

- **Multi-brand resale platform.** These work as e-commerce platforms, like ThredUp or The RealReal, operating mainly as consignment shops, buying and storing products until they are sold. These services often claim to have better and more curated inventory than peer-to-peer platforms as they are taking physical possession of each item sold on their sites. Consignment platforms typically claim a big share of each sale. The RealReal takes an average of about 36 per cent.

- **Brand partnership with multi-brand resale platform.** Working with a third-party established reseller as a partnership is the dominant trend for luxury brands because it involves lower risks and resources. Examples are Stella McCartney with their The RealReal partnership, or the more recent Gucci and Alexander McQueen. However, for a brand it also implies lower margins, no data gathering on consumer preferences and no increased loyalty, since the clients develop the relationship with the resale platform. Recently, some brands developed partnership with wholesale physical distributors, to ensure the brand's certification on pre-owned products.

- **Peer-to-peer resale platform.** These are marketplaces where buyers and sellers find each other and negotiate deals. Vestiaire Collective is an example of this model in the luxury space. Peer-to-peer platforms are betting their leaner model – no warehouses full of unsold inventory – will make it possible to operate in the black, and to charge a lower percentage on transactions compared to multi-brand resale platforms (for example, Poshmark's 20 per cent and eBay's 9 per cent).

- **Partnership with B2B resale business models or white-label services.** Most of the operations of resale are outsourced to third-party services, and enable brands and retailers to enter in the secondary market without being overwhelmed by its operational complexity, creating a much less capital-intensive solution (e.g. collecting, sorting, cleaning, pricing, connecting buyers and sellers, fulfilling). A recent example is the partnership between Reflaunt and Balenciaga, which allows the brand's customer to list their pre-loved Balenciaga product through Balenciaga's platform and other existing platforms, which the brand can monitor.

- **In-house resale.** Building an in-house resale retail programme offers the ability to directly control the product life cycle, as well as to manage the client experience, engage with new consumers and acquire information about their habits, build sustainability credentials and dispose of excess inventory. However, it involves several challenges, like sourcing the product, managing the inventory and logistics, and developing the platform.

- **Brand investment.** This involves the investment in resale businesses or the acquisition of established platforms, like the recent acquisition of the B2B platform Luxclusif by Farfetch. This allowed Farfetch to accelerate expansion in the resale sector, to expand product categories beyond bags, to develop technologies in-house, and to integrate first-hand and second-hand sales.

Table 11.2 Business models operating in the fashion resale market (non-exhaustive list)

Multi-brand resale platform	Brand partnership with multi-brand resale platform	Peer-to-peer resale platform	Brand partnership with business-to business resale platforms	In-house resale	Brand investment
1999 • Fashionphile *2001* • 1stDibs *2002* • Watchfinder *2005* • Luxe DH *2008* • Yoogi's Closet • Secoo *2009* • ThredUp *2010* • Second Friend Store (RUSSIA)	*2016* • Roc-A-Fella Records with StockX *2017* • Amazon with Poshmark • Lyst & Vestiaire Collective • Shinola & StockX • Stella McCartney & The RealReal	*1995* • eBay *2009* • Tradesy • Vestiaire Collective	*2016* • Eileen Fisher with Yerdle *2017* • Patagonia with Trove • Rei with Trove	*2018* • MB&F *2019* • Mark Cross • Farfecth launched SecondLife • Style Share launched Ours *2020* • Mulberry • Zalando • Naver launched Kream • Yoox Net-a-Porter launched Mr Porter	*2015* • H&M acquires first stake in Sellpy • Tradesy acquires Shop Hers *2018* • Farfetch acquires Stadium Goods • Merger between Fight Club & Goat • Richemont acquires Watchfinder

(continued)

Table 11.2 (Continued)

Multi-brand resale platform	Brand partnership with multi-brand resale platform	Peer-to-peer resale platform	Brand partnership with business-to business resale platforms	In-house resale	Brand investment
2011 • The Luxury Closet (UEA) • The RealReal *2014* • Rebag *2015* • Cudoni • Stadium Goods • Poizon *2017* • Thrift	*2018* • Reformation & ThredUp	*2011* • Depop • Poshmark *2012* • Vinted *2013* • StyleTribute (Indonesia) • Rebelle *2014* • Grailed	*2020* • Balenciaga with Reflaunt • Cos with Reflaunt • Farfetch with Luxclusif • Levi's with Trove • The North Face with Archive	*2021* • Isabel Marant • Nike • Veepee Recycle • Rent The Runway • Diesel (OTB Group) • Valentino launches Valentino Vintage • Galeries Lafayette open (Re)Store • Cocoon • Hurr	*2019* • Neiman Marcus invests in Fashionphile

2019	2015	2021	2022	2020
• Burberry with The RealReal	• Goat	• Adidas with RaaS	• Yoox Net-a-Porter launched Mr Porter Resell	• Vinted acquires United Wardrobe
• JC Penny with ThredUp	• StockX	• Yoox Net-a-Porter (and The Outnet) with Reflaunt		
• Macy's with ThredUp	• Tinkerlust	• Lululemon with Trove		
• Ralph Lauren & Depop	• GoShare2	• M.M.LaFleur with Archive		
• Selfridges & Vestiaire Collective	**2016**	• Mulberry with Vestiaire Collective		
	• GoTrendier	• Daniel Patrick with The Archivist		
	2017	• Oscar De La Renta with Archive		
	• Plum	• Harvey Nichols with Reflaunt		

(continued)

Table 11.2 (Continued)

Multi-brand resale platform	Brand partnership with multi-brand resale platform	Peer-to-peer resale platform	Brand partnership with business-to-business resale platforms	In-house resale	Brand investment
	2020 • By Far & Vestiaire Collective • Gucci & The RealReal • Richard Quinn & Depop • Vans & Depop • Walmart & ThredUp	*2021/22* Veepee	*2022* • Steve Madden with Recurate		*2021* • Kering invests in Vestiaire Collective • Aglaé Ventures – LVMH's family investment firm – invests in Chrono24 • Etsy acquires Depop • Goat Group invests in Grailed • Farfetch acquires Luxclusif

2021

- Alexander McQueen & Vestiaire Collective
- Farfetch & ThredUp
- MyTheresa & Vestiaire Collective
- Balenciaga, Jacquemus and Simone Rocha with The RealReal
- Burberry & My Wardrobe HQ
- Richard Mille & Ninety

2022

- Vestiaire Collective acquires Tradesy

SOURCE Authors' elaboration, 2022

CASE STUDY   Veepee

Founded in 2001 from the intuition of Jacques-Antoine Granjon, Founder and CEO of the Group, Veepee is the European leader in e-commerce, specializing in flash sales.

Veepee Group is present in 10 European countries, collaborates with over 7,000 partner brands, has 66 million subscribers worldwide, achieves daily traffic of 4.5 million users, and ended 2021 with a turnover of €3.2 billion. Veepee members are 70 per cent women, 30 per cent men, and the average age of their customers is 35 years for 20 per cent and between 35 and 50 years for 50 per cent.

The theme of sustainability, now dominant in fashion and luxury, has also led Veepee, 20 years after its creation, to embrace the logic of circularity, including 'eco-environmental' initiatives in its recent strategic choices.

Starting from the data collected from a recent survey carried out on a sample of over 6,000 members throughout Europe, the company has realized that its customers regularly buy and sell second-hand products (66 per cent), mainly through specialized online sites (78 per cent) and marketplace (41 per cent). The second-hand products are mainly clothing (80 per cent of customers), but also furniture and home decor (71 per cent), fashion accessories (54 per cent), or electronic products (32 per cent). Veepee customers' motivations towards second-hand choices are economic (85 per cent) and ecological (75 per cent).

According to the same survey, 86 per cent of respondents, in their daily lives, pay attention to recycling and eco-responsible actions.

In response to this growing demand for sustainability on the consumer side and to allow its brand partners to meet all the challenges of the product life cycle, Veepee presented two innovative circular economy services in France: Re-turn and Re-cycle.

Re-turn

Re-turn is a service aimed at managing returns through a dedicated C2C platform, which allows the resale, directly between users, of products purchased on the site to avoid generating additional logistical flows and to cope with the problem of returned items. The aim is to promote a new approach to the classic return issue, reducing the operations related to the return of the garments and the consequent environmental impact.

Re-turn is already enjoying great success in France, with around 2 million registered user accounts. In this testing period, 600 to 700 items were uploaded to the dedicated platform every day, half of which sold within three days of being put online. This service avoided more than 200,000 returns. In 2022, Veepee will promote the initiative at the European level.

Re-cycle

Re-cycle is a project that focuses on circularity. It is carried out in collaboration with brands through exclusive events on the platform, as it allows users to send back used products of the partner brand to Veepee. Customers subsequently receive a voucher from Veepee to be used on the brand's site or in the physical store. Based on the conditions encountered, the products delivered with this programme will then be recycled, given to charity associations, resold as 'pre-loved', or subjected to upcycling: the goal is to give them a second life and increase their lifetime value. With the programme, Veepee collected more than 200,000 products; more than two-thirds of the products gathered in 2021 turned out to be in good condition, therefore relisting 30 tonnes of clothes and shoes.

Questions for discussion

- What key points of the resale value chain are affected by Re-turn and Re-cycle?
- Could Veepee also operate in the rental market? Which challenges would be faced?
- According to you, is the Re-cycle project able to fulfil circular economy's objectives or not?
- In your opinion, could the two Veepee services succeed in other countries outside Europe?

Conclusions

Consumers and consumption are changing. Luxury is changing too, under the pressure of sustainability, affordability and self-expression. The new business models that have emerged within the umbrella con-cept of collaborative consumption – renting and resale – embrace consumers' new expectations, and have ample opportunities to grow in the luxury market.

New players flourished and established themselves as those to emulate and luxury brands, sceptical at the beginning, are now trying to choose the best way to tap into the secondary market, in order to not lag behind.

Nevertheless, despite the huge growth and the many opportunities, several issues must be overcome, and a challenge that all the resale and renting players face as the business scales is how to maintain a steady stream of desirable inventory.

Indeed, both big companies and start-ups suffer from the competition in finding high-quality inventory in order to stay appealing and profitable in the future.

Luxury resale players are investing in high-touch services and customer acquisition drives to avoid running into an inventory crunch. As for many luxury retailers in the primary market, a small pool of high-net-worth sellers can often generate a disproportionate share of revenues for luxury resale players. That suggests some companies should cultivate relationships with top luxury consumers. Those shoppers are more likely to have wardrobes brimming with stocks in good condition and hard-to-find products from hot brands. But they can also be the hardest clients to reach, and luxury brands are favoured compared to native renting and resale companies, since these clients are already present in their customers' database.

Another issue is linked to the sustainability and ethicality of the models once more and more people engage with them. The supply chain of renting and resale requires considerable logistic and transport operations, which inevitably implies carbon emissions. Moreover, a secondary market does not necessarily mean a less consumerist society, given that more consumers can access previously unaffordable products and purchase more products; sometimes brands fuel first-hand consumption, offering sellers store credit in return for their pre-loved items.

While the premise of resale and renting is promising, the future of these trends in the luxury market is yet to be written, and it is likely that consumers will proclaim the winners.

Key learning points

1 *Collaborative consumption*
Collaborative consumption is an economic model based on sharing, second-hand purchasing and renting of products and services; the most diffused collaborative luxury consumption business models are resale and renting, which are growing markedly.

2 *Resale and renting*
These business models have deep implications on the concept of luxury, as well as for luxury consumption and for luxury brands, considering that renting and resale make luxury more accessible for aspirational consumers.

3 *Consumers' motivations*
Many different motivations are connected to the growth of resale and renting, including the possibility for customers to preview goods and postpone or avoid the purchasing decision, skipping all the issues coming from ownership. Pre-owned and shared products also give the opportunity to rethink fashion more circularly.

4 *Barriers to collaborative consumption*
All the previous motivations to engage in resale and renting consumption modalities come along with barriers like hygiene concerns, difficulties in finding the correct model, size or colour, and the risks of counterfeit products.

5 *Key points in the value chain*
The fashion collaborative consumption value chain needs some specific attention, compared to the traditional retail business, in some activities: assortment procurement, inventory management, delivery and return logistics, and pricing policy choice.

6 *Different resale and renting business models*
The business models operating in the renting and resale fashion and luxury market can be categorized into multi-brand platforms, brand partnerships with multi-brand platforms, peer-to-peer platforms, brand partnerships with business-to-business platforms, in-house services and brand investment.

References

Armstrong, C M, Niinimki, K, Kujala, S, Karell, E and Lang, C (2015) Sustainable product-service systems for clothing: Exploring consumer perceptions of consumption alternatives in Finland, *Journal of Cleaner Production*, **97** (15), pp 30–39

Bardhi, F and Arnould, E J (2005) Thrift shopping: Combining utilitarian thrift and hedonic treat benefits, *Journal of Consumer Behaviour*, **44** (4), pp 223–33

Bardhi, F and Eckhardt, G M (2012) Access-based consumption: the case of car sharing, *Journal of Consumer Research*, **39** (4), pp 881–98

Bardhi, F, Eckhardt, G M and Samsioe, E (2020) Liquid luxury. In M Felicitas, K Wilcox and S Czellar (eds) *Handbook of Luxury Branding*, Edward Elgar, London

Beard, N D (2008) The branding of ethical fashion and the consumer: a luxury niche or mass-market reality?, *Fashion Theory: The Journal of Dress, Body & Culture*, **12** (4), 447–468

Becker-Leifhold, C V (2018) The role of values in collaborative fashion consumption: a critical investigation through the lenses of the theory of planned behavior, *Journal of Cleaner Production*, **199**, pp 781–91

Beggan, J K (1992) On the social nature of nonsocial perception: the mere ownership effect, *Journal of Personality and Social Psychology*, **62** (2)

Belk, R W (1988) Possessions and the extended self, *Journal of Business Research*, **15** (2)

Berg, A, Berjaoui, B, Iwatani, N and Zerbi, S (2021) Welcome to luxury fashion resale: Discerning customers beckon to brands, www.mckinsey.com/industries/retail/our-insights/welcome-to-luxury-fashion-resale-discerning-customers-beckon-to-brands (archived at https://perma.cc/BT3D-PQYB)

Bernthal, M J, Crockett, D and Rose, R L (2005) Credit cards as lifestyle facilitators, *Journal of Consumer Research*, **32** (1), pp 130–45

Botsman, R (2013) The sharing economy lacks a shared definition, *Fast Company*, http://www.fastcoexist.com/3022028/the-sharing-economy-lacks-ashared-definition (archived at https://perma.cc/NP3G-QBYX)

Catulli, M, Lindley, J K, Reed, N B, Green, A, Hyseni, H and Kiri, S (2013) What is mine not yours: further insight on what access-based consumption says about consumers, *Consumer Culture Theory*, **15**, pp 185–208

Cervellon, M C, Carey, L and Harms, T (2012) Something old, something used: determinants of women's purchase of vintage fashion vs second-hand fashion, *International Journal of Retail and Distribution Management*, 40 (12), pp 956–74

Christodoulides, G, Athwal, N, Boukis, A and Semaan, R W (2021), New forms of luxury consumption in the sharing economy, *Journal of Business Research*, 137, https://doi.org/10.1016/j.jbusres.2021.08.022 (archived at https://perma.cc/LD2X-484Y)

Cline, E (2016) The power of buying less by buying better, *The Atlantic,* www.theatlantic.com/business/archive/2016/02/buying-less-by-buying-better/462639/ (archived at https://perma.cc/5Y4U-9Z6P)

Crane, D (2000) *Fashion and its Social Agendas: Class, gender and identity in clothing*, University of Chicago Press

Cristini, H, Kauppinen-Räisänen, H, Barthod-Prothade, M and Woodside, A (2017) Toward a general theory of luxury: advancing from workbench definitions and theoretical transformations, *Journal of Business Research*, 70

Cusumano, M A (2018) The sharing economy meets reality, *Communications of the ACM*, 61 (1), pp 26–28

D'Arpizio, C and Levato, F (2022) Secondhand luxury goods: a first rate strategic opportunity, www.bain.com/insights/secondhand-luxury-goods-a-first-rate-strategic-opportunity-snap-chart/ (archived at https://perma.cc/J26H-PNN4)

D'Arpizio, C, Verde Nieto, D, Davis-Peccoud, J and Capellini, M (2021) LuxCo 2030: A vision of sustainable luxury, www.bain.com/insights/luxco-2030-a-vision-of-sustainable-luxury/ (archived at https://perma.cc/MG9P-JWWA)

Durgee, J F and O'Connor, G C (1995) An exploration into renting as consumption behavior, *Psychology & Marketing*, 12 (2), pp 89–104

Edbring, E G, Lehner, M and Mont, O (2016) Exploring consumer attitudes to alternative models of consumption: motivations and barriers, *Journal of Cleaner Production*, 123, pp 5–15

Ferraro, C, Sands, S and Brace-Govan, J (2016) The role of fashionability in second-hand shopping motivations, *Journal of Retailing and Consumer Services,* 32, pp 262–68

Fritze, M P, Marchand, A, Eisingerich, A B and Benkenstein, M (2020) Access-based services as substitutes for material possessions: the role of psychological ownership, *Journal of Service Research*, 23 (3)

Gibson, C, Klocker, N, Borger, E and Kerr, S-M (2018) Malleable homes and mutual possessions: caring and sharing in extended family households as a resource for survival, in A Ince and S-M Hall (eds) *Sharing Economies in Times of Crisis: Practices, politics and possibilities*, Routledge, London, pp 35–49

Guzzetti, A, Crespi, R and Belvedere, V (2021) 'Please don't buy!': Consumers attitude to alternative luxury consumption, *Strategic Change*, 30, pp 67–78, https://doi.org/10.1002/jsc.2390 (archived at https://perma.cc/2Z8X-ZZV6)

Hamari, J, Sjöklint, M and Ukkonen, A (2015) The sharing economy: why people participate in collaborative consumption, *Journal of the Association for Information Science & Technology*, **67** (9), pp 2047–59

Holmqvist, J, Diaz Ruiz, C and Penaloza, L (2020) Moments of luxury: hedonic escapism as a luxury experience, *Journal of Business Research*, **116**, https://doi.org/10.1016/j.jbusres.2019.10.015 (archived at https://perma.cc/T4TC-M3ZC)

Iran, S and Schrader, U (2017) Collaborative fashion consumption and its environmental effects, *Journal of Fashion Marketing and Management: An International Journal*, **21**, pp 468–82

Kahn, B (1995) Consumer variety-seeking among goods and services, *Journal of Retailing and Consumer Services*, **2** (3), pp 139–48

Kansara, V A (2020) Should luxury build resale into its business model? www.businessoffashion.com/briefings/luxury/should-luxury-build-resale-into-its-business-model/ (archived at https://perma.cc/L9TF-CG8R)

Kessous, A and Valette-Florence, P (2019) 'From Prada to Nada': Consumers and their luxury products: A contrast between second-hand and first-hand luxury products, *Journal of Business Research*, **102**, pp 313–27

Krekels, G, Kocher, B, Czellar, S and Muller, B (2020) I don't own it but it's mine – the impact of materialism on perceived ownership of rented luxury, in *NA – Advances in Consumer Research Volume 48*, eds J Argo, T M Lowrey and H Jensen Schau, Association for Consumer Research, Duluth, MN, pp 90–93

Kumar, R, Singh, S P and Lamba, K (2018) Sustainable robust layout using Big Data approach: a key towards industry 4.0, *Journal of Cleaner Production*, **204**, pp 643–59 https://doi.org/10.1016/j.jclepro.2018.08.327 (archived at https://perma.cc/AKY6-KH84)

Lang, C and Zhang, R (2019) Second-hand clothing acquisition: the motivations and barriers to clothing swaps for Chinese consumers, *Sustainable Production and Consumption*, **18**, pp 156–64

Lawson, S J, Gleim, M R, Perren, R and Hwang, J (2016) Freedom from ownership: An exploration of access-based consumption, *Journal of Business Research*, **69**, 2615–23

Lee, D and Malik, R (2021) The future of fashion resale, *Business of Fashion*, www.businessoffashion.com/reports/retail/the-future-of-fashion-resale-report-bof-insights/ (archived at https://perma.cc/NN7R-6DD4)

Machado, M A D, De Almeida, S O, Bollick, L C and Bragagnolo, G (2019) Second-hand fashion market: consumer role in circular economy, *Journal of Fashion Marketing and Management*, **23** (3), pp 382–95

Malik, R and Lee, D (2021) Why the resale boom shows no sign of stopping, www.businessoffashion.com/articles/retail/why-the-resale-boom-shows-no-sign-of-stopping/ (archived at https://perma.cc/ZN9K-FNB9)

Marriott, H (2019) Selfridges opens secondhand clothing concession with Vestiaire Collective, *The Guardian*, www.theguardian.com/fashion/2019/oct/31/selfridges-opens-secondhand-clothing-concession-with-vestiaire-collective (archived at https://perma.cc/2H87-AQLC)

Möhlmann, M (2015) Collaborative consumption: determinants of satisfaction and the likelihood of using a sharing economy option again, *Journal of Consumer Behavior*, **14**, pp 193–207

Morewedge, C K and Giblin, C E (2015) Explanations of the endowment effect: an integrative review, *Trends in Cognitive Sciences*, **19** (6)

Needleman, S E and Loten, A (2014) Startups want to be the next Airbnb, Uber, *Wall Street Journal*, www.wsj.com/articles/startups-want-to-be-the-next-airbnb-uber-1399503252 (archived at https://perma.cc/RP76-3S9Q)

Pantano, E and Stylos, N (2020) The Cinderella moment: exploring consumers' motivations to engage with renting as collaborative luxury consumption mode, *Psychology and Marketing*, **37** (5), pp 740–53

Park, H and Joyner-Armstrong, C M J (2017) Collaborative apparel consumption in the digital sharing economy: an agenda for academic inquiry, *International Journal of Consumer Studies*, **41**, pp 465–74

Park, H and Joyner-Armstrong, C M (2019) Is money the biggest driver? Uncovering motives for engaging in online collaborative consumption retail models for apparel, *Journal of Retailing and Consumer Services*, **51**, pp 42–50

Pierce, J L, Kostova, T and Dirks, K T (2001) Toward a theory of psychological ownership in organizations, *Academy of Management Review*, **26** (2)

Pierre-Louis, K (2019) How to buy clothes that are built to last, *The New York Times*, www.nytimes.com/interactive/2019/climate/sustainable-clothing.html (archived at https://perma.cc/7647-SRKU)

Puhak, J (2021) Ralph Lauren 'first' luxury brand to start a clothing rental business, *Fox News*, www.foxnews.com/lifestyle/ralph-lauren-first-brand-starts-clothing-rental-business (archived at https://perma.cc/7S3X-SN52)

Recode (2017) Full Transcript: Jennifer Hyman, CEO of Rent the Runway, is creating the Spotify of women's clothes, www.vox.com/2017/2/9/14566938/full-transcript-jennifer-hyman-ceo-rent-the-runway-subscription-womens-clothe (archived at https://perma.cc/4RHF-TDNB)

Richins, M L (2004) The material values scale: measurement properties and development of a short form, *Journal of Consumer Research*, **31** (1)

Roof, K (2020) Report: Rent the Runway nears funding below last $1 billion value, www.businessoffashion.com/articles/retail/report-rent-the-runway-nears-funding-below-last-1-billion-value/ (archived at https://perma.cc/FP6S-HCHV)

Sherman, L (2018) The end of ownership, *BoF Professional*, https://www.businessoffashion.com/articles/professional/the-end-of-ownership (archived at https://perma.cc/7PXS-4SCZ)

Sihvonen, J and Turunen, L L M (2016) As good as new – valuing fashion brands in the online second-hand markets, *Journal of Product & Brand Management*, **25** (3), pp 285–95

ThredUp (2021) Resale Report, www.thredup.com/ (archived at https://perma.cc/QN5X-E669)

Widlok, T (2017) *Anthropology and the Economy of Sharing*, Routledge, London, UK

Wiedmann, K-P, Hennigs, N and Siebels, A (2007) Measuring consumers' luxury value perception: a cross-cultural framework, *Academy of Marketing Science Review*, **7** (7), pp 1–21

Wittkowski, K, Moeller, S and Wirtz, J (2013) Firms' intentions to use non-ownership services, *Journal of Service Research*, **16** (2)

Yuan, Q and Shen, B (2019) Renting fashion with strategic customers in the sharing economy, *International Journal of Production Economics*, **218**, pp 185–95

Future industry developments 12

Experiential luxury, extreme personalization and bringing back the human factor in luxury branding

ALESSANDRO BRUN

LEARNING OBJECTIVES

- To know the changing habits of wealthy people as a consequence of the Covid-19 outbreak, and how this could impact consumer habits.
- To understand how brands have reacted during the pandemic, and the consequent potential changes in the luxury industry.
- To recognize the different meanings of luxury in the case studies illustrated and being able to discern the different ways to create value in luxury.
- To be able to 'connect the dots' and conceive and design new and unprecedented luxury experiences, leveraging the latest transformations and new trends.

The luxury industry in the years of Covid-19

Bain & Company, in their well-known luxury global market monitor report for 2019, defined the state of the luxury industry as 'the New Normal' (Bain & Company, 2020).

On 31 December, 2019, the first case of coronavirus (Covid-19) was reported in Wuhan, China. In the next two years, the pandemic would have an impact on all of our lives that nobody could have ever imagined. All sectors and markets were impacted by Covid, and luxury was no exception, with the lockdown forcing people to stay home and stores remaining closed. It is no surprise that 2020 was the *annus horribilis* for the personal luxury goods industry, marking an all-time low year-on-year growth (contraction) of -22 per cent since the beginning of the mass marketing of luxury era.

In 2021, Bain & Company announced that the personal luxury goods industry had bounced back to pre-Covid levels. The 2021 rebound has been a crucial pulse check of the status of the luxury industry, and it was interpreted as a strong predictor of healthy growth of the luxury market over the following few years.

In the years from 2020 to 2040, luxury brands will have to cater to the diverse inclinations of the different customer segments – new personas, with changed values – supporting the new circle of desire with outstanding products and services, and creating a connection with customers across a number of touchpoints. The strong geographic and demographic shifts (with China showing a persistent strong demand, also due to an acceleration of the middle class and a consumption upgrade; and Gens Y and Z, accounting for more than 70 per cent of the global luxury goods markets by 2025, are expected to contribute 180 per cent of the total growth in the timeframe 2019 to 2025) should of course be taken into account.

Changes in consumer behaviour

Arguably, the most important implication for the luxury business is that the lockdown has changed the habits of people globally. As the lives of people went gradually back to normal, some of the luxury consumers changed their spending patterns, most likely in a permanent way.

The first important insight is that luxury will keep having a solid customer base of wealthy customers, whereas high earners may be a more volatile segment. '**Wealth, not income.**' If before the outbreak,

HENRYs (High-Earning, Not Rich Yet) would spend a considerable fraction of their disposable income on luxury goods and experiences, after the lockdown several families may have limited cash availability for superfluous spending, while HNWI (High Net Worth Individuals) will see their spending capacity virtually unaffected. The post-pandemic economic scenario, characterized by high inflation rates and the end of the era of negative interest rates, will be a hindrance to the practice of financing the purchase of luxury goods (a practice that is quite common for luxury cars, residential buildings, etc, but in markets such as the United States is popular also for purchasing luxury timepieces and other hard luxury goods) leveraging on future earnings. A more financially savvy attitude will suggest proceeding with the purchase of the coveted luxury merchandise only if the balance in the bank account allows it.

The segment of '**luxury for those who will stay home**' will have big growth potential. It is expected that, for a number of years after Covid-19, people will keep travelling less; this will be due to factors such as governmental restriction, fear of infection, and companies organizing more efficient conference calls in place of face-to-face meetings. Clearly, some people have already switched back to their pre-Covid travel habits, but some other people have experienced the convenience of working from home and will never go back. This will impact negatively on some channels (especially travel retail), specific destinations (e.g. Las Vegas), specific customer segments in the flagship stores of the world's fashion capitals (Chinese customers visiting Milan, London, Paris, and exploiting tax-free shopping), and product categories (suitcases and luggage). On the other hand, many people are rediscovering the joy of cooking – at the outset of the pandemic in Western countries, in March 2020, bread machines were the second-fastest-growing category in e-commerce after disposable gloves (Styrk, 2020). Hence, with the reopening, socialization occasions may happen at home (in an attitude that has already been labelled 'revenge conviviality'), and categories such as *art de la table*, but also gourmet food to be consumed at home, may benefit. Long times spent in the abode, along with the new role of the home – at the crossroad between private life dwelling and office working – meant, for many people, taking the opportunity to redecorate, thus benefitting furniture, interior design and lighting categories, especially in the high-end segments. Spending more time at home, and in particular working from home, means that customers will be seeking more comfort, extended functionality and flexible solutions to create multifunctional spaces.

The slow switch from materialistic possession of physical products to the **'hedonistic gratification of the experience'** has clearly gained momentum. After the sacrifices of lockdown, customers will crave hedonistic products and services to satisfy the need for self-indulgence and personal pampering – shifting away from the 'bandwagon effect' and moving into the 'luxury as a personal affair' area. Premium beauty products, but also home spa and home wellness, and intense sensorial experiences in the fine food and drinks territory, could benefit.

Younger generation and – in general – more sustainability-conscious customers would embrace a **'responsible luxury'** attitude. The pandemic outbreak stimulated deep societal reflections around the main theme of 'where is humanity going?' Consumers will be even more aware of sustainability, and brands and product categories allowing 'responsible consumption' will be privileged. Giorgio Armani penned an open letter to WWD, in which he challenged the current fast-fashion mindset, saying he believes in an 'approach to the design and making of garments that suggests a way of buying them: to make them last'(Zargani, 2020).

Customers are looking for **discounts** and will develop a predisposition for **second-hand** purchases or even luxury goods **rentals.** If, on the one hand, an even more intense wave of anti-consumerism will not be unexpected, the habit of waiting for end-of-season sales and making pilgrimages to factory outlets and buying from off-price channels will be further strengthened by the self-appeal to frugality. If brands and retailers resort to significant discounts to get rid of the unsold SS20 collection, they risk fostering the vicious circle of off-price and bargain hunts. An early-Covid McKinsey study revealed that special promotions were the main reason for purchasing clothing during the crisis for 56 per cent of consumers (Amed et al, 2020). Another important aspect is the boom of second-hand luxury, which for many years has been confined to such categories as timepieces and mature markets such as Europe. If the concept of purchasing a second-hand Rolex – maybe an extremely hard-to-find model – let alone a vintage Ferrari car, is not surprising and doesn't give the perception of a customer who could not afford to buy a brand-new item, the same should happen for a man's silk tie or pair of pump shoes. Altagamma Bain monitor describes it as an 'extended product lifecycle'.

Offline vs online is a comparison that no longer makes sense. Purchasing **online is the new normal**, yet luxury brands and their loyal customers will connect through a variety of touchpoints. The transition to a life in the digital world was accelerated as if through a time warp, and customers are buying more online as well as consuming more digital content. This represents a major change in paradigm. When we started designing the first 'Master in eFashion' at the business school of Politecnico di Milano in the late 2000s, the online penetration in the personal luxury goods segment was only 1 per cent. In 2018, according to a McKinsey study, 80 per cent of the €254 billion total luxury sales were influenced by digital – yet the perspective was still that the brick-and-mortar retail was the 'normal' way to do business (Achille et al, 2018). Whether the perspective post-pandemic will turn 180 degrees, so that the online will be the norm and brick and mortar will be a way to 'support', it's hard to say. We are now in the 'omnichannel' era, in which customers along their journey are experiencing the brand proposition and storytelling through multiple touchpoints, before making up their minds and proceeding with the purchase. But one thing is unquestionable: a brand without a strong online presence, today, is a non-existing brand in the eyes of many a consumer.

We are in a new era of '**un-branded luxury**', or, at least, less prominent logos. Economic theories say that after a 'quarantine of consumption' (as Li Edelkoort defined this unprecedented period of forced, far from conspicuous consumerism (Fairs, 2020)), consumers may switch to 'revenge spending' (Gopalan, 2020). But after the lockdown ended and travel bans were lifted, the world entered into 'stage 2' of the war, in which the Covid-19 enemy is still there in the battlefield, thus reducing the appetite for conspicuous consumption. Before the crisis, brands with a very bold visual identity (such as Gucci) were performing extremely well thanks to the enthusiasm of brand-sensitive customers – but in a climate of 'social thriftiness', luxury consumers could steer towards the quality and intimacy of 'no-logo brands', as they are finally understanding the meaning of

Bottega Veneta payoff ('When your own initials are enough': there's room for feel-good purchases even without a big flashy logo on your t-shirt).

One last interesting trend may be a **renewed pride for local producers**. This may vary in strength in different markets and for different product categories, but we are already witnessing the first signs that are forewarning the rise of fully-fledged 'buy local' movements.

Concluding this overview of the different post-Covid trends that will be affecting luxury consumer behaviour, it is important to remark that, rather than macro-trends – i.e. trends affecting all consumers, globally – they should be considered as micro-trends, shifting purchasing behaviours in specific niches or customer segments. For example, the no-logo trend may be more popular in mature markets, whereas in some emerging markets conspicuous consumption may still be the dominant attitude.

How did brands react?

A survey carried out at Politecnico di Milano, involving supply chain managers, marketing managers and sales managers of Italian personal luxury goods companies, illustrated how brands are facing the 'new twentennial' of luxury, in which the whole industry will be characterized by new fundamentals.

Managers believe that more importance will be assigned to the intrinsic value of the product (with particular regard to the excellence of the workmanship and materials), but not to the detriment of the brand value. There is no longer such a thing as the trade-off between brand and intrinsic value, where formerly luxury brands were categorized as either symbolic (creating value through aesthetical aspects) or technical (due to the intrinsic content of their products). The values represented by the brand will be even more important when they are perceived as credible. The consumer will ask for greater transparency and attention to sustainability issues will become even more central, not only with respect to the product but also with reference to the corporate mission. There is a general expectation of a renewed discovery of interpersonal relationships in purchasing behaviour, with more direct and human relationships. Brands also expect greater price elasticity in demand even in the premium ranges as a consequence of a more conscious purchasing attitude and oriented towards preferring products with recognizable intrinsic value.

Companies expect purchases of luxury consumers to become generally more responsible and aware, due to two main factors: the decrease in spending ability (as a combined effect of declining incomes and growing inflation rates) and the reflection generated by a new situation that has made humanity more fragile and less certain. Brands that have a strong identity, that work with product quality, service reliability, the guarantee of continuity and that represent strong ethical, environmental and social values, will thrive and survive. Those who will not be able to deliver these messages will struggle – even risking disappearing – and Covid-19 has done nothing but accelerate a process of transformation already underway.

Online has 'literally exploded', some managers reported. There will be fewer physical stores but they will all be renovated to give the best possible presence and image to the brands. They will become ambassadors of brand values and customer consultants to enhance their image. Those who will simply be an alternative to online without offering anything more will have no future. The trend that will be accelerated will be linked to the 'maisonization' of the distribution chain. As has already happened for production, several brands have declared a move towards the direct management of the retail chain. It will be a gradual process but some managers believe it is inexorable.

The reaction of various brands will be characterized by continuity: as one manager stated, 'Retail will not be set aside and will remain central in an omnichannel strategy' where customers will experience a seamless integration between the various direct channels (retail and direct e-commerce will count even more), as well as indirect ones (marketplaces and wholesale). The premium consumer, but also the brands of this range, wants fewer and fewer intermediaries, both in physical and digital encounters; this was for several brands an already existing trend that has been gaining momentum as a result of the crisis.

In an integrated multichannel perspective, brands will no longer manage segregated assortments and stocks by store or city, but a single large stock, oriented towards the only result that matters: the sale of the product to the customer, regardless of the location in which it takes place. This will require efforts to modernize management and operational systems, as well as logistical flows and a well-established mechanism for deliveries, shipments and returns. The world of retail stores will also change both in terms of the assortment of collections and in terms of sales experience. The new rules based on respect for social distancing forced the redesign of spaces and points of sale, with a focus on greater separation and distance. However, exquisitely in the field of luxury, this new sales experience also created an opportunity to redesign an experience of further uniqueness and exclusivity for the customer. A one-to-one sales experience, similar to appointments in haute couture ateliers. Once again, some companies were able to reap the benefits – a potential opportunity arising from a new restriction imposed.

Yet even in this new omnichannel scenario, each single channel – independently taken – will have to find a way to reach break-even. A significant managerial challenge for companies who have directly operated retail stores will be how to financially support the network of points of sale and flagship stores, implying massive operating costs, in the face of the increasing share of sales taking place online. Managers believe that luxury retail will forever remain the maximum expression of a brand's visible values and will have to make the effort to change, to make itself less obvious and to prove to the consumer the real benefits and value provided by a store experience. Whether it is with dedicated collections, with moments of pure entertainment through dedicated events or invitations to unique experiences for the most loyal customers, or by offering customers more services – from made to order to image consultancy, to cross-selling support and total look. Certainly, the times in which brands could rely only on the availability of the assortment, while passively waiting for the customer to enter into a physical store, are over for good.

Clearly, although the perfect formula to get out of the crisis does not exist, a good mix of interventions aimed at reducing personnel costs with a view to greater efficiency, combined with the aid allocated by various governments and close collaboration between companies in the supply chain, were the primary ingredients of a recipe that allowed the luxury industry – as a whole – to bounce back so soon to pre-Covid levels. At a time when the cash-in flow was low or non-existent, brands understood the necessity to collaborate in an organic and organized way with all the suppliers and partners of the supply chain, striving for new and unprecedented collaborative solutions. Slower but constant payment times; more favourable discounts for advance payments; small orders spread over time in place of a single large order. Many aspects of traditional supply chain management were rebalanced with a collaborative 'survival mode' perspective, with the first and foremost goal to preserve the system from entering into a stasis situation: this avoided too many small suppliers – and various districts of excellence in Italian regions – literally closing down.

Another significant trigger to a radical transformation in the fashion luxury supply chain is related to the fact that, during Covid, the limited mobility influenced sales campaigns for the wholesale market; as a reaction, brands worked on the creation of digital showrooms that made it possible to avoid trips and physical visits to buyers from all over the world. From this point of view, fashion weeks would arguably change their vocation. 'The fashion shows will manifest the true reality of a show for the public. Values but not products – or products with value. No longer functional to the business', said Giorgio Ravasio, country manager Italy for Vivienne Westwood.

With buyers unable to travel from all over the world to go to showrooms for collection orders, the entire system has suffered a physical stagnation in favour of greater virtual liveliness: appointments in showrooms and virtual platforms to get to know the collections and finalize their own orders, increasing the demand for the production of digital content and sharing platforms able to give an ever-clearer way of rendering the reality of the products. It is possible to consider the two years of the pandemic an experimentation phase in which brands had the chance to understand what works and what doesn't... what is possible to do remotely and what is not possible. Luxury follows a very specific logic that contingency is modifying but which it will not be able to eliminate or eradicate. High-priced luxury products require buyers (but also customers) to pay attention to quality and to every single detail during the selection and purchase phase.

Now that the travel bans have been lifted, while the world has been moving towards 'phygital' processes, there are clear limits and perplexities around the feasibility of remote orders. Even – especially – when the purchase volumes are important. It is easier when the product is already known, but very difficult when the product is not known or in the start-up or negotiation phases of new business opportunities.

Future developments in the luxury sector

Brands should first of all regain full awareness of the true meaning of luxury: go back to the origins of artisanal *savoir faire*, of beautiful things done well, take a break from the incessant rhythms of fast fashion, or at least slow down – and go back to making their customers feel 'exclusive'. As underlined by all the interviewees, the disintermediation of sales channels will lead to a more 'intimate' relationship with customers.

In order not to be out of place, in a climate of social moderation, the approach to marketing will have to be on the one hand more discreet and at the same time responsible. A significant part of the budget for above-the-line communication could be used for cause-related marketing or transformed into a budget for below-the-line communication.

To avoid the risk of financial distress in the short term, it will be essential to start the recovery from those channels, markets and product categories that will restart faster: online and discount channels to bet on; mature economies, and for China to try to meet customers locally (even if Chinese people travelling to Europe are more incentivized to do tax-free luxury shopping); and, in terms of product categories, beauty, fine food and wine, *art de la table*, personal mobility, evergreen items and no logos and, of course, experiences. But to survive in the long run, brands will have to complete the transition from brick-and-mortar player to omnipresent player.

Finally, to overcome the aftermath of the crisis, companies will have to leverage digital technologies, with an impact on both the simplification of processes and the organization of work, and activate collaboration and sharing mechanisms with the various partners in the supply chain, ranging from data to strategies, to be stronger together.

So what could be – in a nutshell – the best lesson learnt from the seismic shift that catapulted the luxury industry from 2000 to 2020 into the 2020 to 2040 twentennial? Established online presence and digital strategy; fluid collections without a real Spring-Summer and Autumn-Winter dichotomy; focus on the intrinsic value of the product and investments in sustainability across entire supply chain: some brands faced the beginning of the new twentennial better prepared than others to deal with the unexpected Covid-19 emergency and the forthcoming Darwinian shakeout of the industry. For all the others, the ability to adapt to the new scenario will prove, more than ever before, essential to succeed in the long term.

The 2000s have been marked by a further wave of democratization of luxury, following the mass marketing of luxury. The 2020s – as the first stage of the 2020 to 2040 twentennial – will be characterized by a mix of strategies evolving in different directions, catering for a variegated and heterogeneous set of target segments.

Those brands who will target the loftier segments of luxury will be aiming at more exclusivity and overall premiumness – not just in the product, but of course in all associated services – trying to make the overall experience absolutely exceptional. Ultra-luxury is a concept that is rapidly developing, from one-off cars to subscription-only restaurants, haute-couture in retail stores, event-based marketing and so on.

Case studies

CASE STUDY Exclusivity – yet within a circle of peers

Subscription-only restaurants

With a large number of restaurants having to close temporarily or permanently due to Covid-19, the post-Covid relaunch may be a new era for a business model that – albeit barely sustainable – is not new. Members-only clubs have been the epitome of luxury for a long time.

In Hudson Yards, *Wine Spectator* – the bible of wine and wine culture – runs the exclusive club WS New York, reserved for members willing to pay a $15,000 initiation charge plus $7,500 yearly. The finest wines and spirits are paired with the menu, curated by the chef Eli Kaimeh, and members are brightened up by a calendar of 'one-of-a-kind cultural events'.

One establishment that appeared in many 'top luxury trends' report is Omar's/La Boite. Located in Manhattan's Lower East Side, it defined itself as a 'speakeasy-style supper club'. Upon paying the $1,500+ yearly subscription – that, *ça va sans dire*, could be conveniently purchased online – guests were able to enjoy special multi-course dinner menus, were granted access to cocktail parties, and would avail themselves of the live shows with dancers, cabaret singers, DJs and more. In 2021, Omar opened a location in Miami: Omar's/La Plage.

Circles such as the CORE: Club, located on 55th in Midtown Manhattan, are so exclusive that – even if you could afford the $50,000 initiation fee and the $17,000 annual dues – your application must still be approved by the club's management.

Occasions to join an exclusive circle of friends are not only on the East Coast, though. There are two interesting locations in San Francisco that you don't want to miss out on. In Battery Street, the heart of the financial district, a $2,400 yearly subscription allows venture capitalists, entrepreneurs and top managers at the big-tech firms, to meet and mingle at The Battery – a social club whose offer is not limited to fine dining and wine. It offers private lectures, book presentations, concerts – and in between business meetings guests can relax in the spa, stay active with a training session at the gym, chill out in the garden and even rest well in the 14-suite luxury boutique hotel – now available also for public booking.

The triple Michelin-starred chef Michael Tusk created a membership programme for his Quince & Co restaurant, located in a small Victorian townhouse in Pacific Heights. In that intimate space, Michael succeeded in creating a deep sense of fellowship and community. People intrigued by the programme will have to join the waiting list until some members decide not to renew their subscription, since at the time of writing this chapter the membership programme is fully subscribed – witnessing the exceptional success of the initiative.

> When meals become beloved stories, they are conjured, retold and embellished, and the experience returns twofold. Pleasure not only comes from the food itself, but from the meal being a part of something greater.
> *Lindsay and Michael Tusk*

https://wsnewyork.com
http://www.omar-nyc.com
www.thebatterysf.com
www.quincerestaurant.com

Don't even try to visit https://thecoreclub.com – you cannot enter the website without a valid member's password!

Discussion questions

- Trivia: what is the oldest private, members-only club still in operation today? Find some examples of members-only clubs in ancient societies, and try to find how modern-day members-only clubs are an evolution of these ancient establishments.
- What is the value of belonging to a members-only club? How can the price (i.e. initiation fee and yearly membership fee) be determined?

CASE STUDY   Living in a luxury residential community... at sea

MS *The World, Utopia, Storyline*, and counting

For those wondering what could be the ultimate travel lifestyle, consider the unique opportunity to travel around the world while enjoying the comfort of one's home:

> You can now travel the globe from the comfort of home, experiencing the ultimate travel lifestyle. Unpack once. You're home... and you're travelling around the world. You can have it all. Work onboard and discover offshore tax benefits. Learn in a truly global classroom. Enjoy the adventure – it's all part of the Storylines luxury global lifestyle.

MS The World is a 644ft cruise ship operated as a condominium complex, hosting as many as 165 large apartments, owned by private families. The residents, from many countries, can live on board as the ship travels. Some residents choose to live on board full-time while others visit periodically throughout the year. The *Utopia* cruise ship will have 190 residences and a hotel. Life on board will be enhanced by attending the exclusive The Club, where the elite residential community will mingle and socialize, while the staff will offer one-to-one bespoke service, to attend and cater for even the most specific requests of each resident, 'without having to ask'.

Nowadays luxury travellers are demanding more than just comfort and convenience: being a conscious globetrotter is also important. For this reason, Storylines believes in (luxurious) sustainable travel, as clearly stated in the official website:

> We believe the world is your playground. We also believe that we have a responsibility to protect that world. Our method of sustainable travel preserves the seas and the communities we visit. We aim to leave no trace on our amazing yet fragile planet by focusing on environmentally friendly sustainability initiatives and responsible social & corporate governance (ESG) principles. We believe that sustainable travel can have a lasting positive impact on societies and the natural world.

To substantiate the claim, the website mentions a number of sustainable initiatives.

https://aboardtheworld.com
http://www.utopiaresidences.com
www.storylines.com

Discussion questions

- What could be the typical day on a residential cruise ship? How would that differ from the typical day on a passenger cruise ship? Could you explain the differences?

- Imagine you are a marketing company in charge of creativity for a residential cruise ship. Prepare a one-page leaflet synthetically presenting the benefits of joining this elite residential community.

- Discuss the pros and cons of creating a homogeneous community (e.g. similar age range, similar family composition – young couples with kids vs empty nesters – same geographic provenance, wealth…) vs a more heterogeneous one, on board a residential cruise ship.

CASE STUDY   Extreme personalization

A way to justify luxury status and keep the soaring prices trend, notwithstanding increased price elasticity

In 2022, Balenciaga opens its first haute couture boutique in Paris, at an extremely significant address for the brand: 10 Avenue George V. It is the very same location where Cristóbal Balenciaga opened his first French store in 1937:

> The concept of this shop is a gateway to haute couture, which remains a very closed universe, especially for the younger generations.
> *Cédric Charbit, CEO of Balenciaga*

This store retails the haute couture collection, which is strictly produced to order, and will also offer to Balenciaga's exclusive clientele special collections and customizable garments and accessories.

Bespoke and tailor-made are not only synonymous with high fashion. 'Tailor Made' is the name of Ferrari's personalization programme, through which lucky customers can personalize their *Rossa di Maranello*, with the attentive support of a 'Personal Designer', competently guiding them through the countless personalization options arising from the ongoing research of the Ferrari Design Center. Everything starts by visiting the 'Atelier', which is described as follows on the company's official website:

> The Atelier Ferrari is a special studio to which all of our clients may come to make their Ferraris even more unique and moulded to their personal tastes. Designed to ensure the client feels absolutely the centre of attention, the Atelier is a truly exclusive, sophisticated space where our guests can create their very own bespoke car with the assistance of a team of experts.

After the first Atelier, opened in Maranello in 2011, Ferrari opened the second and third Ateliers (quite unsurprisingly) in Shanghai (2014) and New York (2019). The Tailor Made programme carries on a tradition that dates back in time, as the Maranello factory has manufactured personalized models, and even one-off vehicles, since the 1950s.

Following the trend of boat-inspired supercar designs, Horacio Pagani and his team conceived and realized the beautiful Pagani Zonda HP Barchetta. It is a lovely Riviera-style, roofless carbo-titanium monocoque, hosting a brutal Mercedes AMG V12 7.3lt engine, with horsepower to push the 1,250 kg car to barely street-legal limits, that the Argentinian carmaker designed for himself. Eventually, the supercar company from San Cesario sul Panaro realized three units of this special model, which – to date – is the most expensive car in the world. The Zonda Barchetta paved the road for a new series of one-off cars designed for Pagani's most demanding customers.

Besides personalization, few-offs and one-offs, there are also supercar programmes that offer exclusive experiences to their owners.

Boasting a large number of imitation attempts, Ferrari's XX Programme, launched by the prancing horse's brand back in 2005, allows owners of very extreme Ferrari models to race on track at private events, with the supervision of the highly skilled engineers of Ferrari's racing team, for a one-of-a-kind, memorable experience.

A very interesting aspect of the XX Programme is that it allows the supercar manufacturer to collect a wealth of telemetry data, supporting the research and development of innovative solutions that will then be implemented in regular production models. Not only participants in the programme are well aware of this: knowing that your passion can contribute to better your dream car's new model can be a source of pride for any *Ferrarista*.

www.balenciaga.com
www.ferrari.com
www.pagani.com

Discussion questions

- If you were purely observing the business model from an industrial (i.e. production management, supply chain management) perspective, how much more would a personalized item cost, compared with a standard one, produced in large lots? Which elements are justifying the difference?

- From a marketing point of view, which other aspects would you mention, that would make a bespoke item more pricey than its standard counterpart?

CASE STUDY Interpersonal relationships in the shopping experience

Expanding the network of directly operated stores, emphasizing personal selling, customer engagement in co-creation, and creating event-based marketing and sales

The personal luxury goods sector is – quite obviously – a very concentrated one, with the top 10 players of the 100 'Global Powers of Luxury Goods' accounting for 51.4 per cent of the sales of the top 100 (Deloitte, 2021).

If you look at the three top players in fashion luxury – LVMH Moët Hennessy Louis Vuitton SE, Kering SA, and Compagnie Financière Richemont SA, who, taken together, own more than 100 of the most famous luxury goods brands in the world – the share of their sales coming from directly operated stores has been constantly increasing in the past few years.

The largest groups could benefit from the cash flows of the 'cash cow' brands in their portfolio, to finance the growth of the 'stars' and to keep opening new directly operated stores in the best locations of the famous shopping streets in the fashion capitals of the world.

As of December 2021, there were a total of 501 directly operated Gucci retail stores worldwide. The strategy of reinforcing the network of stores dates back to the early 2000s, and this direct-to-consumer strategy is now definitely back in fashion.

In total, Kering SA owned 1,433 directly operated stores throughout the world in 2020. This wide retail presence would be obviously impossible for a smaller, independent brand.

The direct management of the retail chain is not only relevant in terms of better margin: arguably, the most important reason for luxury brands to directly operate their retail outlets is to create a better experience for their most loyal customers. As the patron of LVMH, Bernard Arnault, famously put it, 'If you control your distribution, you control your image'.

Luxury concierge services have been around for quite some time. The London-based Quintessentially is probably the most famous, and for more than 20 years has pampered millionaires, organizing their travels, nightlife and private parties, granting them access to the most exclusive events and more. Luxury hotels and credit card companies are offering concierge services to their loyal members.

Now this kind of support is also offered directly by luxury brands. The Milanese flagship store of the jewellery brand Bulgari, located at the very beginning of Via Montenapoleone, mixes quintessentially Italian architectural elements and construction materials, interior design and art. Designed by the archi-star Peter Marino, the boutique is an homage to Milanese interior design masters such as Gio Ponti, Portaluppi and Mangiarotti. Top customers may be invited into a private room, an inner orangery, natural light coming in from the conservatory, to enjoy the shopping in such an amazing surrounding that many a bridegroom decided to propose in this very space.

One of the golden rules in service operations management is to 'build commitment through choice' (Case and Dasu, 2001). A very interesting study, reported in Chase and Dasu's paper, proved that blood donors reported having perceived a significantly lower level of pain when they were offered the opportunity to choose the arm from which to donate blood. Luxury brands have learnt to apply this principle, even if the control they hand to the customers is largely symbolic. Offering the choice of the method of payment, whether the goods will be picked up at the store or conveniently delivered at the customer's home, nicely packed or simply put in an anonymous shopping bag, and whether customers may want to drink some still or sparkling water, ristretto espresso coffee or a tall cappuccino while they are waiting to be attended by a sales assistant, are simple ways to create customer engagement in the retail store, making the customer 'encounter' with the brand more memorable.

At the time of writing this chapter, on 27 August, 2022, I was enjoying the OMEGA European Master golf tournament in the fairytale Swiss Alps town of Crans-Montana. All of a sudden, my wife started sending me urgent messages summoning me to join her *at once* at the OMEGA boutique in the Rue Centrale. A huge crowd was gathering outside the flagship store, as – unannounced – the American actor George Clooney, a brand ambassador for the Swiss watch brand, popped up to enjoy the golf tournament and take some pictures with customers. Imagine being an OMEGA customer and finding George Clooney in the store. The subsequent presence of George on the golf course definitely brightened up an already amazing day.

Event-driven marketing is a way to seamlessly integrate a luxury brand's presence into (potential) customers' daily lives. Today, it's hard to name a major sports event which is not sponsored by a watch brand, whether it is OMEGA (official timekeeper of the Olympic Games), Rolex (supporting, among others, 'The Championship' at the Wimbledon temple of tennis), or Longines, partner of many equestrian sport competitions.

www.omegawatches.com/stories/george-clooney-in-crans-montana

Discussion questions

- In the light of the above-described trends, discuss the role of the retail (brick and mortar) store of the future, also keeping in mind that online will be a key channel for the time being. (Hint – consider these keywords appearing on Altagamma's monitor: Brand Booster, Omni Enabler, Customer Explorer.)
- Why do we need interpersonal relationships when purchasing a (luxury) good?
- What are the contributions of personal touchpoints with the customer, within the overall luxury business model?

References

Achille, A, Marchessou, M and Remy, N (2018) Luxury in the age of digital Darwinism, McKinsey Report, February

Amed, I et al (2020) The State of Fashion 2020: Coronavirus Update, McKinsey, www.mckinsey.com/industries/retail/our-insights/state-of-fashion (archived at https://perma.cc/2GGL-Q5BR)

Bain & Company (2020) 2019 Luxury Goods Worldwide Market Study, www.bain.com/insights/eight-themes-that-are-rewriting-the-future-of-luxury-goods/ (archived at https://perma.cc/MP27-8TML)

Bain & Company (2021) 2021 Luxury Goods Worldwide Market Study, www.bain.com/insights/from-surging-recovery-to-elegant-advance-the-evolving-future-of-luxury/ (archived at https://perma.cc/2F7R-W2TA)

Case, R B and Dasu, S (2001) Want to perfect your company's service? Use behavioural science, *Harvard Business Review*, June, https://hbr.org/2001/06/want-to-perfect-your-companys-service-use-behavioral-science (archived at https://perma.cc/G5R4-64QY)

Deloitte (2021) Global Powers of Luxury Goods 2021: Breakthrough luxury, www2.deloitte.com/content/dam/Deloitte/global/Documents/Consumer-Business/gx-cb-global-powers-of-luxury-goods-2021.pdf (archived at https://perma.cc/8Z83-8VHS)

Fairs, M (2020) Coronavirus offers 'a blank page for a new beginning' says Li Edelkoort, *Dezeen*, 9 March, www.dezeen.com/2020/03/09/li-edelkoort-coronavirus-reset/ (archived at https://perma.cc/E2C9-5SHY)

Gopalan, N (2020) Revenge is a dish that's off the China menu, *Bloomberg*, 21 April, www.bloomberg.com/opinion/articles/2020-04-20/china-luxury-revenge-spending-surge-is-likely-to-fade (archived at https://perma.cc/ZHT2-EC6V)

Styrk, J (2020) Top 100 fastest growing & declining categories in e-commerce, *Stackline*

Zargani, L (2020) Giorgio Armani writes open letter to WWD, *WWD*, https://wwd.com/fashion-news/designer-luxury/giorgio-armani-writes-open-letter-wwd-1203553687/ (archived at https://perma.cc/29BH-Y3Q7)

INDEX

From 4 December 2025 the EU Responsible Person (GPSR) is:
eucomply oÜ, Pärnu mnt. 139b – 14, 11317 Tallinn, Estonia
www.eucompliancepartner.com

www.ingramcontent.com/pod-product-compliance
Lightning Source LLC
Chambersburg PA
CBHW041207220326
41597CB00030BA/5071